CBI
Top Cop
Recalls

Attention Authors

Manas Publications is fighting a war to tell the world that India can win the battle not only by the bullet but also by pen. We are converting fighters into writers. There is no dearth of intellectuals in our country, however, their knowledge is confined to them only. No sincere effort has been made by any other publisher to channelise their knowledge, that is why the talent of every intellectual remains latent. An author always presents the raw material in the shape of a manuscript and it is the job of the publisher to convert it into a finished product. Manas has been continually motivating intellectuals and publishing their manuscripts for more than two decades and would like to publish your manuscript too. If you or your colleagues have a manuscript ready for publication or are working on it, contact us with a detailed synopsis and list of contents. Manas can also suggest you a suitable title for writing related to your area of expertise. Manas is known for its publishing quality. We take utmost care in publishing and also give wide publicity to the book and its author through our national and international distribution network.

Acknowledgements

This book is dedicated to the honest and brave police officers who are never tempted by the tinge of corruption.

My gratitude to my parents who instilled in me my value system.

I express my deep regards to my only living elder brother Satyen Dutta, who was a very senior journalist in *The Statesman*, inspired me to write this book. He even at the age of 82 took the trouble to check the first draft of this book.

I am thankful to many officers of UP police and especially Premlal Yadav who helped me by providing materials relating to his brave brother Dhrub Lal Yadav. Dhrub Lal gave his life fighting with Omer Sheikh gang to rescue three British nationals from a hideout in Saharanpur district of UP. He had earlier worked in Jhansi range where he emerged as the hero in liquidating armed gangs of dacoits.

Thanks to my wife Krishna and daughter Sushmita who coerced me to purchase a laptop, to facilitate my work. My niece reshaped the original manuscript into two parts i.e. Career and Spiritual Quest which was a difficult task for me to handle. She taught me some new features of the laptop. Thank you Amrita.

I owe every thing to Sathya Sai Baba, as I was fortunate enough to be drawn into his fold gradually. All these events have been mentioned in the book.

Dedicated To

All brave and patriot police personnel who sacrifice their lives for Mother India.

Preface

I strongly believe in destiny and the cosmic power that shaped my life. I have crossed 75 years of my life. The idea to write my memoirs came from a strange request from my friend SNS Murthy, a dear batchmate who took on his shoulders to bring out a coffee table book for our reunion in December 2009 held at the Police Academy, Hyderabad. He allotted 'My life in CBI' as my theme subject. Writing such a story in two months was an uphill task. I then decided to write on a peculiar subject: 'My life as ADC to the Governor of UP'. While recording on my laptop I realized that I could as well write my memoirs that would include my professional career as a police officer and my spiritual quest.

My intention is not to project myself as a great achiever, which I am not. I never believed in image projection as my icons avoided publicity. They were, namely, the late DP Kohli and the late D Sen. They believed in hard work and anonymity. I recall a small incident. One day D Sen rang up at my home around 8 am. My wife told him that I was in office. When he talked to me in the office, never did he ask me why I was in office so early. He was not in the habit of pampering officers, but he kept a mental note of events and happenings.

I did not maintain a diary in my service life. As a result, my memoirs are based entirely on memory, which is still quite strong. It is not my intention to hurt anyone by way of revelations of certain facts. I nurse no grievance against anybody even against those who attempted to harm me, as I believe in *loka samastha sukinu bhavanthu*.

This book is for young police officers, criminologists, crime fiction readers and for those who are interested in spiritual quest as beginners.

SK Datta

Introduction

My life as a police officer gave me an opportunity to face various challenges, meeting many people at the grassroots level, injustices inflicted on Dalits and weaker sections of the society, unimaginable corruption in public services, reign of terror in Bundelkhand by armed gangs of dacoits including a thrilling life story of Phoolan Devi, flawed budget formulation for UP police, gross evasion or avoidance of payment of income tax and excise duty while serving in the ministry of finance.

My last tenure in CBI was one of unique experience in supervision of the most famous cases like Syed Modi murder case, dealing with terrorist cases, diamond merchant kidnapping case, brutal assassination of Rajiv Gandhi and security scam cases that rocked the nation with a new variety of bank fraud that was never heard before. The success stories reflect the CBI mantra of teamwork under close supervision of able leadership of senior officers.

My philosophy of policing was always for innovation. The Management Information System [MIS] was one of them. By introducing the system, I could locate easily slow or non-moving items of work. Mere preparation of such fortnightly reports was enough to make such items move fast. I developed my own idea of zero budgeting by freezing budget at one constant level by a new method of generating savings to be retained.

India is yet to build up many athletes of world standard. As a young commandant of a battalion I found out that the main reasons were lack of motivation and practices. My battalion could produce many athletes of all India standards by taking care of these two factors.

I had the opportunity to work under outstanding police officers like Satish Dutt Pandey, Gary Saxena, who became Governor of Jammu and Kashmir twice, Shanti Prosad, D Sen, Rnenison and many others.

My spiritual quest was always a secret. I benefited by meeting spiritual giants like Deoraha Baba, Swami Rama and many others. Sathya Sai Baba came to my life gradually. His amazing story is unbelievable. Many are not aware of spiritual science. How many of us are aware of *Parkaya Pravesh, Kayakalpa, Khechri Mudra*? I have attempted to inform those who had never heard about these highly developed secrets still available in India.

In spiritualism, personal experience matters more than sermons. 2012 end or beginning is another matter of interest to many. I have just introduced the topic as the nature has its own way dealing with for over-exploitation of the Mother Earth. I believe in mother Teresa's definition of God. 'God', she had described, 'as love in action'.

One chapter is devoted to Ayurveda and Yoga. From personal experience, I have narrated how Ayurveda treatment cured me of many ailments. *Astanga Yoga* i.e. eightfold path of *Raja Yoga* is area of my interest. It might create interest for beginners. Kriya Yogis, Brahma Kumaris, *Sahaj Yoga* and many others, practise *Raj Yoga*. The restless mind with five senses has tendencies to go outward. As stated repeatedly by Sai Baba that by practice a die-mind stage has to be reached to attain a stage of bliss with full realization of the self. All *Raj Yoga* practices are designed to reach the die-mind stage.

1

How I was Selected in the IPS

My life in police service was a blend of pain and pleasure. My selection in the IPS was providential. I scored high marks in the interview. Going through my papers, one of the members of the All India Service Board found that I had written cycling as my hobby. This prompted him and other interviewers to ask me what I had achieved in this field. Perhaps they thought that cycling meant going round and round the city and nothing more. When asked to narrate my experience, I said as a student of BA (Hons) five of our school friends once decided to travel to Agra by cycle, carrying with us a stove and utensils to cook our own food just to save money as we belonged to middle class families. I lost my father when I was a student of class eight. My brothers were supporting me. We all had enough experience in cycling. I used to reach Delhi University from Karol Bagh by cycle and return home. Thereafter, everyday I had to go out for errands for the family. On an average, the distance covered would be around 20/25 miles per day. One day we started our journey from Delhi early in the morning. At Delhi-Punjab border— there was no Haryana then—policemen hiding behind the bushes, jumped at us blowing their whistles. We were taken aback. They checked our belongings and asked a few questions. We were soon let off. Later, I learnt that this was called, 'naka-bandi' to check border crossing by suspicious characters. This naka bandi is rare nowadays. Our next stoppage was Palwal where we settled down to prepare tea and frugal breakfast. Again, two local constables accosted us to ask few questions. We were again let off. We were surprised that police were so effective to spot strangers and question them. Later, I learnt that this was called the beat system in the police. I wonder if our present police system is currently as effective. Our next stoppage was Kosi Kalan in UP. The police was nowhere to be seen. From Kosi Kalan, we reached Vrindavan and stayed in Birla Dharamshala which we found to be a good place for night rest. The manager was very kind to us. Next day after a visit to Mathura, we left for Agra. We stopped in the evening in a village for a while, where the locals told us not to undertake the journey at night as the highway was not safe. They provided shelter and food for our night stay. This hospitability and simplicity of the village folks have left an abiding impression in our minds. The soul of real India was well absorbed. We visited the Taj Mahal for the first time. We returned home by the same route. I narrated to the Board Members the distances between the places accurately and that must have gone in my favour. They perhaps thought that I was fit to join the police service. The interview was in 1958 and call to join the service came in 1959. Thus, we are called fifty-niners.

2

The Police Training

The first feeling of empowerment was when I entered the office compound of Central Police Training College (CPTC), Mount Abu where the smartly dressed sentry at the gate gave me a smart salute. At once, I realized I was a different person with a huge responsibility ahead. There was a peculiar feeling of self-satisfaction and empowerment. Like me, many others of my batch might have felt in the same manner.

The satisfaction of empowerment has a story behind it. In those days in Delhi, the police for double riding on cycle often harassed us. They would deflate our tyres. Once I found pillion riding by two constables. I was agitated and I rang up Dr Katju, then the home minister of India. He was kind enough to listen to my grievance and advised me to lodge a complaint with the Mandir Marg police station, which I did. I was impressed that even a cabinet minister had the courtesy to listen to a complaint of a school-going youngster like me. During service, I always instructed my staff to allow me to talk to people bringing to my notice some special information he might be holding. Effective police officers of all ranks should interact with them. At times, this may cause irritation as some people have the habit of displaying their closeness to such officers before their admirers.

Some of us reached Mount Abu on the day of joining. We rushed to office only to find to our embarrassment that the

Commandant Gopal Krishna Handoo, an IP officer, was addressing the IPS probationers, who had reached Mount Abu a day or two earlier. We did not know what to do as we went by the instructions in letter and spirit. Seeing our pathetic condition, Elizabeth, daughter of a senior officer of the Academy, Devenport, told us to enter the hall quietly. We sneaked into the hall. Commandant Handoo took notice of our surreptitious entry. He got the finest opportunity to shower on us the choicest abuses without giving us an opportunity to explain our conduct. He even went to the extent of telling us to go back home for which he would be too happy to pay for our return journey. The situation was tense and unbearable. After sometime he cooled down. Later, we learnt that such severe dressing-down was part of hardening up training so that we remain calm and cool in adverse situations. I profited from this experience. I was never late in my work. Punctuality is very important in life. I also learnt to cope with adverse situations.

Training schedule was very tough as we were fresh from universities. One probationer fainted on the very first day while running around the ground several times. There was hardly any show of sympathy for the poor probationers. Immediately after the rigorous morning drill, there was one hour break for bath and breakfast. The classes would start from 10 am. Many of us would doze off while listening to the lectures on law, procedure and the like. Some smart trainees would wear dark glasses to keep up the appearance of being awake and when they woke up would ask questions giving the impression of being keen listeners. One enterprising probationer from Bihar distributed a pinch of a mix called *tamaku* mixed with *tambul* to be kept in the mouth for stimulation. We soon got addicted and many could not get out of this bad habit for years together.

Living together, two in one room, was the first experience of inter-cultural interaction. We were instructed to wear dressing gowns while in hostel. The Deputy Commandant Eric Stracy, a renowned officer of Tamil Nadu, would appear in the mess to locate defaulters at odd hours. On the second day of our stay, Deputy Commandant Stracy gave us training in table manners, how to handle several spoons, forks and knives laid on the dining table. He made it clear that this practice of picking up right spoons, forks and knives would help us in future. In my case, it did when I became ADC to the Governor of UP. At times, I stayed in the Rashtrapati Bhavan. In later years, I had no difficulty in attending international dinners in India and abroad without feeling awkward. The simple rule is that the forks and knives are to be picked up from outer to inner after every serving. I found many political leaders were not conversant with table manners and created awkward situations before the foreign dignitaries.

Stracy was very particular the way we drink water or tea. Indians, mostly, drink with lot of noise resembling gurgling. We had to practise soundless drinking. When we take food, we open our mouths much before arrival of spoon with food. The mouth opening should be simultaneously with spoon coming into the mouth. In the language of Stracy 'this was not just done'. We also learnt to keep our mouths shut while chewing food. Eric Stracy was called 'Etiquette Stracy'.

We were given lessons in ballroom dancing. Our partners were mostly the wives of senior police officers or wives of Indian Army battalion stationed in Abu. We learnt Waltz, Foxtrot, Tango and the like. Some avoided attending the club on Saturdays for learning the dancing lessons in the club and went hungry as members of the mess were served food only in the club to ensure maximum attendance for ballroom dancing lessons. Jackson Jacob was one of them who never attended Saturday mess nights in the club. He was a deeply religious person who would like to remain alone at leisure times. Perhaps on his own request he got a separate small room to himself. He soon was named Father Jackson which reputation he carried throughout his police career. He never deviated from the path of virtue. He was an honest officer. Before joining service, police verification is required. The head constable who came to meet him for verification found nothing adverse against him, but still he demanded a sum of Rs 20 only as 'bakhseesh'. Jackson had no other option but to pay the amount. The head constable told Jackson that he would retire before Jackson joined the UP police service. The fear of Jackson taking action against him was not there. This story was narrated by Jackson personally.

As part of training, we were taken to Jodhpur, a district in the state of Rajasthan, to watch a real-life hanging of a person accused of murdering his wife's paramour. This visit was again part of toughening up exercise for young probationers. In the early morning before sunrise, the convict, looking fresh after bath, was brought before a magistrate to record his last wish. The convict said that nothing should be paid or given to his wife. Then he said that he did not commit any crime by killing the paramour of his wife. He was innocent in the eyes of God. As he was taken to the gallows, he looked at us and asked if any one of us would like to convey to God any special message. He showed no nervousness as he stood on the wooden plank blindfolded. He was shouting repeatedly 'Jo Bole So Nihal'. The executioner did not look at him when he pressed the lever. The jail inmates were in tears. The whole atmosphere was so calm that even whispers were audible. We too felt some strange feeling inside us. Many of us were in tears. The whole act was repulsive. At that time, the concept of rarest of rare case for awarding death sentence was not a part of judicial decision process. Perhaps, now such a case would have resulted in life sentence only. Many of us could not take food on that day, as the scene of hanging was still vivid in our minds. We were told that many inmates of the jail behaved the same way. The line between a living and a dead person was so thin that the convict perhaps thought life and death had lost their meanings to him. After execution, the body remained in that position for 30 minutes. Later, a doctor examined the body and declared the person dead. This jail rule possibly incorporated this provision after an event when a hanged person survived after hanging and demanded his release. Till date I have not been able to collect an authentic report on the subject.

Often mess nights were organized to provide an opportunity to show our talents in any field of our choice. Sial was a good singer and was much in demand. There was one from Tamil Nadu who was a great 'ghatam' player. Once I too had to perform a magic. I had a plain one page of a newspaper with me and showed it to the audience. I folded it and brought out materials like currency notes, napkins and similar objects. This trick I had learnt from a book authored by the great magician PC Sorkar. For mess nights, we were dressed as per dress code in those days and were told to escort ladies by lightly touching their shoulders. I believe this practice has since been discarded. This western etiquette does not suit our eastern cultural milieu.

The daily parade used to be supervised by Devenport, an Englishman to the core. He was a strict disciplinarian. His daughter Elizabeth became famous for discus and javelin throws. Every morning before sunrise he would check if any one of us was unshaved by touching our cheeks. The chief drill instructor Spadigham from Malabar Special Police was a terror. His shouts on high pitch kept us on our toes. Jumping over the wooden horse lengthwise, especially was a great challenge. It required a great deal of courage and right timing for a take-off from the ground. Many failed in their first attempt. Rope climbing was equally difficult. Climbing two ropes using both the hands is called first-class, which was beyond any of us. The second-class rope climbing requires climbing one rope with the help of two hands only. One or two of us perhaps could do it. Most of us were in the third-class category where both hands and legs are used for climbing one rope.

For me, horse riding was a pleasure. On one occasion, I fell down and was under the belly of the horse. The horse realized my condition and stood still that saved causing any injury to me. Horses have great intuitive powers. They are very intelligent. Due to old age, the police horses are put to sleep by firing through the front portion of the head. We were shown a live case where the horse was put to sleep in this manner. This type of killing was called 'humane killing' as the death was instantaneous. The horse to be killed was given a ceremonial garlanding and a *tika* on the forehead. As soon as that was done, the horse started shedding tears as if it knew death was imminent. We witnessed a cruel drama of killing of a horse that had served many probationers with tears in our eyes. There is no old-age pension for such lovable animals. We just kill them in their old age, though they deserve better treatment.

Between PT and drill, we had to change our dress in a very short time. We used to call it 'putty parade' as we were to wear putty for drill around the ankle wearing khaki pant and shirt. It takes time to wrap the putty around the ankle. Our orderlies used to keep the change over clothes ready for wearing. One orderly was attached to two officers and the probationers paid him. Most of the orderlies were Bhills who were simple folks. They maintained themselves with small amount of money they received from us.

Our mess bills were more than our pay, which was Rs 390 only. Our normal food would include both South and North Indian food. The probationers gradually started relishing both. At times western dishes were also served to familiarize us with another food habit. Handoo was keen to see that the probationers must live with all the money they could obtain from home. Frugal living was beyond him. Handoo was a great narrator of his real-life stories. Whenever he exaggerated stories of his achievements, his charming wife would cough a little, to alert him from crossing the *lakshman rekha*. Handoo was earlier the security officer to Nehru and became famous for Goa operation. His son Asoke became a General of the Indian Army. He took a leading part in Gen Sunderji's Operation Brass Track Exercise that unnerved the Pak Army fearing a possible attack.

We had a cooperative store for purchase of items of daily use. The store manager was a simpleton. A middle-aged woman visited the store once to know if the store was keeping sanitary napkins. The manager knew nothing about this item but napkin was a familiar word to him. He produced plenty of napkins that are used in dinners. She continued to demand sanitary napkins. The manager yielded ground and said that he had never known about this item in his lifetime. The store manager was a favourite of all of us. He was simple, hard working and honest. With the shifting of Academy to Hyderabad, he too shifted to the new location.

Mount Abu was not a popular tourist spot then. The day a foreigner was sighted, there would be a lot of discussion on the subject. Some even greet them for visiting Mount Abu. At leisure especially on holidays many of us would go to Nakki Lake and see the sunset. Abu is very different now with hotels and tourists all over. It is now a crowded place brimming with activities. In our days enterprising probationers would go down to Abu Road which is in the plains just for little outing and eating out. Brahma Kumaris were few, but all sorts of stories were spread about them. We had never interacted with them. Now Brahma Kumaris have beautiful buildings in Abu and many distinguished personalities visit the place for conferences. There is no stigma attached to them now. All Brahma Kumars and Kumaris wear white clothes only. They practice with concentration on *bindu*, an imaginary point between the eyebrows focusing all attenticn on it.

The Governor of Rajasthan was Sardar Gurmukh Nihal Singh, a well-respected gentleman and a freedom fighter. Abu was a sort of summer capital of the state of Rajasthan. He came to Abu and the probationers were invited to meet him by way of a courtesy call. No doubt, he was a great freedom fighter, but did not show style and sophistication required of a Governor. He was in the habit of openly belching to the embarrassment of others. We were all amused. He just did not bother. Years after, I happened to read BK Nehru's book where he too mentioned the same embarrassing situation in a dinner party held in honour of Mrs Kennedy in Jaipur. 'The Governor was not eating but he was continuously belching.' Mrs Kennedy refused to ride with the Governor next morning to visit other sites. The problem was solved by making BK Nehru sit between the Governor and Mrs. Kennedy, as a buffer. I had seen many senior officers belching. When asked why they could not prevent it, the answer was that belching was good for health. Belching is more common in North India than in other parts of the country.

At the passing out parade, I was dressed up half in *dhoti*, a *pyjama*, a *kurta* and a shirt to highlight national integration in an evening cultural programme. This funny looking dress attracted the attention of Dr Radhakrishnan who was the chief guest. He said in his final day parade address that national integration was in the hearts and minds of the people. That was the real bonding of Indian people.

Out of a batch of 42, eight have passed out. Dear Ramu [SK Ramchandran] was my roommate in Abu and his premature death while in service affected me intensely. He was very friendly to me. He was very fond of his wife and would communicate with her telepathically every night before going to sleep. It is now for his wife to confirm whether she had received such telepathic messages. Ramu was a fun-loving person and became a good painter. I attended his painting exhibition, which was inaugurated by Jyoti Basu, the then Chief Minister of West Bengal. Ramu helped me when I reached Kolkata to become SP CBI Kolkata in 1970 by vacating his garage to keep my luggage. I was under the impression that SP CBI would have a dedicated house as is the practice in UP. KPS Rathore died recently. He was a great horse rider and got a first prize in riding. We used to call him Raja as he was from a princely family. A P Varma was tall with a baritone voice he would argue endlessly on any subject. He was called Canadian or Dicky Varma as he had done some studies on Canada.

We fifty-niners still cherish with admiration and love the memory of Commandant Handoo, Dy Commandant Eric Stracy, Devenport and other junior instructors for their total dedication to groom up the budding IPS probationers. Handoo gave us a piece of advice not to nurse a grievance. It is a spiritual truth as it is self-destructive and makes a man burn within. Field Marshal Manekshaw practised this, as he never punished those who tried to harm him when he was holding a junior post. Sai Baba has said that evil utterances should be paid back with thanks. Evil begets evil. To the best of my ability, I did practice even in situations where people were trying to harm me. To practise positive thinking and healthy lifestyle one may utter 'Loka Samastha Sukinu Bhavantu' before sleep. I hope the IPS probationers are given the same sound advice even now.

Prof Ramakrishna Dev was our chief law instructor who came on deputation from West Bengal. His teaching method of a dry subject like law was unique. While lecturing on conspiracy, he would combine elements from the IPC, the Evidence Act, and the Criminal Procedure Code. Section 10 of the Evidence Act was the most difficult to understand in the context of proving conspiracy. Conduct evidence before and after the crime was clearly explained. In real life cases, it is my experience that evidence of conduct is hardly taken seriously by the courts as a result, many escaped punishment. Dev was always ready with the rulings of the high courts and the Supreme Court on all sections of law. He wrote several books on law, investigation and prosecution, which proved useful to many police officers. I personally benefited whenever I faced difficulty in giving my comments on a case.

Captain Gopal Krishna taught us driving, wireless communication and related subjects. Many became his fans as he would speak more on sex and other interesting things of life than the subjects allotted to him. This may be due to his previous army background.

Our attachment with a battalion of Rajputana Riffle for a brief period was equally rewarding. Col Tandon was the CO of the battalion. We were taught how to ambush an enemy convoy. Enemy party was taken by surprise by rapid firing by three ambush parties separated by a big distance so that none could escape. Col Tandon held an orderly room to punish a jawan who sneaked out of the camp at night and was found missing. Col passed a dismissal order. The badges and his belt were taken off. In Army, if one is caught he is not spared.

The emphasis on physical side of training, now perhaps being neglected, gave us the strength to withstand long hours of hard work. As SP and DIG in UP I used to take boys for long-distance walks covering at a time more than 20/30 km a day.

We, probationers came from all parts of India with diverse backgrounds. We realized the beauty of oneness of India. This togetherness is deeply felt in the police, central police forces and defence services.

Training at Moradabad, UP

I was allotted UP cadre. Every probationer was required to undergo training in his or her respective state training centres. Training was again in drill, indoor studies etc. Our principal of the training college was Qamrul Hasan, DIG who was very fond of riding. We used to go with him for cross-country riding. He was very fond of flowers. He found our knowledge of flowers limited only to marigold and roses. He used to show us each flower telling its botanical name. My knowledge of flowers helped me to lay flower beds in the Raj Bhavan compound in Lucknow when I was ADC to the Governor of UP that pleased the gardeners as well.

With state training there was district training also. I was attached to district Aligarh. The UP tradition was that probationers used to stay with SP. GC Saxena alias Gray Saxena was the SP of Aligarh district in those days. Once there was bereavement in his family, so he arranged my stay with the District Magistrate Dileep Kumar Bhattacharya who was a bachelor then. The remarkable thing about him was that he would take meals with me. His servant Chottu told me that his boss was not particular about lunch and often skipped lunches. However, that never happened during my two months stay with him. He was an erudite scholar hailing from Banaras. He believed in straight talk and did not yield to unreasonable demands of the politicians. During district training, I was attached to the Police Station Sasni. Once I took Station House Officer's horse for a countryside ride. While galloping the horse, I soon realized to control the horse, the straddle was breached. I pulled the leash and that too gave way. I was just thrown on to the ground unconscious. The horse returned to police station without the rider. When I became conscious, I found myself in a small hospital and was soon transferred to the district hospital. I broke my collar bone and was on plaster for almost six months. That exempted me from attending drills. I faced such accidents on many occasions and my DIG wrote in my character roll that I was 'accident prone'.

ASP Mathura

My SP RN Sheopuri was a Kashmiri who was thorough and methodical in his work. He taught me to draft a report to be sent to higher officers. His command over language was superb. He once exposed a superior officer for corruption for which he had to suffer. He ultimately went on deputation to CRPF as SP and never returned to UP.

I was initially accommodated in a regimental mess by the efforts made by my SP. In those days, SPs were very concerned with the welfare of junior officers. In the Army mess, we were treated very well and were always invited to mess nights. My counterpart in the IAS was Inder Mohan Sahai. We two became good friends. Sahai was not very conversant with dress code of the Army. Once he came to the mess in his casual dress. He was politely told to change over to formal dress.

We soon got accommodation. Sahai lived in a two-room farmhouse. I lived with Bhargava in his bungalow in two rooms with separate entrance. Bhargava was a good landlord. I had a Vespa scooter to use as government vehicle was not supposed to be used for going to office. We were bachelors and sought every opportunity to go to Delhi to visit parents. Sahai was a pillion rider. On Saturdays we used to leave for Delhi after office hours and would reach Delhi around 9 pm. Sahai's father was in the Air Force. He used to give us small pegs of drink to kill our tiredness of a long scooter journey. Every Monday we would leave for Mathura early in the morning to reach office by 10 am. As a young man, I used to drive fast, overtaking trucks and buses. This was too dangerous. I met with serious accident for which I had to be hospitalized once.

Inder Mohan Sahai had brilliant educational qualifications with two masters' degree. He was a Stephenian and was a simple soul. We two had fun in giving names to many. My landlord's daughter was LLD. There was an officer who in the afternoon would greet everyone saying 'good night'. We used to call him Good Night. LLD later married to Raj Bhargava an IAS officer of UP cadre. Sahai married Malati, a fashionable charming lady, who had a variety of interests and gradually opted for the glamorous world of cinema. I believe she wrote a book on film actor Raj Kapur. She joined government service and rose to the post of the Director of Film Festivals. Inder Mohan never believed in saints and astrology, but his wife later became a Sai devotee. Sahai too had to visit Puttaparthy. They were rewarded with Sai rings and developed faith in Sai. I did not get a chance to know from them the reasons for their total transformation. Sahai, who was junior to me in age, died some three years ago in sleep. He was in good health. I lost a dear friend. I have studied many deaths and I find that death is an act of destiny independent of state of one's health.

My knowledge of law was tested by a PP who did not recommend prosecution in a rape case, as there was a delay of perhaps seven days in filing the FIR. That agitated my mind. I just opened the book authored by Prof Dev and looked for decisions of higher courts on rape cases. As luck would have it, I found that there were several rulings where delay in filing FIR was ignored if there were valid grounds for the delay in lodging the FIR. One reason cited was the absence of the rape victim's father from his place of residence. The case in question was similar. Citing the case law, I ordered prosecution. The PP was amazed by my knowledge of law. There is always a tendency in police service when junior officers try to test the competence of superior officers. Application of mind is one of the attributes of good leadership.

Intuition and application of mind help one to take correct decision. This happened with me in a case of receipt of a warrant of arrest from a court in Bihar by post. I wrote on the margin of the warrant that the same should be executed after verification of facts. The local police without verification executed the warrant of arrest on the day of marriage of the arrested person's daughter. This was a well-planned conspiracy to humiliate the person concerned. There was an enquiry into the incident. The warrant was false. My career was saved as I had written that warrant should be executed only after verification. I realized that intuition played a big role.

Revenge Killings

I encountered an extraordinary case of revenge killings between two families in a remote village in Mathura district. Periodically, one group would kill the residents of another village. It so happened that while travelling in a village, some persons made complaints against people of another village. I was staying in a rest house. Being a summer month, I was sleeping in the open. At midnight, a truck came to the rest house and driver handed over a chit written by the SO intimating about the incident of mass killing. I rushed to the police station and learnt that a group of another village had ravaged one village. The SO had gone to the village of attackers. I decided to visit the village of the victims.

When I entered the village, there was nobody to be seen. They all fled into the fields. Even the dogs were not barking. At the break of dawn, seeing the police the villagers started returning from their hiding places. The women folks were crying for loss of lives of their loved and dear ones. Some young boys told me that when they grow up they would take revenge. I was shocked to hear this. Later, I learnt that revenge killings had been happening for generations. The persons who met me earlier were the accused of the case. My visit to victim's village was written in the case diary.

I received a summon from the sessions court for recording my evidence. I was then ASP Aligarh. I was not cited as a witness. As soon as the hearing started, the defence counsel objected that my evidence was not admissible. The learned judge snubbed the defence lawyer saying that I was called as a court witness. I identified some of the accused who had met me earlier. I forgot all about this case. As ADC to the Governor, I found the case file of the same case on the table of the Governor. It could be for taking a decision on mercy petition of some of the convicted accused. Many told me that I should not have rushed to the village first. There is a joke in the police that prudence lies in the absence of body in such situations. I have never believed it.

My new SP of Mathura was Satish Dutt Pandey, of the same batch as that of Riberio. He was sober, empathetic and kept a dignified appearance. Nothing would perturb him and he always maintained his cool in all situations. He as DG CRPF sought premature retirement, two years ahead of due date. After retirement, he and his wife went to his Guru's Ashram in Mitrola in Almora.

ASP, Aligarh

My next posting was as ASP Aligarh, which I enjoyed because of many challenges. GC Saxena was my SP. His friends called him Gary. He was a man of style and etiquette. He introduced me to the staff as Chota Kaptan. In UP, SP is still called Kaptan Sahib. Maybe this was due to history of British Army Captains holding charge of the districts. He was dapper and spoke English like an Englishman. He would keep me with him in his camp office in the morning to show how *Dak* should be disposed of. His marginal notes on each paper would give clear directions to the subordinates. Report writing was his forte. He used to tell me that good drafting of reports would prove your worth before your seniors who like to read a crisp and succinct report. Later on this training proved useful to me.

Gary would always take me along with him whenever he went to rural areas for inspection of police stations. In such outings, he and I would occupy a room and his wife and children another room. He rejected my request to stay with the family. After dinner, he would ask me to retire to bed. I pretended sleeping and observed that just before sleep; he meditated on the bed for sometime. Next day I could not hold back my curiosity and asked him if he was praying. 'Yes' he said and also told me that prayer was useful in life. Here, I got another side of his life, which was not known to many police officers as he never discussed spiritual matters in public or made his belief public in cosmic powers.

Gary was a shikari. He would take me along to jungles and bushes where there were partridges in plenty. My task was to throw stone into the bushes to make the birds fly and shoot at them. At that age, it was a thrilling experience to me, as I had no previous experience in shikar.

When SP was out of the district, the charge of SP would be given to ASP as per old tradition. In one such situation, I faced a serious problem of communal nature. A Muslim vegetable vendor wounded a cow for eating his vegetables meant for sale. There was immediate reaction from the Hindus and a riot-like situation developed. I rushed to Kotwali to take charge of the situation. My direction was clear that the situation must be brought under control at any cost. The strong attitude of the police force was required to deal with the situations. Nothing untoward happened. Aligarh was a communally sensitive district. Many SPs had to face even suspensions for failing to control riots in Aligarh. Divine power saved me from that situation.

The social life in Aligarh was different from other districts. There were many Nawabs such as the Nawab of Chattari. Often they would invite us for dinners. The Nawab of Chattari liked me. He once told me rather frankly that they were Hindu Rajputs who converted to Islam, many of their extended families were still Hindus, and they followed many of the Rajput traditions in marriages. The same story I heard from JN Dixit who was our High Commissioner in Pakistan. A part of the Pataudi family migrated to Pakistan. One of them became a General in Pakistan Army. Dixit attended a Pataudi family marriage in Pakistan. He found some Rajput traditions being followed. When asked, he too got the same answer. Indian Muslims are different as most of them are converts. Many of them call themselves Ranas, Saigals, Sethis, Chaohans and the like to show their higher status before their conversion to Islam.

Gary became a highly successful police officer to become chief of RAW. He became the Governor of J&K twice. Such successful officers are rare in the police service. I have taken the liberty to write about him as I feel that he had shown great concern to train junior police officers so that they too could achieve success in their career and motivate the present generation of senior officers to train the new generation of police officers under their charge.

My residence in Aligarh was almost adjacent to Joint Magistrate Vinod Dikshit's residence. Since I was a bachelor, Vinod and his wife Sheila Dikshit would often invite me to dinners and lunches. Sheila would often urge me to marry and even went to the extent of finding a good girl. I was advised by Islam Ahmed my DIG not to marry before I become SP as pay of an ASP was not enough to support a family. Our friendship with the Dikshit family grew stronger and stronger. A son was born in their house in Lucknow when we stayed with them in their Lucknow residence. Vinod died in the eighties. Sheila is now the chief minister of Delhi. She is a popular figure by dint of her own merit. She has been successful in changing the face of Delhi. Even now whenever she meets us in police functions, she hugs my wife in the presence of people. Many ask me the reasons for this. I would avoid telling them that our relationship is based on a long-standing bond forged between the two families.

3

My life as ADC to Governor of UP

It was my good luck that the governor once selected me for visiting Badrinath and Kedarnath along with him and large staff of the Raj Bhavan. Our first stop was Joshimath where we stayed in an army guest house. The town was well lit. The reason was that the Army had its own captive hydel generation plant well enough for the township. Joshimath is named after one of the four famous monasteries, each named as *math*, established by Adi Shankaracharya, a saint from Kerala, who spent his life in the hills of Himalayas. The Brigadier in charge of the station took us to brief the governor about the situation on the Chinese border. On a sand model, he showed us troop concentration on the Chinese side. In his thundering voice, he told us that in the event of a future war, the Chinese would receive a befitting reply. His knowledge of the topography of the Chinese side impressed us. We knew that any future mischief by the Chinese would be dealt with severely and there would be no repeat of 1962 War.

The distance from Joshimath to Badrinath is nearly 24 kilometers. From Joshimath the journey was on foot as roads were still under construction by the Border Road Organization. The governor and some ladies were carried by palanquin. Each day we covered 10 kilometers and took rest in a government rest house. Badrinath lies at the confluence of rivers Rishi Ganga and Alaknanda. The mules carried our luggage and one mule just slipped into the fast flowing

Alaknanda River and could not be traced thereafter. I was given a *tattu*, a small sized horse, so that I could oversee movement of the front and the tail-enders. It was risky to ride a horse as anytime the horse could slip into Alaknanda.

The popular belief is that word Badri derives from the word berries, which grew in numbers in that region once. Badrinath is almost guarded by two mountain ranges Nar and Narayan. At some distance, one can see Neelkanth peak. There is hot water spring called Taptkund where a pilgrim can refresh himself by taking a hot water bath, a rarity in that cold climate. This is nature's gift to pilgrims. The Badri temple is called Badrinarayan that is the temple of Lord Vishnu. For thousands of years people have been visiting Badrinath and Kedarnath. Only a few yogis stay in Badrinath during winter months. Great Yogis, Rishis, and Mahatmas sanctify this place for years to attain a state of higher consciousness. Mahavatar Babaji is said to be alive in this *tapo bhumi*. The sacred mountains of Himalayas are believed to be the powerhouse for transmission of blessings of great souls to the seekers. We could see only one yogi with *veena* who reportedly stayed in Badrinath around the year and never spoke. He was called *mauni baba*.

Kedarnath can be reached by first climbing down and then up. The road was *kaccha*. Efforts to build all-weather roads could not succeed, as the soil was sandy and unstable. Kedearnath is dedicated to Lord Shiva. I was in a tent and found there was no water in liquid form as had turned into solid snow. Using toilet was difficult. There is some cosmic attraction in the region. People feel happy here; many describe it as spiritual vibrations. I too felt different. My prayer to Lord Vishnu at Badrinath was to keep me on the right path. This was a simple prayer and I strongly believe that God did answer. I did not have another chance to visit these two shrines again.

One ADC to governor used to be on duty and the other was supposed to look after the wife of the governor but since our governor was a widower, one of us would have a free day. The job was to usher in dignitaries before the governor as per scheduled appointments. Before that, the governor used to be briefed about the dignitary and the purpose of his meeting the governor. On tour, the ADC was supposed to brief the governor all the required details of the district. All the paperwork used to be done by the

Governor's secretariat based on reports received from the districts. This required a lot of fast reading of all the materials.

The governor being a spiritual person would often speak on spiritual subjects. After hearing him for sometime, I could say beforehand the words and sentences he would use in his speeches. The job of the ADC was to remind the governor about the next appointment by sending a chit five minutes before. At times, the governor would make a joke of it. He told the audience that his time to speak was being controlled by his ADC. He did this by showing the chit received by him from me.

The governor did not know where to sit in the midst of a social party. The Secretary to the Governor told him to speak to the ladies also by way of courtesy. Thereafter, he used to rush towards the ladies and sit with them throughout. Our old generation leaders, barring a few, hardly knew the etiquette of the modern times. The governor, however, refused the secretary's suggestion to wear black *achkan* during dinner parties. He used to wear dark brown knee length *achkan*. My governor late BN Das was honest and simple. He ran his own kitchen at his own cost. His spending habit was just minimal. Once I accosted his private servant who brought fish from the market. He purchased only 250 grams of fish. We had poultry and eggs which were sold at cheaper rate for the staff. Once he called me to know who from his family had ordered for substantial purchase of eggs. This he found from scrutiny of bill presented to him. The reply was that the order came from his household. He ordered the quantity to be delivered each month for consumption of his grandson only. A big part of his salary used to go to a trust. He lived a simple life although I found later that his landed property was huge in Ganjam district of Orissa. Twice I had gone with him to that district. He knew Bengali as well but never spoke to us in Bengali. I picked up a bit of Oriya language in Ganjam. I found that the food habits of Orissa and Bengal were similar. Bengali '*jhol*' is also called by the same name in Oriya. Cooked rice is called *bhato* similar to *bhat* in Bengali.

We attended a function organized by Swami Sivananda in Rishikesh. President Dr Sarvepally Radhakrishnan and my Governor were present. Swami Sivananda was a spiritual giant and was a doctor before taking *sanyas*. He was a highly realized soul and wrote several books in simple language for the benefit of ordinary people. He was tall and healthy. His personality was overpowering. After the function, we left for Delhi in President's special train. The Governor was supposed to stay in a guesthouse of UP government near Okhla. President requested the Governor to stay in Rashtrapati Bhavan as his guest. The President's ADC Bindra and I became good friends. He was from the Indian Navy.

In Rashtrapati Bhavan, I was allotted the Mysore Room, which was decorated with Mysore touch. Sandalwood cot, furniture, and paintings were the basic features of the room. Smell of sandalwood filled the air. In the morning, the housekeeper would find out my preference for food and if I would like to invite any one for lunch or dinner. I invited JN Dixit IFS for lunch. Dixit and I grew up together since our school and college days. We used to go out for long walk after dinner. Plato and Aristotle were his pet subjects. Because of my association with him I scored more marks in the UPSC examination in political science than economics in which I did my Honours. The Rashtrapati Bhavan has several rooms bearing the name of each State.

The ADCs were in great demand in social circles as they were bachelors. They would often receive invitation to clubs and parties. One car was earmarked for each ADC. On off-duty days, he could go out in style in Raj Bhavan car without numbers. Capt. Ranade, my counterpart from the Army, was a man full of life and enjoyed his stay in Raj Bhavan. Despite his bohemian lifestyle, we became good friends. We had parallel telephone lines and could hear what the caller was talking. The ground rule was that personal talks should be avoided. The pleasure in the life of ADC was aplenty. The ADC used to live in the Raj Bhavan and was considered part of the family. I believe this tradition is now extinct. An ADC had the advantage of coming in contact with political leaders. Some of my own experiences are worth recording.

Pandit Nehru

As ADC to the governor, I had the opportunity to see great leaders and observe their behaviours from close quarters. Pandit Nehru and Lal Bhadur Shastri impressed me the most. Nehru was very particular about his breakfast time. The breakfast must be served immediately after his bath. The steward of Raj Bhavan made the mistake of not knowing his preference for boiled egg or omellet when Nehru was waiting for his breakfast. Nehru lost his temper and left the room in anger. At that time I was taking a round and found staff taking shelter behind the walls and pillars. I too was told to do likewise. Fortunately, I saw only Nehruji from behind muttering 'kiya tamasha' as he entered the lounge where there was a large congregation. As soon as he saw those people, he became normal. For damage control, I met Indiraji, who said there was no cause for worry, everything would be normal. After the 1962 war with China, Nehru was deeply hurt by the Chinese betrayal and soon his health deteriorated which we too observed. Much later I found from our Ambassador Purnendu Banerjees's book that Nehru would often ask Banerjee "where did I go wrong?"

Whenever I visited Teen Murthy residence of Pandit Nehru along with the governor, I would sit in the lounge and Indiraji would always come and talk to me and asked the staff to provide snacks and coffee for me. She would engage me in small talks. This showed her character of humility and concern for ordinary guests like me. This is rarely seen nowadays. I received a letter of good wishes from her in response to my marriage invitation card.

Nehru had a personality much different from others. His overbearing personality was so strong that many avoided even talking to him. On one such occasion, I found something unusual. It is still vivid in my memory. Once a dinner was arranged for Nehru in Raj Bhavan. A table was laid for six persons of eminence. Pandit Nehru, the governor and the chief minister were seated. It was a difficult task to persuade others to occupy the remaining three seats. I persuaded senior ministers but they gently declined. I requested Vizzy, the great cricket commentator, to sit beside Nehru. Another two individuals, now erased from my memory, occupied the two remaining seats very reluctantly. Nehru was mostly talking to Vizzy. After dinner Nehru took out a cigarette from the inside pocket of his *achkan* and enjoyed his smoking. Thereafter, he went out in the verandah to enjoy Col

Ram Singh's band music. Nehru had the courtesy to pay due attention to Ram Singh and his band members. In service, this is a normal practice. Thereafter, Nehru started walking up and down and all others were just following him keeping themselves at a safe distance. He went up and down alone. After sometime he retired to his room. At midnight, I found him dictating matters to his stenographer. Later, I came to know that it was his daily routine. Here, I must mention that Col Ram Singh was a veteran of the Netaji's Indian National Army. He remained a lifelong admirer of Netaji.

Lal Bahadur Shastri

Lal Bahadur Shastri was both short in height and weight. As minister, he stayed in Nainital Raj Bhavan twice during my tenure. Once he wanted to visit the Nainital lake area and enquired from me if he could use the official car. As the governor was using car to go to the lake area, I told Shastriji that it was permissible. He did go out in a car but on return, he reprimanded me for giving him wrong information. I pleaded that he was a VIP and the rule would not apply to him. What he told me was amazing. He said he was no VIP and the rule would apply to him. Then and there I realized that he was not an ordinary leader and destined to play a big role in nation building by projecting a vibrant ideology of personal honesty and propriety in public life. He proved his mettle in 1965 war with Pakistan. He soon became an ideal leader. He was a swadeshi to the core. He terminated PL 480 agreement with the USA as wheat dispatched to India was not even fit for animal consumption. He advised people to fast on every Monday to tide over the food shortage at that time. Even today, many people fast on Mondays.

Shastri was a simple soul. Once he had to rush to Delhi from Nainital on an urgent call from Nehru. As he reached the portico, we requested him to take his weight on a weighing machine and he obliged. His weight was only 65 kg or even less as kg was yet to come in use then. He had a hearty laugh. His weight was recorded in the Visitors Book. As the family was left behind, his instruction was not to give any special attention to them. Any leader nowadays barring a few cannot match Shastriji's standard of probity and integrity.

He did not promote his children professionally or politically. As a result, his two sons are rarely visible in public life.

Shastri once arranged a private dinner for our governor at his Delhi residence. I was astonished to see him serving food to guests personally. Shastri never prevented me from asking him questions even when I was a just young officer. I asked him why he was not taking food with all of us. He said that tradition had it that the guests should be served first. He took his meal only after the guests had finished their dinner. Here was a leader with a difference. I am mentioning these incidents only to show that the first generation of leaders after independence were different from the present leaders.

Once Shastri in his convocation address in the Gorakhpur University, which was also attended by the governor, described his early days as a student with no pocket money. He lived like a poor student. This caused laughter in the audience. That provoked him to say that the students of the new generation had no idea what poverty was. His concern was to remove poverty from India by helping the poor and the needy. His slogan after the 1965 war 'Jai Jawan Jai Kisan' was an apt reflection of his concern for the poor and Jawans who fight for the country. The Jawans in the Indian army were largely drawn from the rural India. Jai Kisan and Jai Jawan slogans are interlinked bonding together a vast majority of Indians.

Dr Zakir Hussain, Vice-President of India and the then governor of UP were in Agra circuit house in November 1963. I carried a new brand of Phillips gramophone with radio set with me. It was quite big in size. In the morning of 23 November 1963, I switched on the radio and heard that President John F. Kennedy was assassinated on 22 November at midday in Dallas. He was shot dead. I carried the gramophone-cum-radio to the governor to listen to the radio announcement. He heard the news and together we went to Dr Zakir Hussain with the set. Dr Zakir Hussain too heard the news. It was news that shocked everyone of us. All of us remained silent for sometime. Kennedy was pro-India and admired Indian democracy. He played a big role in helping India during 1962 war with China by providing all possible help. Mrs. Kennedy had previously visited India in her private capacity before the Chinese attack. The culprit who killed Kennedy was soon apprehended. He was shot dead by a security man. He too was shot dead by another security man. All the leads were thus destroyed and till today, the murder of Kennedy is a mystery.

My governor was fond of fish as he hailed from coastal Orissa. He wanted a pond in the Raj Bhavan compound for pisciculture. That was in January 1964. He called experts including Professor Kaul, an eminent agricultural scientist and a brother-in-law of Nehru. They estimated an investment of Rs 1 Lakh. The governor was not agreeable to spend such a big amount. I accosted him in his evening walk and found him dejected. I asked if the engineers had given their estimates. He said that the estimate was too high and he had dropped the idea. Being young and enthusiastic, I asked if he would permit me to recalculate the cost based on my own method of calculation. He readily agreed.

I called the junior engineer of Raj Bhavan and asked him to calculate the cost based on materials to be used. The labour cost was not to be included. He gave a calculation, which was around Rs 2000 only. The labour would be provided in the form of *shramdan* by the staff of the Raj Bhavan. In lieu of free service, all of them would receive produce from Raj Bhavan garden in plenty. The Raj Bhavan mason would involve in brick-laying and cementing. I conveyed the proposal to governor and wanted to know if he would take the risk of spending that small amount. He readily agreed. The soil structure was sandy. Therefore, I asked the junior engineer to design the pond in layers and brick laying at the base and brick lining on the sides to hold the sandy soil. I enquired if in due course the soil structure would change. The junior engineer confirmed that in due course the soil structure would become more stable. The work started in full swing. In the meantime, my marriage date was fixed for 29 February 1964 at the age of 28 years. This date was fixed as the IG UP Shanti Prosad told me that my promotion was due in February. DIG Islam Ahmed had already advised me not to marry before becoming SP. Many including my IG Shanti Prosad knew this. Therefore, the work had to be completed much before my marriage. It happened that way. Fishlings were released in the water-filled pond. It takes *rohu* fish to become one kg in one year. *Rohu* is vegetarian and feeds on left-over food. The minimum depth of the pond has to be 6ft to 8ft at least and the running length of 80 metres. This experience proved that cost reduction is possible if there is will and determination. I subsequently came to know that governor relished the fresh water pond fish. I replicated this experience elsewhere. Many police officers have ventured to do the same in their areas of jurisdiction successfully. My view is that all lands under occupation of defence and police services be used for water harvesting. This would result in a tremendous rise in ground water level within a short time with much less cost. It is a matter of pride that BSF, the CRPF and Police schools are stories of success to be replicated by other public service units. Funds are no constraint as no government funds were involved. If there is a determination to do some useful work for the society, there is no constraint. I wonder if the central and the state governments have taken up this pressing issue with the defence and police authorities. There is a pressing need to take up water harvesting on a war footing to avert water crisis in future.

Capt Ranade was my army counterpart. He was a jovial man full of humour. His attractive personality was a point of attraction for ladies irrespective of age. He could make friends quickly. He had his own way of leading a life of his own. He, however, remained a bachelor until he retired as a Brigadier. We became good friends and remained in touch for many years.

Once I faced a peculiar and an embarrassing situation. A young student from Allahabad came to meet me with the request that he would like to meet the governor for some financial assistance to get admission in the Allahabad University for higher studies. The amount was not much. I asked him how he had reached Lucknow. He said he came by train without a ticket. I was taken aback. I then asked him how he managed his food. He said he had not taken food for the last few days. In any case, he looked hungry. My final question was what he would do if the governor refused to help him. His answer made me nervous. He said in that situation he would commit suicide. In his looks, such determination was visible. I prepared a note for the governor for helping this student from his discretionary fund. Perhaps the governor did not realize the gravity of the situation. Before his reply came, I told a staffer to take him to my room, give him food and allow him to sleep.

In the meantime the governor's rejection came. I started thinking how to fend off the suicide threat. I worked out a plan. The boy came in the evening and thanked me for food and rest. I told him that fund had been arranged, but would be paid in two instalments. I obtained the name of the Dean of the University who would help him in admission. I gave him some money for return journey. I sent the first instalment with a personal letter to the Dean requesting him to admit the boy. Next month the second instalment of money was sent. The Dean was a pious person who did the needful. He appreciated my gesture and thanked me. After a few months, the boy came to Lucknow and met me. He profusely thanked me and learnt from the Dean that money was paid by me. The boy was from Rajasthan and he had sisters to be taken care of. His father died long ago. He wanted to achieve some position in life. He maintained contact with me for few years. I am sure he must have achieved success in life.

I was married on 29 February 1964 in Kolkata. My wife Krishna was born in Faridpur, a district in Bangladesh. She was educated in India and abroad. She was a good singer of Rabindro sangeet. Her relatives in Kolkata speak East Bengal dialect. I being a man from Delhi never knew that way of speaking Bengali. To tease me on the day of marriage, they spoke in their dialect. I pleaded with them to speak the language I could understand. The answer was "Mother Bhasa Chadbo Kan". It meant that why should they give up their language. Until then I had no idea of cultural differences between two Bengals. The most amusing event was that KL Watts, an IPS officer of UP, was then in Kolkata on duty. He visited my in-law's place a day before the marriage. He was served with sweet and *labda*, which was mixed vegetables with small fish pieces. As soon as he consumed a bit of *labda*, he vomited. Watts has been my well-wisher in service and after retirement as well. I always respect him, as he is senior to me by three years. He is man of humour with ready wits for every occasion.

4

Commandant of a Battalion

My first posting as SP was in 1964 as Commandant of a newly raised Battalion in Sitapur, a district near Lucknow. The idea of IG UP Shanti Prosad was that a newly promoted SP must be first posted as a commandant of police battalion called Provincial Armed Constabulary [PAC] to develop professional and leadership qualities and office management. Each PAC battalion normally had five companies of 100 men and officers of the rank of Inspector were in charge of each company.

This was a challenging task, as the force, men and officers, had to remain engaged in useful activities more because the boys were young. Events like football, hockey, and athletics were of special interest. I found athletics as one area of showing immediate results. This would require rigorous practices under close supervision. I learnt from books that for long distance running six months were required to take part in competitions and for short distance one year of practice was good enough. In six months, two boys were found good enough to go for marathon. Soon the boys were found to achieve timing of 2 hours and 40 minutes. By any standard, this was a creditable performance. For short distance run of 400 meters, one of the boys could score a timing of just less than 50 seconds. In other athletic events performance achievements were equally good. The battalion secured first position in State level competitions for years. I also learnt some interesting tricks of the trade. One was to make slightly longer

400 meters track without the knowledge of trainees. As a result, the trainees build up an extra strength for 10 meters. The main problem was to provide special diet for the trainees. Finance was the problem as there was no state funds.

As funds was a problem, the same was solved by advancing interest-free loans from the battalion private funds to athletes to buy cows or buffaloes. The mess leftovers were found good enough to feed these animals. Where there is will there is always a way. For several years, the seventh battalion remained in the top position. During sixties and seventies sport events were greatly encouraged in defence and police forces. Now things have changed.

Pandit Jawaharlal Nehru died in May 1964 just a few months after my assuming charge of the seventh battalion in Sitapur. I heard the news on All India Radio. I immediately ordered for 'bussing' operation. Bussing and debussing exercise is a part of a drill for any paramilitary formation. Each operation should not take more than 30/40 minutes. Bussing exercise means getting into vehicles with all tentage, food materials and the like. Each company must be self-sufficient in every respect so as not to depend on outside help.

I anticipated that my unit would be ordered to send a few companies to Delhi for Nehru's funeral. There was no communication of orders from PAC Headquarters. Orders came in the afternoon and our companies departed immediately because of our completion of bussing exercise previously. A thinking officer always anticipates what is required in a developing situation. Reaction time must be reduced to bring the situation under control. This should happen in case of hijacking, hostage taking or attacks mounted by terrorists on Akshardham and Parliament attack. In anticipation of possible attacks, the trained commandos have to be in readiness 24 hours a day. The government in its wisdom has now taken such a decision by positioning them at various locations in India. This was recommended by many think tanks years ago. I would recommend that police officers during training should be trained to anticipate in a given developing situation. Orders are given after much delay. In fact, I would recommend that in a developing situation the head of the formation should seek orders on his own from the competent authorities. This would avoid the usual blame game after the event as it happened in hijacking of IC 814.

In 1964, I was sent to East Pakistan border as CO of UP PAC battalion as the Pakistanis were firing into Indian side relentlessly. Our boys were never battle trained. Therefore, the boys were kept in the firing zone for some days and soon they learnt how to enter bunkers through long tunnels. They soon took up bunker positions and started firing in retaliation. The interesting thing was that Pakistani and Indian sides were listening each other through wireless sets and at times, the language was abusive. I also learnt that a War Book had to be maintained to record events and happenings. The Army was far behind us. Within a month or so, there was ceasefire and we returned to UP. The Army could not be sent back to Siliguri as their movements were regulated by a cabinet decision. This was my first understanding of a decision making process in a democracy in peace and war situation. The defence services do war game in case of potential threats.

Our boys were getting ration allowance in cash. That came from West Bengal Government on a weekly basis. When we were ordered to return, one week's payment was due. The boys were keen to get that money. So I approached Ranjit Gupta, then DIG in Siliguri and who used to camp in the border area along with us. He and the Commissioner Ivan were great friends. They used to play war games anticipating a Pakistani attack. Each would have his own views and argue endlessly. I benefited, as the concept of war game was new to me. When I pleaded for release of ration money, Ranjit Gupta took no time to release the money. Later, I learnt that the money was obtained from a battalion private fund. Subsequently he had to face audit objection. Gupta was famous for taking unusual routes for solving the problem. Under him the anti-Naxal operation in Kolkata was highly successful. He was known for taking prompt decisions on his own.

As commandant of the seventh battalion, I had faced a situation which convinced me of cosmic power that guides every one of us. Everyday I used to go home for lunch. On a particular day, I told the driver to take the longer route to reach home. The decision was intuitive and not based on rational thinking. After lunch, I used to rest for sometime. Then I used to visit the battalion office for disposing of some urgent *Dak* and go to the playground for games with the boys. I knew each boy by name, a must for man management. On that particular day, I just felt that I should remain at home. I was not sick or feeling unwell. It was again an intuitive decision for which there was no reasoning. I told my stenographer on phone to come to my residence with *Dak* for disposal. After sometime he reached home. He was trembling and told me not to go out. He narrated the entire story. A dismissed constable was hiding near a culvert with a sword on the route I used usually. He missed me in the afternoon and was waiting for my visit to office in the evening. He spotted my stenographer going towards my residence. He charged him with the sword to know why I failed to turn up. My stenographer pleaded with him to spare him, as he was just an employee. He found him roaming around with a naked sword around my house.

The SP Sitapur was informed and our subedar major of the battalion apprehended him. Subedar Major was called Kala Colonel in British Army as he used to be a native with dark colour. The dismissed boy's father came to meet me after a few days. He had served in the Indian Army and said that he had not come in support of his delinquent son. He said his son's conduct was deplorable and he deserved to be punished. I felt here was a father who did not come to me to plead for his son. This small incident made me realize that there was something called destiny and we were mere tools of the cosmic game. My decision to take a different route and not to participate in the evening games was not a conscious decision. Some force saved me from sure death or severe injury.

Social life in a small town like Sitapur was limited to few families. Whittle and Thompson, owners of a plywood factory in Sitapur, were the centre of social activities. They had big bungalows with well-maintained gardens and swimming pools. The SP of the district was Samarendra Nath Ghose. In short, he was called Sam. My first name is Samit. Therefore, I was called Samti. Three eye specialists from Sitapur Eye Hospital, a private hospital of great repute, were in the same social circuit. Their names I failed to recollect. Mani and his sweet wife were in the social circuit. Mani was from the royal family of Kapurthala. He had huge landed property in the outskirts of the district. He lived in style. He was a fat man and on doctor's advice, he used to take long walks with a stick in hand. Parties would last until midnight. From Mani I learnt about *Bhrigu Samhita*. Rishi Bhrigu had reportedly prepared the life history of every individual in the world. Mani once took out a notebook containing his life story. He claimed to have lifted it from the *Bhrigu* manuscript. It was predicted that his wife would separate from him and he would marry again. This happened the same way. The *Bhrigu* manuscript that he had consulted was available in Hoshiarpur, a district in the state of Punjab. The Hoshiarpur family had only some parts of the manuscript. The correct pages could be found out on the basis of horoscope. I have subsequently found out that only a few have genuine *Bhrigu* manuscript. My time of birth was not recorded as a result I gave up the idea of approaching anyone claiming to have *Bhrigu* manuscript.

Whittle would often recall how he once arrested Nehru who behaved well. Mrs. Thomson was a great dog lover. She had many dogs of different pedigrees and would take them out for long walks. I had picked up a newly born puppy from the battalion. Out of pity, I took the small creature to my house. When it grew up it became very lazy. In those days wheat used to be washed before it was sent for grinding. Our dog was supposed to watch the wet wheat placed in an open area for drying. We found that the dog was sitting still while monkeys were eating wheat happily. Mrs. Thomson always advised us not to keep pie dogs in the house. Impulsively we decided to release him in a far away place. Surprisingly the dog would come back after a long period. This happened three times. Then one day the man who was engaged in this task turned up to say that our dog would never return. He said that he had confined the dog in the toilet of a local train and he jumped out as soon as the train started moving.

We forgot all about the pie dog. After a year or so, the same dog ran into our house. A couple of bird catchers were running behind the dog and pleaded with us that the dog be given back to them. We asked why. Their reply was that our dog was an expert bird hunter and they required its services. When told that the dog was very lazy, they disagreed vehemently and said that the dog was a money earner for them. Finally, we agreed to give back the dog to them. We realized afterwards that a pet needs to be trained to make it hard working and efficient. Hard training is applicable to humans as well as to pets.

5

SP Deoria

In 1966, I was posted as SP Deoria bordering Bihar. As SP, my ninety per cent time was spent on complaints against the police. Some political leaders were unreasonable. One leader turned against me for not giving an adverse report against an IAS aspirant who qualified for the post. The politician was so persistent that he almost forced the then Chief Minister Charan Singh to visit my district. Charan Singh made his own enquiries. At the time of departure at Kushinagar airport, he called me aside and wanted to know why the politician was hostile. I explained the case. He heard me and appreciated my stand. He advised me never to yield to such unreasonable demands. I was impressed by the boldness of this leader knowing fully well that he was leading a coalition government. Charan Singh was never called a corrupt politician. Such leaders are rare now. I would bracket Charan Singh with Gopi Nath Bordoloi, the former chief minister of Assam. When Bordoloi died, his wife had no money for his cremation. Pandit Nehru sent some money to his family. This is on record.

The first thing I noticed was acute caste politics in the district. Every politician was keen to know my caste. Dattas like me are sometime considered Brahmins like Narain Dutt Tiwari or Punjabi Dattas. The dominant classes in the district were Brahmins, Bhumihars and Thakurs. I was born in Delhi and our family had been in Delhi for few generations. Never anyone talked about caste in my school and college days. I was very ignorant of my own Kayastha caste. I decided to give evasive replies. I have been wearing *kada* i.e. an iron bangle in my right hand, which my wife had obtained from a Gurudwara. I used to show my *kada* to those enquiring about my caste. They thought I was a *mona* Sikh. That helped me to overcome caste factor in Deoria.

KL Watts, a 1956 batch of IPS, told me many stories how he dodged the caste hunters in UP. Many thought him to be Christian as his name sounds that way. When he was posted as DG Nagaland, even the chief minister thought him to be a Christian. Opposite also happens as it was in the case of the famous super cop Riberio. A Christian in Punjab where he was DG police in turbulent days of terrorism, he was generally perceived as a neutral officer. Most of the public were happy that he would be impartial between two communities. Now the trend is to drop surname like Srivastava, Trivedi. I consider this as a healthy sign of maturity. Inter-caste marriages are happening on a scale unheard of before. I always tell my North Indian friends that caste is not a problem in Bengal. Negotiated inter-caste marriages are happening in Bengal. Hindu reform system was first initiated by stalwarts like Iswarchandra Vidyasagar, Swami Vivekananda, and Raja Ram Mohan Roy almost two centuries ago. Sahas are the richest segment of Bengal although they have been included under the category of scheduled caste.

I knew nothing about oppression against Dalits. As a student, I was inspired by Gandhiji's teachings and used to visit the so-called Valmiki colony where Gandhiji used to stay in Delhi. Along with a pahari friend of mine, we used to take classes there in evening. JN Dixit, former foreign secretary, and I were selected while undergoing BA [Hons] course at Delhi University to attend a special course on Gandhian philosophy at the Wardha ashram run on Gandhian teachings. Eminent persons like Jayprakash Narayan and Acharya Kripalani gave lectures on Gandhian values. One day we were taken out for toilet cleaning in the Wardha city. All of us cleaned the toilets with the help of implements barring Modi, who came from South Africa. He used his bare hands for cleaning. On that day, we realized that the whole system of manual cleaning of toilet was repulsive. The stench was disturbing and poor Modi could not use his hand for taking food for a day or two. We then realized that safai karmacharis deserve a better deal. They were untouchables and derived no benefit from our democratic system as they were physically prevented from casting their votes in those days. Miss Madeleine Slade, who was known as Mira Bhen, daughter of a British Admiral remained a lifelong companion of Gandhiji. She too used to do latrine cleaning in town and huts in Wardha when Gandhiji was alive. Here, I must quote Gandhiji who had said that 'I may not be born again, but if happens I would like to be born in a family of scavengers so that I may relieve them of the inhuman, unhealthy and hateful practice of carrying night soil.'

A delegation of Dalits came to meet me in my camp office in the morning, as was the routine. When asked what their problem was, they said that daughter of one of them was to be married. I innocently asked if they had any problem. What they told me was amazing. They said that the *baratis* would use a palanquin for the bridegroom. I said it was their right to do what they liked. This prompted them to say that I was not aware of the ground realities. The Dalits were not allowed to do so by the Thakurs in the area as it would be considered an insult to their prestige and authority. I was taken aback. On their petition, I gave a clear order to the local police of Saleempur to ensure their right to use palanquin in the marriage.

After a week or so, I found the same group appearing before me. They were in bandages. They told me that the Thakurs beat up *baratis* and the local police did nothing to protect them. Being young, I took few constables in a jeep and thrashed Thakurs of the locality, an act that was just impulsive. There was no complaint against me for my being so reactive. I started wondering whether true democracy had taken roots in India at all. There was no concept of social engineering then. I have never forgotten this incident ever since. Things are changing fast as Dalits have realized the power of vote. When Mayawati became the chief minister of UP, Narasimha Rao, then prime minister described it as ‘miracle of democracy’. It is my personal opinion that Dalits must enjoy the benefits of quota in services especially those who are in the lowest rung of the society for years if we wish to change the outlook of the society. This evil must be rooted out as fast as possible. My argument is based on the Gunnar Myrdal theory on reservation for Negroes in USA where he found that there was a vicious cycle of poverty leading to deprivation and resultant stagnancy of the socially deprived people. Now, many Dalits are occupying high positions and proving their worth. A friend of mine in police, a batch junior to me, used to abuse the high caste Thakurs during the lunch time. The reason was that he had seen torture inflicted on the Dalits in UP villages. He used to narrate how they were beaten up if they remained seated on their cots when a high Rajput crossed their way. The outlook of the second generation of Dalits are different. The US has shown the way by electing for the first time an African-American as the President of America, which is bonding the country together.

The image of police was corrupt and brutal. I never imagined that the image of an SP could be the same. An air force man of the lowest ladder met me in office. He narrated woes of his family being harassed by villagers in his absence. I was always helpful to such complaints and assured him that the family would be protected. He was happy with my reply. Then he came near my table and handed over an envelope. I opened the envelope and found a 100-rupee note. That made me mad. I immediately called staff and told them to call the local police. He was arrested. I thought that there was a conspiracy to damage my reputation. When asked why did he do so. The airman said that he was advised by his fellow villagers that without giving money nothing happens in the police department. I felt ashamed of our image in the eyes of the public. I now feel that my action was rather harsh in punishing the airman. In a sense, he was a misguided simple man who deserved no punishment. Upholding of the law was uppermost in my mind. The police image is worse now than before at cutting edge level where ordinary people come in contact with the police.

The people of eastern UP were politically conscious. Once an ordinary looking person wearing a *dhoti* turned up and gave me a long lecture on Communism. I asked him from where he had derived this knowledge. He said that he had worked under Ajoy Basu who was a veteran communist leader. The CPI's office is named after him in Delhi. Another prominent leader of north Deoria, a minister himself, demanded my presence with him during the election period. In those days there were no conduct rules of the Election Commission. I declined the invitation on moral grounds. He became annoyed with me. In UP, the administration used to play a significant role in influencing elections. People would seek advice from daroga and tehsildar on the choice of candidates. I believe their advice was given due consideration by these voters. The politicians were patronizing this lower rung of bureaucracy. In a case, I remember a sub-inspector was ordered to be posted at a particular police station from Lucknow. Soon things went wrong. Now all posting orders are perhaps issued from elsewhere. This undermines the position of the SP of a district.

Many leaders were also men of character. Dr Sitaram from Deoria was a minister for many years. He was handsome and soft spoken. He was a member of the scheduled caste but was popular in all for his fair dealings. During his visits, he used to receive hundreds of representations and would hand them over to me whispering into my ears that only genuine grievances need to be addressed. He was above caste politics rare now in UP. As he was well educated he did not suffer from inferiority complex. If Dalits and poor are educated, India will emerge as a big power as many talents are yet to be tapped. I have found many Dalit officers who have entered service on merit and not through quota system. India needs social engineering on a massive scale.

Being a border district there was an inter-state gang of dacoits operating in the district. One such gang was led by a person called Babu Shaib of Patna. The task to deal with this gang was given to Zalim Singh, not his real name. He was SO Kotwali. He was a man of courage holding the fort of Kotwali. He managed to obtain as much information on Babu Shaib as possible. In due course, he through his sources found out all the details of the gang. One day he came to me to inform that Babu Shaib would commit decoity and take shelter in a particular village. As expected, the dacoity was committed and he did arrive at the place of shelter. Here, it is necessary to mention that Babu Shaib used to worship *Ma Kali* before committing dacoity. He believed that during the puja he would receive signals from *Ma Kali* to commit or not to commit dacoity. If the signals were positive, he would go for the kill.

Babu Shaib while resting found himself surrounded by Zalim Singh and his men and firings were exchanged between them. Babu Shaib was killed in the encounter. When his body arrived in the district HQ a huge crowd came to Kotwali to have a glimpse of the body. He looked like an athlete, tall and handsome. His range of operation was from Gorakhpur to Tinsukia in Assam. The only mistake he committed was to take small time local dacoits in his group for commission of dacoities.

This was my first experience in anti-dacoity operation. Zalim Singh, I believe, was posted at the end of his career in Faizabad and was in touch with Gumnami Baba. According to many he became close to Gumnami Baba, who many believed was Netaji Subhas Chandra Bose. I could not locate him for confirmation of this story. Gumnami Baba died in 1985 in Faizabad.

Justice Mukherjee presided over the last commission on Netaji. Before that, the Shahnawaz Committee and Justice Khosla Commission came to the conclusion that Netaji was killed in a plane crash near the Taipei airport just after the take-off. They never visited Taiwan to find out the truth. Justice Mukherjee report came to the conclusion that as there was no plane crash, Netaji could not have lost his life in the crash as held by the previous reports. In a TV interview, he said that he believed that Gumnami Baba was indeed Netaji.

I was summoned by the Mukherjee Commission in Delhi for recording my statement as I had written perhaps more than 20 articles on Netaji's mystery for *Dainik Statesman*. That did create some interest and I did come in contact with Dr Purabi Roy, an expert on Russian affairs. The articles were mainly based on materials provided by a young journalist Anuj Dhar as he sought my help to understand the documents written in Bengali. Dhar subsequently published a book '*Back from Dead, Inside the Subhas Bose Mystery*'. This book is worth reading as it has more material than could be possibly collected on the subject by any other person.

My writings were based on evidence provided by people who came in contact with Gumnami Baba. There was no doubt that Gumnami Baba was a Bengali. Netaji's style of writing was peculiar. Gumnami Baba's handwriting matched with that of Netaji's. The handwritings were compared by AB Lal, a famous handwriting expert. He proved that the specimen writings of Gumnami Baba matched with the admitted writings of Netaji.

Close associates of Netaji in the INA days used to visit him on 23 January i.e. the birthday of Netaji every year. Dr Purabi Roy was able to obtain oral evidence of a retired Soviet General who reportedly had seen a file dealing with Netaji when he was a junior officer in the Soviet Russia. The Mukherjee Commission could not examine the General as he was shifted to another country. Was it difficult for the Indian government to secure the presence of that General through diplomatic channel?

On a petition filed by a close relative of Netaji before the Allahabad High Court, the belongings of Gumnami Baba were inventoried and kept in the custody of the DM Faizabad. Some of the items included the photos of the parents of Netaji, his writings and notings in the margin of some books on 1962 war with China. My contention was that objects touched by Gunnami Baba contained his fingerprints. For the benefit of readers, I must inform that such fingerprints remain intact even after 40 years if not more. This has been established by international experts. It was my argument that the Mukherjee Commission should undertake this exercise. The Commission failed to locate competent fingerprint experts for the job when such experts, serving and retired, are available in plenty. Unofficially, I wanted to furnish such names.

The second point that was crucial was to organize DNA test of the remains of the ashes and bones purported to be those of Netaji kept in a Buddhist temple in Tokyo. Many readers may not be aware that Government of India has been paying money for its upkeep annually. Perhaps modern technology is available to prove the age of the bones necessary to prove or disprove the theory of substitution by the bones of some of the relatives of Netaji. The Commission failed to do so for some reasons. For credibility, two groups of experts drawn from reputed international community should have been engaged for this task.

My personal view is that a multidisciplinary task force headed by a competent serving or a retired police officer can solve Netaji's mystery and the job can perhaps be completed within a year or so. Even now, the government or court, which is seized of the matter, can take such a worthwhile initiative.

The Deoria Police Line was about 400 metres from my residence. I was very particular in attending parades on Tuesdays and Fridays. The SP is supposed to visit the barracks and check the quality of food served in the mess. I found water scarcity in the police lines. I decided to bore a tube well without seeking government money as that might not come during my tenure. I decided to approach the local dealer in the district. He agreed to install the tube-well taking payments in instalments. The tube-well came up in record time. It enabled us to cultivate vegetables for the mess and supplied these at much cheaper prices. The villagers in the neighbourhood requested water for their fields at a price. Thus, income was generated to pay back the money due to the supplier of the tube-well. The total cost of the tube-well came to about Rs 3000 only. Boys liked to take bath in the tube-well water. This became popular. I believed in self-help. Now, I believe this tube-well has become a government property.

In those days, the Socialist Party was a big political force in Eastern UP. They organized anti-English agitation by demanding all establishments public or private should carry only Hindi signboards. The agitation remained under control with no violence. It was limited to slogan shouting only by small group of people. Once I had to go to Gorakhpur for a meeting with the DIG Lal, a good-hearted Christian. I told him about the agitation. He said my DSPs were good enough to deal with the situation. In the midst of the meeting, we came to know that a mob had burnt a railway coach and was still there in strength. My DIG immediately asked the Railways to provide a platoon of the Railway Protection Force (RPF) to reach my district along with me. On reaching the station, I saw police officers highly agitated as two DSPs were not giving any orders. The magistrate was there; he too avoided taking any action. In fact all these officers were in a room bolted from inside. Some constables were bleeding as they were stoned by the mob.

I got hold of the magistrate to give me in writing an order for use of force that he did. I just asked the boys to chase them out. They rushed out in no time and beat them up and the mob was dispersed in no time. I learnt that the district magistrate, hearing about the situation, left for another location. Even now, I have not found any cogent reasons as to why my own officers failed to use minimum force or seek my orders on phone. There is a laid-down procedure for dealing with violent mob.

Bonded Labour

Feudalism was rampant when I joined the service in UP. The British colonial regime introduced the Zamindari System. The indebtedness of small and medium farmers pushed them to clutches of moneylenders who pushed them into a desperate situation to earn their livelihood. Soon, they became bonded labourers who became just prisoners of captivity of powerful people.

I received a telephone call from a senior police officer that his father-in-law or his relative would require help in some labour problem in my district. When the father-in-law met me, he explained that he had a brick kiln in my district. His labourers had fled. All his labourers were poor people who had taken advance money. After questioning, I learnt that they were in captivity for meagre amount of money. This was a new revelation to me, which I had not known before as I was born and brought up in Delhi. I refused to help him as I thought that the system was unethical and morally wrong. There was no act on bonded labour. He thought his case fell under the category of cheating and the police would register a case and put pressure to bring back his captive labourers for running his brick kiln. The Bonded Labour System (Abolition) Act was passed in 1976 with penalty provisions like imprisonment and fine. If the Act were there in mid-sixties, I would have urged the district administration to act.

I always believed that for social and economic engineering, the police should act as an agent of change or else the nation will stagnate or deteriorate into abyss of exploitation and social evils. Even in the absence of specific law, the police should act on the basis of moral and ethical grounds. The second type of unusual request came from an erstwhile Zamindar, who under the UP Land Ceiling Act parceled out his land in the name of his servants or tillers of land while virtually holding such lands under his control. Servants and tillers soon asserted their right and gave no share of their produce to the Zamindar. He too wanted police help to evict them. I again refused to help him in his illegal act.

6

SP UP Vigilance

From Deoria I was posted as SP Vigilance UP in Lucknow. Only corruption cases were investigated there. The Director of Vigilance NS Saxena was known for honesty and integrity. He never knew me before. KL Watts, who was already in the organization, proposed my name. Watts was the only police officer of UP who attended my marriage in Kolkata where he was sent with a PAC contingent. Our bonding remains strong till date.

In the vigilance department, I learnt how corruption cases were required to be investigated. Much time was spent in the investigation, as there was no concept of team investigation and fixed time limit for completion of investigation. The UP Vigilance had no power to initiate a case on its own. The Vigilance could send a detailed report to state government seeking orders for registration of a case. This was possibly done to keep the agency under leash and at the mercy of the state government. Even state government was to be provided with progress reports periodically of each case giving enough scope for leakage of information to the interested parties. Almost all cases ended in departmental action, which in reality meant nothing. A toothless organization without powers can achieve little. I however learnt how the First Information Peport (FIR) was to be drawn up and various provisions of law like the Prevention of Corruption Act.

I do not recall any case where searches or arrests were made. We had many SPs in the organization. There was hardly any worthwhile investigation, which I can recall. Some cases were to find out proper utilization of government funds. I felt frustrated. We expected that the vigilance organization would be vibrant and play active role in weeding out corruption from public life. The director was no match to his brother D Sen, who was a pillar of strength to the CBI.

Social life in Lucknow was dull and boring. Hazratganj was the only shopping area that we used frequently. In popular parlance, this was called Gunjing. Tripuresh Tripathy, IPS, was in the ground floor of our apartment. Once his old gracious mother requested my wife to give her a full grown fish for performing puja. We were amazed that fish could be part of a puja ceremony. She explained that in Eastern UP fish was considered auspicious.

Small towns have fewer opportunities for serious discussions on subjects of importance. There was no concept of think tanks. Club going was beyond us. The local club was dominated by the defence services. The popular shopping area was Hazratganj where officers with wives often used to visit for shopping or window-shopping.

Some of us decided to play rummy in the evenings with our children in our laps. The participants were Prabhat Kumar, Tripuresh Tripathy and some other IAS and IPS officers. Prabhat Kumar retired as the Cabinet Secretary. He was a voracious reader of books and had read the *Autobiography of a Yogi* written by Sri Yogananda. He was so thrilled that he would discuss the subject with others interested in the subject. I escaped from this drudgery when I was selected SP CBI Kolkata by a stroke of luck. At that time, Naxalism rocked Kolkata and West Bengal under leadership of Charu Mazumdar, a man from Siliguri area. No West Bengal officer was available for deputation to centre. Thus, I was selected for this.

7

SP and DIG CBI Kolkata

I was in Kolkata from 1970 to 1980 as SP and thereafter as DIG CBI. This happened, as I have already said, that West Bengal was not in a position to spare officers as the state was facing acute Naxal violence. In Kolkata, traffic constables were being killed while performing their normal duties. When I disembarked at the Howrah railway station and got into car, the driver, a Bengali speaking Bihari, asked me why I decided to opt for a posting when Bengal was burning.

Professionally, it was a rewarding experience for me especially in areas of investigation of acquisition of disproportionate assets and bank frauds. Many, who were searched for possession of disproportionate assets, were found to have kept detailed account of purchase of assets like houses, daily household expenditure etc. That made our investigation easy. Depending upon the status of public servant, the searches would be supervised by an officer of the rank of SP and above. Special care was taken to select two respectable local witnesses as per the requirement of law. All searches, barring a few, were carried out after obtaining search warrants from a competent court. The judges or the magistrates kept all papers in a sealed cover until the searches were complete. I found the judiciary very cooperative in maintaining secrecy. The searches were carried out mostly in the early morning. Only one member would know about the place and persons to be searched. Each team leader would be provided with a briefing note to be read and explained to other members while travelling in a car on the day of search. This secrecy was adopted to avoid possibility of leakage of information to the suspects. Local police were informed only after entry into the residences of the suspects. The founding father of the CBI, the late DP Kholi, laid the foundations of this strong and efficient system. He was the first Director of CBI and remained in the organization for several years.

Disproportionate Assets

A public servant is punished for possessing of disproportionate assets in his service career. This penal offence was introduced in 1964 only as a substantive offence based on recommendation of the Santham Committee Report. Many public servants have been punished by courts or in departmental proceedings for possession of disproportionate assets. The method of calculation of disproportionate assets is very simple and has been tested in courts. A check period is fixed for calculation. Normally, the check period begins from the date of joining the service. At the time of joining the service, a public servant declares his assets. Assets acquired before joining the service are excluded from total assets found at the end of the check period. The total income earned by a public servant consists of his salary, rent obtained from the tenants of his house, bank interests, dividends or other legitimate income. Thereafter, his expenses during the check period are calculated mostly based on documentary evidence. These expenses are deducted from total income. The surplus, thus generated, is available for explaining acquisition of assets. If the value assets exceed the surplus income by a substantial margin, then a case is made out for prosecution or for departmental action. In a sense, there is an attempt to conceal ill-gotten income.

There is an interesting case worth recalling. Every year an officer has to declare his assets movable or immovable. This officer had declared large tracks of land at the time of joining service. The quantum of land held by this officer as found from seized papers was less than the annual declaration made by him.

The searching party was intrigued and asked the officer about this discrepancy. The officer with a straight face said that at the time of joining the service, he had fixed a target for acquisition of land during his service period. Because of the unexpected CBI search, he said he could not achieve the target he had fixed for land acquisition. In services, such declarations are taken as true. Here, he decided to be corrupt before joining the service. This is a unique case of criminal propensity from the very beginning of his life.

I recall another interesting case of a Revenue Service officer who was on the CBI scanner for a long time indulging in corruption. Every year an intelligence file would be opened against him for showing favour by way of duty clearance and he escaped, as the matter was too technical and could be explained away. He used to boast that the CBI would never be able to catch him. I decided to read all the previous files. After deep study, I found that he had a farmhouse away from Kolkata and that was a declared asset. The money spent for acquisition of this farmhouse was very nominal. It did not match with the valuation of our own junior engineer, which was much higher. I called the junior engineer to revisit the farmhouse again and submit a fresh valuation report based on prices of the year of acquisition cautioning him to calculate the value of the farmhouse on a conservative side. His report had shown a discrepancy of nearly thirty thousand rupees. That was a significant amount in the early seventies.

I could locate a CBI circular that authorized the CBI to register a case of disproportionate assets in case of significant discrepancy between the declared value and the actual value of any property. On this basis, the case was registered, as we had no other information on unreported acquisition of any other assets. The only requirement in that circular was that there should be enough evidence against the concerned officer for initiating a regular departmental action for major penalty. The case was registered yielding documents of shares and bank deposits and the like. The officer was ultimately charged for possessing of disproportionate assets. I do not know the outcome of the case.

Assets are mostly hidden. Superficial searches are useless exercise yielding hardly any tangible results for further fruitful investigation. I always held the view that 'nil' recovery in searches is an exercise in futility. Searches require deft handling. In one search I found the suspect officer was very nervous and frequently visited the toilet to smoke as he was a chain smoker.

During his brief absence, I found a blank letterhead pad of a share broker. If he were asked to explain the presence of the blank letterhead pad, he would have explained it by saying that some broker might have left it behind by way of a visiting card.

When the suspect officer came from the toilet, I just asked him how many shares he had with him without disclosing the recovery of the blank letterhead pad. Such a direct question gave him the impression that we had definite information of share holding by him. With a straight face, he admitted of holding of shares of some companies of minimal value. He said as those shares were with his chartered accountant, he would produce them next day, which he did. He did not realize that he had been trapped, as such purchases of shares were not declared to his office.

By way of verification, we wrote to the concerned companies without mentioning share particulars of the shares he had of those companies. The verification result was startling as he had more shares than what he had revealed to us. We realized that the concerned officer was in the habit of bluffing and would require further proof by widening the net by addressing more blue chip companies. Again, the result of this roving investigation yielded more discoveries of shares of the suspect officer. On the basis of product advertisement in a newspaper by a well-known company, a letter was issued to them. The company also gave details of shares held by the suspect officer. For want of staff at one point of time the IO was exhausted, as he was single handedly investigatng the case of this magnitude. IOs in CBI are burdened with verification of complaints, intelligence reports, *pairvi* of cases as IO or holding IO in the absence of the original IO.

Can anyone imagine that discovery of a blueprint of Salt Lake area in Kolkata in a search can lead to discovery of a plot purchased by the suspect officer? There were no documents to show such a purchase of a plot of land by the suspect officer. During the temporary absence of the suspect officer, his wife was asked why they did not construct the house in the Salt Lake area. She being a simple housewife said that the house would be built in future. When the suspect officer appeared, he flatly denied any such plot. He was then told that his wife admitted having such a plot of land. He sarcastically said that she might have purchased the plot of which he was not aware. It took months to locate the plot of land by examining all the documents of the Salt Lake area. No clue should be left out during the searches. I always used to tell young officers in the CBI that an investigating officer should develop a third eye and sixth sense while conducting searches.

Voluntary Disclosure Scheme

I knew about the scheme from newspapers. The reality of the generation of black money came to my notice by way of an incident that is worth recalling. We received a tip-off that a particular branch of a bank had issued fixed deposits receipts in the name of fictitious persons reportedly owned by a public servant. All the fixed deposits were checked. Some were found in the name of fictitious persons, mostly in the name of women. We had no other alternative but to write to the bank not to release the fixed deposit money by way of encashment. None came to claim the ownership of those fixed deposits for a year or so. Subsequently we received a written communication from the Income Tax that the actual person holding those fixed deposits had filed an application under the Voluntary Disclosure Scheme of 1975. The tax authorities checked the genuineness of the person. We had to allow the encashment. He was not a public servant as we had initially thought.

In all, four VDS were tried out, one in 1951, two in 1965 and one in 1975. These schemes were an attempt to induce the tax evaders to declare their concealed income or wealth by way of taxation at concessional rates and immunity from penalty and prosecution. In the first three schemes, the disclosed amount was only Rs 267 crore. Total tax realization under these schemes was only Rs 61 crore. Under the 1975 VDS income tax realization was Rs 241 crore and wealth tax realization was Rs 8 crore. This better realization may be because the country was under emergency.

Bribe money is partly consumed and partly held in the form of black money. All the studies on black money, starting from Prof Kaldor to Prof Chelliah, did not include bribe money in the estimation of black money on the ground 'such inter-individual bribes do not swell the total of gross personal income—that an income should be counted only once and not twice over as bribe received by the recipient was already taxed in the hands of donor'. This is not at all true as bribe is paid out of black or tax evaded income. The fact of the matter is that bribe income is a significant component of black money. This task of calculation of generation of bribe money or money derived from crime can be well performed by a unit of the Central Statistical Organization annually by sample checking and inputs provided by all anti-corruption agencies based on cases registered by them.

Black income and black wealth follow the concept of stock and flow theory where black wealth in the form of assets are to be considered as stock and black income by way of bribe or fraud is the flow of annual generation of black money. For dealing with these problems, as explained earlier, anti-corruption agencies have adopted legally tested method of calculation of black wealth by taking into account of durable assets and extravagant lifestyle expenditure. I found that Income Tax department does not adopt the same method of calculation of concealed income in the way the CBI does. My question is, why the Income Tax department should not adopt this method to calculate concealed income, which is a severe offence under the Income Tax Law. Earlier, for concealment of income over one lakh of rupees, attracted the punishment of seven years rigorous imprisonment. Strangely, this well-tested legal method is not adopted for those who do not fall under the category public servants. Only receipts not reflected in tax returns are considered as concealed income. The logic of this argument has not convinced me so far. How a family owning a big house, four cars, spending fabulous amount of money on education of children, spending huge money on electricity should not be caught in the tax-net same way as is done in the case of a public servant for possession of disproportionate assets. This has never been discussed by politicians or by economic experts dealing with tax evasion or tax avoidance. If the government is determined to clean up the system, the approach to this problem has to change. This, I agree, might make the government unpopular. Only thing that is likely to happen in future is that some PILs would be filed by someone for a clear ruling on this subject. Double standards in dealing with the same offence of concealment of income are likely to be brought to the notice of the higher judiciary as discriminatory and unequal.

Demonetization of high value currency

At the initial stage, bribe money is paid in cash and thereafter it is transported and stored again in cash. This is the critical area of giving and taking bribe. As of now, bribe money transactions are in crores of rupees. High value currencies provide a comfortable method of bribe giving and bribe taking. You may recall how high value currency notes were recovered from the residence of a former union minister stacked in pillows. A few crore of rupees can be easily carried in a brief case and handed over to the bribe taker. If the same amount of money is carried in low denominations, the bribe giver will have to carry the money in several trunks attracting everybody's notice. So will be the case of bribe taker. In several raids and searches by agencies, the recoveries were in high value currencies. As for storing the low value currencies, the bribe taker would require time to convert the bribe money into durable assets or purchasing high value items of luxury. His entire house will be used to store that kind of money. In that situation, nothing will remain secret.

There is a strong public pressure to demonetize high-value currencies like Rs 1000 and Rs 500. This is also necessary as the ISI of Pakistan through land and air routes is pumping fake Indian currencies of high-value into the country. Indian fake currencies are being used for terrorist funds. In developed countries, high cash transactions are minimal. In the USA the highest note denomination is $100, and in UK, the same is 50 pounds only. In 1978, the high value currency of the face value of Rs1000, Rs 5000 and Rs 10,000 were demonetized. To the best of my knowledge, the experiment was successful. The bulk of these high value currencies were not converted into low value currencies as many would have been caught for possession of illegal money. There was no visible destructive effect on the economy. If such steps are taken now, the purchasing power of the rich and the well-to-do will come down and there will be immediate effect on inflation. The parallel functioning of the organized black money lending system will be highly dented and RBI's credit policy will have effect on stock holding of finished goods and raw materials as businessmen would prefer obtaining loans from banks against holding of stocks of raw materials and finished goods.

Howrah station car parking scandal

By way of digression, I feel that I must narrate a true story of corruption at Howrah railway station. People could take their cars inside the platform area after paying an entry fee of Rs 5. In those days, Rs 5 carried a high purchasing power. I took my private second-hand car and paid the required amount to the man managing the booth. I was given a half ticket on which the person managing the booth noted my car number. When I reached the platform, I was told that train was late by two hours. I felt sorry for my wife and children for their late arrival. I had enough time to go around and found that every car owner was given half ticket. That baffled me and I entered the booth to find out why this was being done. The booth man had a ready answer. He said that the man in charge of the entry gate had not arrived and he was doing his job by issuing half tickets retaining the other half ticket on his behalf. The answer was logical and I was initially convinced. I paused for a minute or so and then asked him to show me the other half ticket. He enacted a drama of searching my other half ticket. That could not be found. Then I asked him to show me the closing ticket number of the previous date. The man was taken aback. He realized that my knowledge of the working of the railways was profound. He touched my feet for mercy not knowing who I was. The fact was that the half ticket issued to me was sold previous day. Therefore, this was a clear case of fraud. All these activities in the booth were then known to many people. I had no option but to call CBI officers many of them had come to office in the early morning for a raid. The clinching evidence was the booth man's own handwriting on the half ticket given to me against my vehicle number. Later, I heard that the practice of writing the vehicle number was given up perhaps to help the evil practice to continue. This is a classic example of looting from within. Many readers may perhaps recall how they too were paying Howrah station parking fees without realizing that money was going into the pockets of individuals. I was wondering how this could happen right in front of the station master's office and his staff. This small area of corruption was perhaps yielding thousands of rupees everyday. Someone told me that Lal Bhadur Shastri had once said that if there were no corruption in Railways, the railway tracks could have been converted into golden tracks.

Berth Reservation

Berth reservation was another area where people at large were greatly affected. The organized racketeers were involved in bulk booking of seats in fictitious names. Agents sold such tickets to people at high premium. There was a system of joint checking of tickets by CBI and Railway staff when the train left the Howrah or Sealdah station. The children were travelling holding adult tickets. When asked by someone they, out of nervousness, gave their real names. For safety of their luggage, some paste their genuine names on their luggage. All those people were dealt with as per railway rules. Ticket holders sometime noticed genuine mistakes. I wish to narrate a true but an embarrassing case that happened with a CBI legal officer.

Avtar Singh, Deputy Legal Advisor of CBI posted in Delhi, came to Kolkata for appearance in a court case. He requested Inspector Subhas Bose to purchase his return journey ticket for Delhi. Subhas gave the money to a constable. The constable purchased the ticket in the name of Subhas. Subhas in a hurry handed over the ticket to Avtar Singh. When the Ticket Checker asked his name, Avtar Singh gave out his real name. The ticket checker hauled him up for travelling under a false name. He was handed over to GRP and Avtar Singh landed up in the GRP lock up. When DIG CBI Lahiri came to know about the incident, he settled the matter with the railway authorities. After all, it was a genuine mistake. Avtar Singh, a tall bearded Sikh, was honest to core. He was a respected lawyer with vast legal knowledge. Out of this small experience two lessons can be learnt.

When a task is assigned to a subordinate, the officer concerned should brief the subordinate and ask him to repeat the instructions. After completion of the task, the officer concerned should obtain debriefing from the subordinate. This is well practised in Defence Services. This practice is relevant to civil services also but is rarely followed as this simple procedure is not a part of training.

The second lesson is that as far as possible instructions should be in writing. This was well practised in CBI. In today's parlance, this is called transparency. Every instruction in CBI was in writing. This gives confidence to subordinates in conducting their work. I have noticed that some tricky officers blame the superior officers for doing wrong because of oral instructions.

Avtar Singh's case is a real time anecdote. Such funny jokes and anecdotes are in plenty in every service. Such interesting anecdotes were compiled by ITBP [Indo Tibetan Border Police] in 1993 under the guidance of my batchmate RK Wadehra in the form of a small book. I am tempted to recall a wireless miscommunication. The original message was; COMMANDANT BHATTACHARYAJI REACHING DEHRADUN RAILWAY STATION, REQUEST TPT. TPT means transport. At the receiving end the message was read as' 'BUTTER, ACHAR, CHI REACHING DEHRADUN, REQUEST TPT'. Bhattacharya on reaching Dehradun station found a three-tonner truck instead of a car.

Master File

When I became Additional Director CBI, someone well versed with office management gave a suggestion that as a senior officer

I should maintain a Master File to keep copies of letters and file noting for easy retrieval of files from the office. I followed the advice with immense benefit. The master file remained in my custody. It came to my rescue when someone claimed to prove that I did not issue a particular instruction. His trick was exposed by locating my instructions from the master file. In CBI and may be in other offices there is a tendency to open part files for dealing with a particular matter concerning a case. These small part files may remain untraced and only the master file can easily locate the part file number. The only precaution to be taken is that the master file should be handed over to the successor. In addition, the officer should not retain copies of the master file in his personal custody.

Bank Frauds

At a time 'Kite flying' in bill purchase facilities in the banking system was rampant. The banks were nationalized in 1969. By early 70s, bank frauds surfaced in the nationalized banks in a big way. The bill purchase facility was the easiest way to induce the banks to part with their money. What was needed was to open a couple of fictitious accounts and raising bills against each other for supply of goods. There was no system to obtain identification documents for proper identification of account holders. Mere introduction was considered good enough proof of the identity of account holders. Most of the introducers took the stand that they just signed on the request of people whom they had never met earlier. This enabled many to escape the clutches of law, as they remained untraceable.

The most important kite flying case registered by the CBI Kolkata was of the Central Bank. The fraud was to the tune of around Rs 60 lakh, quite a big amount in the early seventies. A certain group under the control of Chandrana committed the fraud. Under the bill purchase scheme these group of firms raised bills against each other for supply of goods. Such bills would be sent to local branch of the bank for realization. The fraud could continue if payments were made as there was arrangement to provide three months for settlement. After a good length of time, there was stoppage of payments to the bank. A smart group of bank inspection team detected the fraud. Not all the entities existed.

The same group also obtained loans against stocks of raw materials under lock and key arrangement. That means that the stock of goods, finished or raw materials, can move in or out under the supervision of bank officer. The finished or raw materials were nothing but cow dungs, ashes or plain water as chemicals.

After a week or so, the press reported the story in a big way. There was uproar in the Parliament and a Call Attention Motion was tabled. As the Government was kept informed by the CBI head office there was no difficulty to give answers. The accused bank manager was arrested, but could secure bail from the high court. Thereafter, the principal accused Chandrana, who was evading arrest, ultimately surrendered. The investigators carried out his custodial interrogation.

Chandrana made an unusual request to meet the SP. Initially I was hesitant meeting such a person, but he made repeated requests. I agreed to meet him. What he told me was amazing. He did not plead for mercy or weakening of the case. He wanted to narrate his story of going underground for a good length of time. Firstly, he tried to find if the IO could be purchased. He found the CBI inspector was beyond such temptations. Then he tried to find out if SP could likewise be influenced. This too was a futile exercise. Thereafter, he met a lady saint living near Birla Jute Mill. The lady saint told him that he had no option but to surrender. What he wanted to convey was that CBI was a corruption free organization and he almost appreciated the honest duty it performed.

In a biennial conference organized by CBI in 1972, I proposed that all bank account holders must provide photographs as part of documents to banks for opening of bank accounts of any type. This was because in many bank frauds the account holders could not be traced as they provided fictitious names with false addresses. My concern for bank frauds in nationalized banks happening in future did evoke adverse comments on the ground that banks were not police offices, but were in business to earn profit. After more than 30/35 years now, no bank account can be opened without photograph of the account holder. The gestation period between an idea and its implementation is too long in our country. This happens, as new innovative ideas are never encouraged by the older generation. There should be a system to reward implementable ideas in the system of governance. Much has changed now with the introduction of computer. Data collection has become easier. There is now a great possibility of cross analysis of data for spotting persons who indulge in various malpractices or even crimes. The integrated system of data collection is yet to be evolved as a tool for good governance for prevention of crime, detection of crime, spotting targets for surveillance, tax evasion or avoidance and the like.

Telephone Exchange Trunk Call Fraud

Our head office in Delhi informed the Kolkata branch that too many complaints were being received in trunk call billings. We knew that anybody's telephone in those days could be used to book long distance or international call. This used to happen with the connivance of staff that used to tamper with the telephone junction boxes. When a telephone line is not used especially at night, the same could be connected to another person's line on regular monthly fixed consideration. I know of a person's telephone bill contained a call to Australia when he had no friends or relatives there. We decided to find if more could be done in this area of corruption. At that time Charlu was the vigilance officer of Kolkata Telephone Exchange. He was a technical man who knew his job well.

After deliberation, he suggested a novel method of checking false billing in area of long distance calls. All calls originating from district exchanges for long distance calls outside West Bengal will be routed through Kolkata Telephone Exchange. The originating telephone exchange would prepare a call record card for the purposes of billing the customer. Kolkata Exchange would prepare a transit call card for purposes of record only.

Charlu suggested that we should first collect some transit call records from Kolkata Exchange and compare them with the district call records. We never expected a startling discovery of a virgin area of corruption. Long distance calls recorded in Kolkata transit records were shown in the district exchanges as local or short distance calls. For example, call from Siliguri to Mumbai was shown as a call from Siliguri to Kolkata or a local call. A series of cases were registered. There was loss of revenue and gain mainly to businessmen and telephone staff. This was happening for years without being detected by the entire system of internal or external audit.

We soon realized that in case of shortfall in the registration of cases, we just tapped this virgin area for registration of cases. Based on our experience we submitted a note to the head office for the benefit of all the CBI branches.

False Medical Reimbursement Claims

In seventies, there was a scheme for the central government employees for reimbursement of money spent for the treatment of employees or their dependants. Private doctors were empanelled to prescribe medicines after examining the patient for which they charged consultation fees from the patients. It was a progressive scheme that benefited the genuine patients.

Soon the scheme was subverted by employees by submitting false medical claims as genuine claims. There was a steady rise of expenditure under this head. Everyone knew that many false cases were entertained and payments were made. Many departments made complaints to CBI for investigation. The investigations led us nowhere. The doctors certified their prescriptions, the chemist shops certified sale of medicines. In some cases, the patient suffering from serious ailments was found attending schools and the like.

I deliberated on the issue with some officers of the affected departments. We hit upon an idea to find out the names of some doctors who were earning substantial amount of money by way of consultation fees. The list of some 20/30 doctors was circulated to some departments to report the consultation fees paid to such selected doctors in two financial years to coincide with Income Tax assessment years. The result was startling as many of them earned fabulous money by way of consultation fees. A constable working with me compiled manually total earnings of each doctor. The computer could have done this job more quickly and perhaps we could then have covered more departments.

The consolidated list was sent to Income Tax Commissioner to report if such earnings of these doctors were reflected in their Tax Returns. It took time for income tax department to locate individual return files of these doctors. After a series of reminders for early reply, we did receive reports, bit by bit, that the earnings were not reflected in their tax returns. Thereafter, we pressed for total realization of tax due from such doctors and penalty imposed on them for concealment of income, which is a serious offence under the Income Tax Act. Recoveries from such doctor were substantial. We felt satisfied as only my constable and I were involved in the entire exercise. I cannot recall the name of the constable, may be Tapash, who eventually became an Inspector by dint of his merit.

The lesson from this experience was that a big exercise was possible with no extra workforce. It is very easy to detect cases of evasion of income tax or excise duties if we just apply innovative methods of investigation. Such more cases would be discussed when I joined the Central Economic Intelligence Bureau in Delhi.

Management Information System (MIS)

My understanding of Management Information System (MIS) was evolved out of demand for instant information by CBI's head office. After taking charge as SP CBI for a fortnight, MP Singh, then joint director visited Kolkata for inspection. DIG Lahari left the office along with John Lobo, DIG from Delhi for some urgent work. I was facing an officer who would ask questions on each pending case. After all, I had no time to review each case in-depth. After answering a few questions, I pleaded my inability to answer all queries thrown at me. I decided to take a tough stand telling him that he should give me time for in-depth study of cases. Then, I just told him to send me back to UP. My next salvo was decisive. I asked him whether he was aware of my problem of getting a government accommodation that was readily available in UP. Private accommodation was out of question as no property owner was willing to rent out an accommodation to a police officer who was the target of attack during the Naxal period in Kolkata and West Bengal. This posture of mine brought down his tone and temper. He became very friendly. I subsequently learnt that his nick name in Bihar was Danda (stick) Singh. Thereafter, I was keen to develop a system for prompt reply. I also learnt that most powerful officer next to Director would ask the newcomers in CBI if they could mention the oldest item in the malkhana. Not a single officer could answer such difficult questions.

In management, the critical areas are to speed up functioning at all levels and bring to light slow movements of non-moving and sticky items. It is similar to management of inventories in a factory. Our police management system should take care of non-moving or sticky areas. They in CBI are:

1. Investigation of regular cases
2. Pending enquiries of complaints
3. Pending intelligence reports
4. Pending court cases
5. Pending malkhana items

These areas of work are required to be speeded up by chasing sticky and non-moving items. Therefore, all those dealing with these subjects from respective desks (mainly clerical) would provide inputs to my steno who would prepare a consolidated report fortnightly. The requirement was that only ten oldest items are required to be shown. The reasons for delay were also mentioned. For a few months, I would issue my observations on sticky and non-moving items to the concerned officers. As a result, there was awareness to speed up the oldest items so that they do not appear again. These reports became a self-correcting mechanism. The results of introduction of this system were impressive. Pending items moved fast. My own awareness improved and I could inform HQs promptly if there were enquiries. When I became DIG CBI Kolkata, I introduced the same system for EOW branch also. The same system was introduced by me in UP as DIG Jhansi in all the five districts. From MIS I could locate a car lying in a police station in Laitpur, a disrict in UP, for more than a decade. I saw the car myself. The police failed to find out the owner of the car. I told the SP to write to Hindustan Motors giving them the engine and the chassis numbers of the car. Soon the reply came from the Hindustan Motors giving me the name of the dealer. The dealer on being approached provided the name and address of the owner of the car. He was not found at the given address, as he had become a *sadhu* staying in Vrindavan. He was contacted in Vrindavan. He was totally surprised to know of recovery of his car. He rushed to Lalitpur and identified his car. He was simply surprised by the efficiency of the police and thanked each member of the police station staff for his wonderful work. As he had renounced the earthly world, he did not take possession of ramshackle car.

8

A Brief History of CBI

When I became joint director of CBI I introduced a management system to speed up the functioning in all areas within my jurisdiction. The system, I was told, was adopted by Bedi also in UP with some modifications. However, the tragedy is that any innovation is resisted and discarded after departure of the officer. It was never institutionalized. A proper management system is a sound concept for good governance. Speed has to be maintained along with good delivery system which was lacking in our system from the colonial period whose only priority was maintenance of law and order.

The reason for non-inclusion of MIS was that the CBI manual does not provide for this. The CBI manual is well drafted to cater for strict supervision of all activities of CBI. This was the gift of Late DP Kohli who had vast experience of UP CID. UP CID was very efficient and solved many complicated cases. CBI's origin can be traced back to 1941 when the government realized that unscrupulous persons were milking money out of purchase of war materials, which included many items required by defence services. The government, in its wisdom, created by an executive order the Special Police Establishment (SPE) with its HQ in Lahore. The first officer to head this organization was Qurban Ali Khan, a Pathan, who was then a DIG. I could get this information from the National Archives, New Delhi.

The Delhi Special Police Establishment Act was executed in 1946 by British Government to look into the charges of corruption in defence services. Slowly the economic and some of other offences were included within its ambit. After independence, it was renamed as Central Bureau of Investigation (CBI) under a resolution in 1963. It remained dependent upon DSPE Act, as all its powers emanated from that Act only. Simultaneously, it was made more broad based and the scope of cases that the CBI could take up, was widened. Every case is required to be registered under the written orders of SP in certain category of cases, DIG in respect of certain higher rank of officers and Director again in category of most important cases. In such a situation, there has to be total application of mind or else he will face an awkward situation in his long career. Let me cite a real case in which home ministry wanted a politician to be booked under TADA. As usual on verification, it was found to be otherwise. The Governor of Punjab with his legal knowledge ultimately agreed with the CBI and the case was not registered. There were many other cases which CBI did not register even when those cases came from state governments. No case of terrorism could be registered in CBI without the orders of the Director.

CBI's inbuilt system of checks and balances

During investigation, case diaries are written by the IO with details of investigation he does on each day. It is a time consuming process, but necessary to avoid future manipulations. A copy of the case diary is received by the SP who is required to read it and give his comments to be communicated to the IO. I met SP GOW and Santunu Sen as SP EOW Kolkata who had to carry these case diaries home for study and write our comments on the margin of the case diary itself. Such comments were typed by our stenographers to be delivered to IOs. D Sen as Director of CBI, while visiting a branch, would call for case diaries of any case of his choice only to see if case diaries were promptly submitted by the IOs. That kept us always busy with this important item of work. I still remember that some IOs were always lagging behind. At times, they were kept in office for long hours to ensure submission of case diaries. A DIG or IG or even the

Director inducted in CBI for the first time will take sometime to know the working of CBI. The SP CBI is the most important functionary in CBI. His performance needs to be closely watched by officers who have previous experience of working as SP CBI.

In all cases, progress reports are to be submitted by SP to higher officers giving analysis of the case from the point of view of collection of evidence and what remains to be done. It has to be written personally by SP so that he becomes fully conversant with the case under investigation. Some easy going officers manage to obtain a draft from the IO, which is totally against the spirit of close supervision of a case. A period is fixed for completion of a case. If the cases exceed the time frame, such cases are reported in a statement called 'statement five'. Any visiting officer inspecting the branch will call for the statement five and the SP and DIG will explain reasons for the delay.

After completion of investigation, the IO submits a Final Report 1. The PP of the branch submits a report, called Final Report 2. He is required to critically analyze the case and his recommendation may or may not agree with the recommendation of the IO.

The SP is required to study the case and submit his comments. In minor cases, his orders are final. In other cases, the reports would go to DIG for his opinion and orders. In major cases, all the reports go to head office for final orders. This inbuilt system is designed to ensure highest degree of fair investigation. My Joint Director, Renison used to joke that the Kolkata branch never gave unanimous recommendation creating difficulties for the head office to give final orders. This independence of view was the strength of the CBI.

The story of supervision does not end here. In court cases, the public prosecutor has to submit court diaries to show the progress of trial in court and hostility of witnesses if any. In that event, he recommends calling another witness to prove the fact in question. The SP is required to read the court diaries and to give his comments. Because of close supervision, CBI could achieve higher conviction from courts.

The most difficult are the areas of appeal. I do not wish to discuss, as many may not be interested. The point that I am making is that the system of working in CBI is as perfect as possible. Higher level officers due to lack of knowledge of CBI manual and working can subvert the system if there is non-performance. Thus, CBI needs to be staffed at the higher level by those who had worked as SP and whose performance was impeccable. I have narrated all these only to highlight the crucial part that SP plays in the functioning of the CBI.

Vindictive Officers

There are officers, who by temperament, take sadistic pleasure in spoiling the character roll of their subordinate officers. Some of them genuinely believe that officers should fulfill all the tasks assigned to them. In CBI Kolkata, good officers had good reports but would receive ifs and buts for not collecting intelligence reports, for which no minimum requirement was laid down. When I joined the CBI Kolkata, the officers complained that because of such lukewarm reports they did not earn promotion. I decided that any officer collecting two intelligence reports in a year would not receive adverse reports. That satisfied the officers. Because of good reports, many of them were promoted eventually.

Now, let me narrate another type of vindictive attitude of an officer of the rank of a member of the Central Board of Direct Taxes [CBDT] who inflicted utter humiliation to a very senior officer of Income Tax department. The case is still fresh in my memory. At midnight a high-ranking Income Tax officer attached to Johnson, a member of the Board of Direct Taxes, rang the doorbell of my residence. I woke up from my deep slumber and opened the door. The officer introduced himself and said that he was under instruction of Johnson to get a case registered against one Tiwari for receiving a huge amount of bribe on that very day and that has to be recovered by registration of case and followed by a search in the morning. It was a tall order. The CBI would first require verification of the allegation and a search warrant from a competent court giving adequate reasons for conducting a search. This argument did not impress him. I also told him that in a case of this nature the DIG Kolkata was required to pass orders for registration of a case and a search. He then wanted to meet the DIG who was living in the vicinity.

At that hour of the night, we reached at the flat of the DIG Lahiri and pressed the doorbell. After sometime Lahari opened the door with his wife behind him holding a 'dhaw' to be used in case of danger. The said officer explained the case to him. Observing the adamant attitude of the visiting officer, he told him emphatically that in that situation Johnson would have to give us in writing a complaint taking full responsibility for the correctness of the complaint.

We reached the Nizam Palace where Johnson was staying and learnt that he was enjoying a drink party in a famous hotel in Kolkata. After sometime he came back and I explained that he would have to give a handwritten complaint against Tiwari. The correctness of the allegation would have to be vouched by him. He did likewise and a case was registered. It may be mentioned here that the CBI office always remained operational. I personally called CBI officers living in Kolkata and all of them appeared in no time. Johnson or his officer did not know the address of Tiwari. With great difficulty, his address could be found. I called two well-respected vigilance officers as witnesses. We all used our personal vehicles, as there was no time to call the drivers and the cars.

With fears of uncertain future in our mind, we entered the residence of Tiwari in the early morning as per the practice of the CBI. As soon as we entered the house, we realized that the information was wrong and malicious. Tiwari's style of living was below par of an officer of his stature. Even he used the charpoys and not the wooden beds. There was hardly any furniture in the house. He was an innocent looking man. Nothing was found at his residence. I left the place with a heavy heart and mentally cursed Johnson for inflicting torture to a poor soul for no fault of his.

A day after the incident, the news spread like a wildfire in the Income Tax department. There were demonstrations at Income Tax office with 'murdabad' slogans against Johnson and

'Zindabad' in favour of the CBI. During enquiry the shocking truth came out. A girlfriend of Johnson in Kolkata was acting as an agent for parties or pressuring parties for payment of commission for settlement of their tax cases or the like. She fed Johnson with stories against Tiwari, as he was not acting the way she wanted. Tiwari perhaps knew her relationship with Johnson. He was wise enough to record in writing all the wrong things she wanted him to do. Several files contained such notings, which came to his rescue. The role of Johnson and Kolkata lady became apparent. The case was finalized within no time and report was sent to the Government.

Strangely enough, Johnson was almost selected as the chairman of the CBDT. The *Blitz* magazine published a lead story quoting the CBI's damaging report. That prevented the attempt to promote him. Instead of punishing him, the government was attempting to promote him.

The CBI officers are often under threat by corrupt officers. They have to uphold their standards of integrity or else someone is ready to find out something that would go against the officer. In 1975, my children pressed me to purchase a TV to see some world sport event, may be the Olympics. I had no money to purchase the TV. I obtained a loan of Rs five thousand only from a nationalized bank to be paid in several instalments. The dealer received the cheque from the bank for installation of TV at my residence. After a couple of months, the dealer rang me up to say that some inspectors of the Income Tax department wanted to see the documents of purchase. As my transaction was open and transparent, I told him to show them all the records. The matter ended there. I still believe that some high level officer must have given the clearance for such an enquiry. This possibly happened, as some income tax officers were booked for possession of disproportionate assets to their income.

This is how the Left Front managed to Win Elections

Here, I am making a little digression. I used to travel to Shantiniketan to reach a village for fetching special oil for healing joint pains for my mother. She had read somewhere that such oil was good for joint pains. I used to go to that village by train from Howrah. As these visits were private, nobody knew about such visits. I used to reach that small village by rickshaw from Shantineketan. I have the habit to talk to people to know the ground realities, their problems in life etc. On one such occasion I casually asked the rickshawalah which party he had voted and why. He was frank enough to say that he and others always voted for Left Parties. To my question 'why' he said that, if he did otherwise he would be deprived of his rickshaw and his earnings. He also said that he would be deprived of rations, kerosene and other benefits. This was perhaps how the rural Bengal remained under the grip of the Left Parties.It is equally true that the Left Front introduced land reforms which benefited landless tillers of land. I learnt a new lesson of political mass management. Much later I learnt that there is a book called R Documents, wherein the same technique was also recommended for big corporates to bind all the employees together by a series of leverages to be used to keep the flock together. Rigging and booth capturing are not the only methods to win an election. Higher mass management tools are required for winning an election in rural India. In urban area, a different method is required to keep the intellectuals and opinion builders under perpetual obligation by operating a finely tuned quota system, which works well. All that is required is to allot plots of land, shops etc to such vulnerable people who would otherwise be deprived of a decent life. Most of the Indian political parties have never studied the subject in-depth.

The manner of mass management of diverse elements by the Left Front by a combination of threats, inducements and obligation were so fine-tuned that the Front continued to rule West Bengal for three decades. The cadre was maintained by allowing them to fend for themselves. In Kolkata, for example, they need to be paid by suppliers of building materials and building contractors have to purchase the materials from their suppliers. In rural Bengal, they might have used crude methods to raise money.

9

DIG Kolkata

In 1977, I was promoted as DIG, Kolkata, and was also looking after the Economic Offences wing of the CBI. This area was new to me. I found that most of the cases pertained to violation of export-import rules and regulations. For obtaining import licences, export was one such facility. False exports were shown to obtain import licences. Imported items were in great demand. Small-scale units were entitled to obtain import raw materials. False units managed to procure import licences. All court cases were prolonged. The accused were sentenced 'till rising of the court' and a small fine, which the accused happily payed. For CBI it was a conviction and for the accused a great relief.

MCBI had great reputation for integrity. Once I was in the EOW office at around 9 am. I received a call from a person who was running a small business in central Kolkata. He enquired if CBI had ordered a search of his office. I said no, as any search could not be conducted without the knowledge of the DIG. I requested the caller to keep the man posing as a CBI official engaged. Soon CBI officers arrested the man and brought him to office along with the complainant. I talked to the complainant to find out how he suspected the man. What he said was very interesting. He knew that no CBI officer would even accept soft drinks during searches. This impostor was consuming soft drinks at the cost of the complainant and that aroused doubts in his mind. Such was the reputation of CBI in the minds of the public.

Fake CBI officers

There was a case of an impostor who would stay in the house of the father of a girl for marriage negotiations. He picked up such targets from newspaper advertisements. He used to stay in the house for a good length of time enjoying lavish food. He would raise the confidence of the father of the girl by means abusing lying that DIG CBI as his nephew and the police commissioner as a close relative. Whenever he was absent from the house, calls would be received and caller introduced himself as DIG CBI or the police commissioner, Kolkata. This initially raised the bonafide of the cheat. At the time of his departure to far away places like Delhi or Mumbai he would request for train expenses and the like. In this way, he had cheated many who were genuinely trying to get their daughters married to respectable grooms from respectable families. One day I received a telephone call from the father of a girl inquiring if I had such a nephew. I said that my nephews were school-going children. Then he told me all that had happened. I requested to bring him for confrontation. The impostor looked much older than me, and persisted that he was my nephew. It was useless to argue with him. I picked up the phone to call the Director of the the Fingerprint Bureau and asked the cheat to reveal his real name or else I would send his fingerprints to check his antecedents. Realising that his game was up, he promptly gave out his fingerprint number. He confessed that he had been in this business for years and was caught several times before. The case was handed over to the local police. I secretly asked the father of the girl what raised his suspicion about this man. He told me that so-called telephone calls emanating from DIG's or Commissioner's office would come whenever he was absent from the house. He was wondering why no such calls were ever received when he was present in the house.

Before the Durga puja and the New Year, a number of impostors used to carry out fake searches and swindled money from small business people. A businessperson from Chetla informed us that the CBI was harassing him and threatening him with a raid on a particular day. The CBI decided to catch the culprits in a trap. The genuine CBI officers took position in a nearby house. Lo and behold, the impostors came in private vehicles posing as inspectors and constables of CBI and entered the residence of the person concerned. The genuine CBI officers then entered the house to confront the impostors. Each party was calling the other fake. Since it was an early morning raid, the early morning walkers took notice of this drama and were genuinely confused. The CBI called the local police and as a result, the impostors were arrested.

The CBI Kolkata started releasing press notes alerting people not to allow any such search in their premises as CBI searches were backed up with warrants of search. Despite this, small business people paid money to impostors. One of them told me that even knowing them to be impostors, he felt safe to handover some money by way of safety and peace of mind.

Political Interference

Some CBI officials are susceptible to corruption. Such cases used to be dealt with promptly and drastically. No compromises were made by any senior officer. Many CBI officers were charge-sheeted in courts or faced departmental action. This is unique, as it is not usually found in any other organization. This strictness should continue as it is in tune with the CBI motto i.e. impartiality, industry and integrity.

On political interference, there were clear instructions. In the event of meeting a politician or receiving a telephone call from them the officer concerned was required to report to the head office with details. One day, I received a call from Joytirmoy Basu, who was a powerful politician of the Communist Party, asking me to meet a public sector official. The official rang me and wanted to meet me at my residence. I told him that I would meet him in my office. I suspect this man must have spoken to

Basu and complained against me. Basu rang me up to know why I wanted to meet him in office only. I told him that it was the CBI tradition not to meet complainants or informers at residence for reasons of transparency and to avoid public gaze. This apparently did not satisfy him. Perhaps he took it as an insult. I immediately brought this incident to the notice of the Director, CBI. Basu then complained against me to the Prime Minister Morarji Desai. The PM took up the matter with the Director who explained the long held tradition of the CBI. The PM was satisfied. The concerned public sector officer threatened that I would have to face music. For a day or two, I was disturbed. Thereafter, I was given the impression that Basu made detailed enquires about me and perhaps that satisfied him. The matter ended there. I wonder if this tradition is being followed now. None was allowed to meet a minister unless authorized by the head office.

AG Office fraud

Before I end this chapter, I must narrate an interesting case of swindling government money for years without being caught. A low ranking official in the office of AG West Bengal used to introduce a bill in the name of a fictitious firm for supply of items like tents to central police organizations based in West Bengal. The unit concerned was not aware of it. The bill would be around Rs one lakh or so. The cheques used to be collected by the AG official by signing the cheque receipt register in bogus name. This could have been detected at the time of reconciliation. Strangely, the concerned official never showed this amount at the time of reconciliation statement. The case was detected by chance as the concerned official was absent. During this period the reconciliation statement showed the discrepancy. AG office took serious notice of this fraud, suspected that it was the work of an insider. A senior AG officer brought all the records to us to find out who could be the possible culprit. After cross-analysis of records the name of a possible suspect surfaced although there was no oral or documentary evidence against him to nail him. The CBI decided to check his residence and within an hour or two the officer came back to report that the concerned official, perhaps of the level of a clerk owned a big house, a car and a good lifestyle. There were no declared assets of this official. Thus, we found enough grounds for registration of a case against the concerned low level official.

The AG office had already found out the name of the branch of the bank where the cheque was deposited. Wisely, they did not request the bank for details of the statement of accounts. The bank was in south Kolkata miles away from the residence of the suspected official. The official anticipated a raid, as documents of the fictitious firm were not found in the first round of search. The clerk stoutly claimed that he was not connected with the bogus firm. Unfortunately, one letterhead of the bogus firm was recovered from one corner of the house of the clerk. He knew that his game was up.

When his fictitious account in south Kolkata was scrutinized, it was observed that such big amount cheques were regularly deposited, may be for a period of ten or fifteen years. The dimension of the fraud became serious and mind-boggling. Oral evidence was available from the bank staff that he was operating the account. However, CBI was required to prove his handwriting on cheques and pay-in-slips. The handwritings did not match with his admitted handwriting as found in the AG office. The style of writing was very different.

The investigating officer brought the suspect official before me. I had only one trump card to extract his admission. I proposed that I would call his wife for her specimen writings as the writings in bank documents were that of a lady. That made him nervous and begged that she should not be called. He agreed to write the way he did in the bank. He wrote a specimen writing to prove the point. The investigating officer called two witnesses and in their presence his specimen writings were obtained. He explained that over the years he developed a different style of writing for operating the bank account where cheques were deposited.

10

The Central Fingerprint Bureau

The Central Fingerprint Bureau [CFPB] was located in Kolkata. Previously, it was under the control of the Intelligence Bureau and subsequently came under the charge of the CBI. The supervisory officer was the Deputy Director [DD] of CBI's Coordination Wing in Delhi. In the late seventies, the officers of the CFPB stopped working almost like an unofficial strike. The DD could not handle the situation as they refused to talk to him in his room. I was told to visit the CFPB office to restore normalcy or else there will be lockout, a step too drastic for a state like West Bengal.

When I entered the office, I found the Bureau officers in a room and they refused to move out to meet anyone of us in the room of the Director. I realized that there was an ego problem from both sides. I decided to meet them unannounced in their room. This was a surprise to them, as they never imagined that officer of my rank would meet them in this manner. Some of them refused to speak, but the majority snubbed them, saying that I had taken the initiative to do something positive. I heard them patiently for a good length of time. Their major grievance was simple. There was acute stagnancy and for years, there were no promotions from the rank of sub-inspector to inspector. There were more posts of sub-inspectors and only a few of inspectors. I immediately realized that ratio has to be changed to provide free flow of promotion.

The cease-to-work situation was called off. I explained the situation in a report to Director with a proposal to create more posts of inspectors by keeping some posts of sub-inspectors in abeyance. This was done to avoid rejection of the proposal on the ground of economy by the ministry of finance, as it happens when any demand is made for increase of staff strength. Eventually, this happened as PC Sharma chased the file from desk to desk in the various departments. Sharma was then wearing custom-built cane hat that he does even now. He took fancy to the hat while he was a probationer in Assam. He retired as Director CBI and presently is a member of the Human Rights Commission.

The officers of the CFPB, independent of their ranks, were highly educated and qualified. Matching fingerprints was a mechanical job. I thought some of them could be encouraged to take up some innovative work. I had read an article written by Prof. Astrom, perhaps in the *Time* magazine, focusing on research on migration in Europe on the basis of fingerprint science. I wrote to him to know how the same could be done in India. Due to his suggestions and our own understanding, we decided to work on two areas of interest.

One such area was to find out if fingerprints were found from the excavations in Lothal and other areas. Promptly, a reply came from Dr Rao that plenty of such prints were available, gave us some copies of such prints and wanted to know why we need them. We informed him that such prints were useful to find out if they were used for transnational trade purposes. Dr Rao wrote a few articles on the subject in the newspapers. I do not think he could find out if such fingerprinted seals could be recovered from India's trade partner countries. I have since found out that legible fingerprint marks are still available on the mummies in Egypt. Fingerprints were used on the potteries and seals thousands of years ago in Egypt, Syria, and China and are still available in museums. This virgin area is open for researchers to do some work on the subject. It has so far not been explained why such seals with clear fingerprints were created. Even objects like potteries bear clear fingerprints at the bottom, maybe by way of identification of creators of such objects. Now the time has come to find out if some of the ancient fingerprints found from excavations in India can be matched with those available in other countries.

The second area of interest was to find if there were some differences between North and South Indian fingerprints. Dikshitlu, our research officer, tentatively concluded that gaps between the ridges differ. The work ended there, as this research project did not receive the approval of higher authorities.

The Fingerprint Bureau is a depository of conviction slips with the fingerprints of convicted persons. Therefore, the states play a major role in building up of data bank of convicted persons. If the states fail to send the fingerprints, the central depository cannot reflect the ground reality. Bihar, for example, was sending only three or four conviction slips a year. Did it show that there were no convictions in Bihar? Many states failed to transmit the conviction slips fully. This reflected the state of affairs in the districts. The whole purpose of building up a data bank of convicted fingerprints is thus defeated.

The fingerprints of arrested suspects received for comparison with the previous records were destroyed as per the Identification of Prisoners Act, on the basis of which the Bureau functioned. This lacuna was supposed to be plugged by an amendment.

I gradually learnt how valuable it was to go in for mass identification programme. I was so enthusiastic that I wrote an article, which was published by the *Statesman*, the editor of which was then an Englishman. B N Mullick, former Director of IB who was then looking after the Bureau, had a vision to include fingerprints of Army deserters, and Tibetan refugees. All these ideas were given up for reasons best known to authorities. My feeling was that this Bureau was the most neglected unit of the government. In India's National Security Annual Review of 2002 I advocated 'a strategy for mass identification programme with interface with all computer systems holding fingerprint records'. Thankfully, this is happening by introduction of Unique Identification Document. I hope the unique identification card will contain fingerprints, as this alone can conclusively prove the identity of a person.

Chopra children murder case

Application of fingerprint science played a significant role in solving the famous Chopra children murder case. Captain Madan Mohan Chopra of the Indian Navy, then residing in Delhi, had a daughter Geeta, 16, and a son Sanjay, 14; they were bright students in college and school respectively. On 26 August 1978, they left home at 6.15 pm to proceed to All India Radio where Geeta was to act in a programme and Sanjay was to participate as a guest. Father was to pick them up from All India Radio at 9 pm. On reaching AIR Chopra did not find the children. He found out that Geeta and Sanjay had never reached AIR. As a worried father, he rang up relatives, wife and friends of the two children with no relief to him. He informed the Police Control Room at 10.15 pm about his missing children. He came to his residence at about 11.30 p.m.

In the intervening period, one Bhagwan Das saw a mustard coloured car near the Yoga Ashram at Gol Dakhana with two children struggling with two men in the front seat. The car sped away before he could intervene. He reported to the Police Control Room at about 6.44 pm. Inderjeet Singh, a Delhi Development Authority Officer, riding on a scooter saw a car overtaking his scooter near Ram Manohar Lohia hospital. He too saw two children struggling with two men in the front seat of the car. He chased the car, but failed to catch them because of the red light signal. He, however, saw the car speeding towards the Shanker Road, a road leading to Buddha Jayanti Park. The children were crying for help. Inderjeet reported the incident to Police Station, Rajender Nagar at about 6.45 pm.

Strange are the ways of real life. One Vinod was brought to Ram Manohar Lohia hospital by a person for treatment of his head injury. His head was X-rayed. As it was a medico-legal case of injury caused by some persons as reported by Vinod, his fingerprints were also kept on record. He was refused admission to hospital, promised the police that he would come back on the next day in the morning. He never reappeared. The addresses given by him and his companion were found to be bogus.

Next day, that was on 27 August 1978 one Dhani Ram saw two dead bodies of a girl and a boy in the jungles of the ridge area and he reported the matter to a police patrolling party of Rajender Nagar Police Station. Rajender Nagar police informed Capt. Chopra and he identified the bodies of his children. As expected, the press rightly played up the matter in a big way blaming the police for inefficiency. From Mumbai came the news that Billa and Ranga might have committed this crime as they reportedly murdered two Arabs.

On the day of kidnapping i.e. 26 August 1978, the government introduced in Parliament a Delhi Police Bill for establishment of the Police Commissioner System in Delhi on the basis of recommendations of the Khosla Commission Report. It was passed without much of debate. JN Chaturvedi became the first Police Commisioner of Delhi. Both the houses of Parliament were rocked by Chopra Children Murder case. The minister of state SD Patel made a statement in the Rajya Sabha saying that the police had made all efforts to alert all static and mobile police posts. A member made a caustic remark that the police medals be given to them. Matter became heated when the minister said that it was of no use philosophizing or giving a sermon. Immediately after this there was heated reaction from the opposition benches that the minister should withdraw his remarks and apologize. The minister made the matter worse when he said that the people get from the police what they deserve. There was demand for suspension of police officers for lack of action despite receving inputs from the public. Some members even mentioned that this crime had happened the day the Police Commissioner system was introduced in Delhi.

On 31 August 1978, the car used in the crime was found abandoned by the residents of Majlis Apartments who reported the matter to the police. Asoke Sharma the real owner of the car identified his stolen car and handed over the keys of the car to police. This was a breakthrough, which was necessary to link the criminals with the crime. I as a police officer in CBI in Kolkata was upset and decided to help the Delhi Police by sending one of our experts without receiving any request from Delhi Police.

This was done in other cases also which would be narrated elsewhere.

Dr DN Das was a seasoned fingerprint expert. He had developed a unique herbal powder to lift latent fingerprints from surfaces of all kinds. The herbal powder was more effective than the conventional powders. He never shared his formula with others, as he wanted to patent it first, may be because of earning some extra money. This was legitimate as otherwise the other experts would patent it in their name. That was why he never gave the herbal powder to anyone for field application. His powder was called D-3.

I realized that the fingerprints would play a big role in identification of the accused persons. The car they used was abandoned. Therefore, the prints lifted from the car would not only identify the accused, but also prove that Chopra children were travelling in the same car. There were no worthwhile witnesses to this dastardly crime. The crime was linked with the criminals.

On his return, Das narrated how he and Central Forensic Lab's experts developed several fingerprints from the car. The fingerprints matched with Blla and Ranga who were apprehended in a dramatic manner by army jawans on 8 September 1978 as the duo forced their entry into their train compartment. They suspected these two as robbers or thieves. One jawan had *Nav Yug* newspaper with him carrying the photographs of Billa and Ranga and they matched with the intruders they had apprehended. Both of them admitted their identity. On 9 September 1978, Billa and Ranga were handed over to GRP Delhi.

The challenging task was to prove that Geeta and Sanjay were in the car. The Police, a mistake that proved costly, did not take the fingerprints of these dead children. As our team members were seasoned experts, they decided to lift latent fingerprints of these children from their books and exercise books. This could be done by Nynhydrin treatment of some of the pages of the book and papers. This chemical treatment would spoil the pages but would bring out the latent fingerprints of the users handling them. It was good luck for the experts to find such fingerprints in plenty for verification of latent fingerprints developed from the car used in the crime. They matched. Thus, it was proved beyond doubt that Geeta and Sanjay were in the car. My observations were made on the basis of what Das had told me. I tried to get a copy of the trial court judgment, but failed.

The question would arise as to how long such latent fingerprints on books and papers would be available for lifting such prints. There are recorded cases of discovery of such latent prints even after forty years. It should be brought to the notice of all police officers. I learnt it by becoming the supervisory officer of CFPB by chance and not by choice.

Many lessons can be learnt from Chopra children murder case. The high court judge at the end of his judgment was 'constrained to observe that the lives of the two children could have been saved if the police had acted promptly.' Non-cooperation by the public is 'a routine excuse'. The police control room acted in routine manner despite receiving several inputs from the public. The dots were never connected. This happens in India as control rooms are not under the control of a senior officer who would direct operations on minute to minute basis. I happened to see Tokyo Police Control Room in the early nineties. CCTVs covered the entire Tokyo city. I was shown a live case of a man stabbing another man. The Control Room had the picture of the accused escaping from street to street and the officer was directing all patrol cars to reach a certain point. Ultimately, police officers from all sides surrounded the suspect. Delhi is yet to be covered by CCTV essentials to track suspects on the run by car or otherwise. Until now control room is not functioning the way it functions in Tokyo. A control room should function as a chasing machine and not as transmission of information and then forget the inputs received from time to time.

The sessions court sentenced Billa and Ranga to death. The sentences were confirmed by the Delhi High Court in 1979 and subsequently by the Supreme Court. The convicted accused moved the Supreme Court again for re-appraisal of the case. The Supreme Court rejected this too. It said: 'we hope that the President will dispose of the mercy petition stated to have been filed by the petitioner as expeditiously as he finds his convenience'. Now, this is not happening as many condemned prisoners are waiting to be executed for years together. I failed to obtain a copy of the police charge-sheet and a copy of the judgment of the trial court. All these documents should be preserved in police training institutions for case study for police officers.

My stay in Kolkata was one of professional enrichment and equally satisfying for my search for higher dimension of life. I had heard before joining the Kolkata branch of the CBI that Bengali officers were lazy, intriguing and the like. This was far from truth. My officers and staff were a dedicated lot, who worked hard and were very conscious of their self-respect. In UP officers preferred to be rebuked rather than to be issued a show cause notice with an adverse report in their character roll. After taking charge of SP CBI, a very seasoned and the most senior Dy SP Mitra met me after office hours. What he told me was very interesting. He closely observed me and advised me that I should not rebuke anyone, but call for explanations in writing, just the opposite of UP culture. Then he told me that in Kolkata everybody should be addressed 'Apni' and not 'Tum'. In UP dear ones are called 'tum'. The third advice was that I should learn good Bengali as I had often ordered 'anda' and 'double roti' for my consumption. In Bengal egg is called 'dim' and double roti is called 'pauruti'. Yes; I agreed that my Bengali was poor as we were in Delhi for few generations. However, I did follow his sound advice, which proved profitable to me. During my stay in Kolkata for more then 10 years, no complaint was received by head office against me. I must admit the level of corruption in Bengal was much less than elsewhere. I had total confidence in my officers and they, in return, gave me their best. My career was largely shaped in Kolkata. I left Kolkata on 1st January 1980 for Lucknow.

11

DIG Jhansi Range

I returned from deputation on 1 January 1981 and had to wait for a good length of time in Lucknow as the final say in the matter of my posting lay with the government. On 10 February 1981, I was posted as DIG Jhansi Range. It is still a mystery why I was selected when I had vast experience in dealing with corruption and economic offences. I was the youngest of the three interviewed by the minister of state for selection for this posting. Perhaps age was in my favour or perhaps the image of CBI would satisfy the public opinion of informed and educated people.

The Jhansi range falls under Bundelkhand, an area notorious for bandits. The intensity of the problem was much more threatening and widespread than what I had earlier read in newspapers and magazines in Kolkata. Within a day or two of my taking over charge in February 1981, I saw a news item in a Hindi newspaper that a gang of dacoits had kidnapped a former magistrate when he was on his routine morning walk. This happened in Jalaun town of 50,000 people. This news was so disturbing and shocking that I immediately proceeded to Jalaun to know how in such a broad daytime crime could be committed without any prompt response from the police.

SP Jalaun Uma Shanker Bajpai was in Lucknow for a meeting. Two Dy SPs briefed me that such incidents were almost a daily affair. 'What then we do?' I asked. They gave an evasive reply that was beyond my comprehension. I insisted that such incidents were too serious to be ignored. I was further shocked to know from them that shop owners put down their shutters much before the sunset. Further, no marriages were performed anywhere in the district during night out of fear of the gangs of dacoits. I learnt that kidnapping was called 'Pakad' in Hindi. There were many cases of kidnapping for ransom. Public resistance was nil and kidnapped person, after his release, would never admit of giving of ransom money or details of the gang that kidnapped him.

Bandit queen Phoolan Devi—Behamai Massacre

Reading a few previous First Information Reports [FIR] on gangs of dacoits revealed the dimension of the situation. At times four or five gangs would join up with 150 members and would operate together. One gang was led by Phoolan Devi. She came to limelight after the infamous Behamai massacre of Thakurs of that village. It happened on 14 February 1981 when I was in district Hamirpur. For Phoolan it was revenge killing as Thakurs of that village had earlier humiliated her.

There is long story behind Behamai massacre of Thakurs. Due to circumstances Phoolan became a mistress of Vikram Mallah, who was the leader of the gang of dacoits mostly operating in Etawah, Kanpur, Jalaun districts. On 13 August 1980 Vikram was killed by two brothers called Lala Ram and Sri Ram, both Thakurs, who where leaders of Sri Ram gang of which Vikram was a member. The Singh brothers i.e. Lala Ram and Sri Ram developed liking for Phoolan more out of lust. Lala Ram and Sri Ram killed Vikram Mallah while he was asleep under a tree. After killing, the Singh brothers forcibly took Phoolan away to Behamai, located on the banks of river Jamuna. It is a Thakur dominated village.

Behamai is in Kanpur dehat (rural). These and other adjoining villages are Thakur dominated. These areas are called Chaurasi [84] villages of Thakurs. The Thakurs of these villages had earlier embraced Islam at one point of time and re-embraced Hinduism. I have not studied conversion or re-conversion of

Thakurs of these 84 villages. This story I heard from the villagers. In history, plenty of such cases are on record. Spain was conquered by the Muslims and remained an Islamic state for nearly four hundred years. Churches were converted into mosques and again mosques were converted into Churches after they became Christians again.

Phoolan, during her captivity, was repeatedly raped by both the Singh bothers and by others. She was humiliated by making her work day and night making her physical condition miserable. Finally, her captors made her free— maybe she was in no mood to join the Lala Ram-Sri Ram gang. She was determined to take revenge. After a few months, on 14 February 1981 she entered the village Behamai dressed in jeans and holding a sten gun with 25 groups of fully armed bandits. She came to kill Lala Ram and Sri Ram and Thakurs of the village Behamai. The Thakur brothers were on that day in another village called Damanpur. She just picked up strong-built Thakurs, 20/22 in all. They were lined up in a row in front of a mud wall. Each of them was killed by bullet shots one by one. It was said one of them survived because when his turn came he just, at the nick of the time, dropped his body on the ground and pretended dead.

Life story of Phoolan Devi

Phoolan was born in 1957 at Gorhapurwa village of police station Kalpi. His father Devidin was a poor farmer owning only two bighas of land, not enough to maintain a family of five daughters and a son. Phoolan was the second daughter. Being poor, father used to work as mason and mother and daughters were making ropes to earn extra money to sustain the family. Phoolan was married at the age of 10 to one Puttilal, much elder than Phoolan. The marriage did not last long. As she grew up Phoolan became an attractive belle. To be an attractive belle in a village means invitation to taking liberties with her. She beat up one such character Sockchand in full view of the villagers. People who knew dreaded dacoit Vikram took her to him.

Vikram Mallah graduated from a petty thief to a gang leader or Sardar, as the gang leaders were called. He was just a part of Lala Ram and Sri Ram gang. These two brothers were caught by the police and sent to jail. Vikram thus emerged as the leader of the leftover gang. Police records show that Phoolan committed a dacoity at the house of Maiyadin, a relative of Phoolan, who had fought against him in village panchyat on behalf of his father. It was said that this was a false case foisted by Maiyadin. She was arrested by Kalpi police as stolen goods of Maiyadin were reportedly recovered from her possession in 1979. She was not photographed by the police or by the jail authorities. When operations were started against Phoolan, there was no photograph of her necessary for any police action in apprehending a suspect of a serious case like murder or dacoity. Only Ramkali, Phoolan's sister, resembled her. Phoolan during trial absconded. Her fingerprints if available on jail records would be useful to find out the correctness of the Nadi Shastra on which I had made a brief reference in earlier chapter on fingerprint science.

Why did Phoolan turn into ruthless killer? This is a subject of interest to sociologists or psychologists. Phoolan faced many tormentors who raped her sometime publicly. One such character was Babu Gujar, who was a dacoit leader under whom Vikram worked. Vikram started to hate Babu Gujar for publicly raping Phoolan. On July 20, 1979, Vikram killed Babu Gujar. As a lover of Vikram, she did not spare the villagers of Baijamau where Lala Ram and Sri Ram killed Vikram. She led a gang of dacoits by looting 90 houses of that village as an act of revenge against Lala Ram and Sri Ram. After Vikram's death Phoolan joined the gang led by Man Singh Yadav. In Bahamai massacre on 14 February 1981, she managed to induct the members of notorious gangs like Ram Autar, Raghunath Mallah, Balwan Gadaria, Jagram and some members of Mustaquim gang. Mustaquim himself was not present. The attackers were in large number.

Phoolan, along with a combined force of several gangs after committing Behamai massacre, crossed over to Kalpi police area on way to reach a village called Mukdalan by crossing the river Jamuna. Dhrub Lal Yadav, station officer of Kalpi police station, was inspecting a PAC unit stationed near Gorhapurwa, the village of Phoolan. Dhrub Lal heard a gunshot, a signal to villagers to send food to them. Dhrub Lal understood the situation that a gang was nearby. He, as per his habit, decided to confront the gang at a place near Mukadalan, which he did by way of challenging them by opening fire. The encounter was brief, but the gang managed to escape through the cover of full-grown Arhar fields. Examining the leftover things Dhrub Lal concluded that the gang was of Phoolan. Dhrub Lal was then not aware of the Behamai massacre. If he had known, Dhrub Lal would have taken more force with him.

The police under Dhrub Lal did not give up that easily. On 23 February, I was camping at Kalpi Fort. As usual, I kept my wireless set on. In the late evening, I was surprised that all wireless sets were silent. This was unusual. I wanted to know the reason for this silence of wireless communication. I called a very energetic Dy SP IP Chand. He soon arrived and was reluctant to disclose a closely guarded secret. On my insistence, he disclosed that Phoolan and Balwan Gadaria gangs were resting on the two sides of a road some distance away from our location. He provided the names of these locations. He also said the police parties had taken positions on both sides of the road. BP Singhal, Additional IG anti-dacoity operation, was at the rest house at Bhognipur, which was in Kanpur dehat. To reach him would just mean crossing the bridge over river Jamuna. It was a matter of travelling 10/15 minutes only. I felt it was my duty to keep him apprised of the situation. I met him at midnight. BP Singhal by habit would go to bed much after midnight. I found he was talking to Rajiv Shukla, a prees reporter of a Hindi magazine and *Daily Jagran*. In Rajiv's presence, I was reluctant to share the information with Singhal. Rajiv was a smart person who realized that a scoop was awaiting him. On Singhal's insistence, I only said that something was in the offing. Singhal was so excited that he wanted more details. I refused. Then it was decided to shift to Kalpi. At Kalpi, I disclosed to BP Singhal all that I knew. Rajiv too was excited for a big scoop. We consulted the maps but failed to locate the exact places where the two gangs would be resting. There was no officer in Kalpi as all had taken positions.

Finding no other officer, we soon found that Inspector Moolchand, station officer Boghnipur, was previously posted in Jalaun district who knew the topography well. He was called and he soon arrived. On being briefed, he told us that he knew the area that we were looking for. There was no need for us to reach the spots as our movements at that hour of the night may foil the encounter. It was wisely decided to reach the spots in the early morning just after the break of the dawn. Moolchand led us to a spot on the road where the raiding parties would return after finishing the job. The party that was to capture Phoolan and his gang members returned with dejected faces. They told us that Phoolan gang had escaped after taking their meals in the late evening. They found enough evidence of her presence as leftover food was found at the site. In villages they used *pattals* or leaves of big trees as dishes. Each of them contained traces of food. It was the normal practice of many gangs to shift to another location after taking food by way of escaping possible police dragnet. This was the strategy always used by Malkhan Singh, the father of all the gangs that operated in Bundelkhand.

As we were listening to stories of Phoolan's escape, we heard a sound of gunfire from the side of Balwan Gadaria's location. We realized that Balwan gang was spotted and engaged. We discussed with a local person. He suggested that gang would escape, as they knew the terrain and were fast runners. This person suggested that we should reach a point ahead of him by jeeps. Inspector Moolchand and others got into the jeeps. The members of my own escort team were too eager to reach the spot ahead of Balwan gang. I allowed them to use my escort jeep for a greater cause.

As expected, the Balwan gang on the run was eventually located near village Parson as Moolchand knew the area very well. It was 32 km away from the first sighting of the gang. All the members of the gang were wearing police uniform. Balwan was wearing the uniform of SP. This did create confusion. Eventually there was a bloody encounter, resulting in the death of Balwan Gadaria and Inspector Moolchand. It was an irony of fate that Moolchand, who was not a part of original teams, was killed. As I have already said that we called him at midnight only to lead us to encounter sites in the morning of 24 February. Balwan and five other dacoits were killed in this encounter. Five policemen including a sub-inspector were injured.

Inspector Moolchand's body was brought to Boghnipur. The chief minister, other ministers and all the senior officers paid their homage to him. He was cremated on the banks of the river Ganga in Kanpur with full police honour. He was born on 22 November 1943 in a village in the district of Etawah. He came from a poor Dhanik family. To him caste was not at all an issue while dealing with the gangs with similar background. Once one takes on police uniform, caste, creed and religion do not matter.

Baba Mustaquim was the most dreaded dacoit leading a gang of his own. He was a father figure to all the gangs of Phoolan, Balwan, Ram Autar and many others. He was earlier a member of Malkhan Singh gang. Malkhan was mostly operating in Datia, Gwalior, Morena, Guna and Shivpuri, all in Madhya Pradesh. Most of the gang leaders initially were members of this dreaded Malkhan Singh's gang. Mustaquim's advice to other gang leaders were heard with respect. He did not participate in Behamai massacre, but some of the members of Mustaquim gang were present. He was carrying a heavy reward on his head. He was on his way to meet his brother on 4 March 1981 to a remote village in Kanpur dehat [rural] as he decided to proceed to Mumbai for his own safety. After Behamai, heat was on him and he wanted a safer place to stay. Mumbai is a place where one can easily melt into the crowd. He was killed in Kanpur dehat by the police in a chance encounter. A relative accompanied him.

During anti-dacoity operations I received request from two journalists of *The Hindustan Times* that Khushwant Singh would like to visit Kalpi to cover a story on Phoolan Devi. Eventually, Khushwant Singh arrived at Kalpi guest house and immediately left for Phoolan's village. He said that he would not require any briefing as he had all the press clippings on Phoolan. The Sardar came back in the afternoon with lot of dust on his body. He took bath to look clean. He was jovial and chatted with us in the evening before dinner. The SP offered him drink, which he refused as it was Indian make whisky. He went to his room and came back with foreign brand. He never shared his whisky with us. After early dinner at around 9 pm, he entered his room to sleep. It was his habit to sleep early and get up before sunrise. He wrote a piece on Phoolan in a US magazine, might be *Playboy* that fetched him a good remuneration. He never met Phoolan, but was impressed with the beauty of Phoolan's sister Ramkali. We never received any letter of thanks from him for the services we rendered to him.

One trait of the character of Phoolan was that she felt injustice being inflicted on the weak women and revenge was in her blood. If she were an educated girl, she could have been a great leader of gender equality. Her rustic background did not give her that chance.

After Behamai massacre, the anti-dacoity operation was mounted against all the gangs who would operate from the deep ravines of Bundelkhand, Kanpur dehat [rural] and neighbouring districts of Madhya Pradesh. The first strategy was to prevent joining up of the gangs. The strategic routes were blocked by posting armed platoons of PAC. This worked well. As a result, the splinter groups were engaged in open daylight encounters as my orders were that no night encounters would be allowed. This policy was highly successful as no adverse reports were published in the Press or magazines. The press reporters were watching each daylight encounter. Rajiv Shukla, who has now graduated into a political leader and a prominent BCCI member, would jump into our jeeps to witness such police encounters. He was a reporter of a Hindi daily then.

In armed battles, some 300 dreaded dacoits were killed and police casualties were nearly 20/35 men and officers including two Inspectors. The government under the leadership of late VP Singh was supportive. He and his minister of state were regularly taking stock of the anti-dacoity operations. VP Singh was determined to eliminate this century-old menace. The Bundelkhand region had a history of *Pindaries* and *Thuggies*. They were in thousands. Col Sleeman became famous for launching anti-*Thuggie* operations from Jabalpur. He wrote various books on *Thuggies*.

Col Sleeman devised his own unique strategy. First, he started compiling details on each member of each gang, their hideouts, associates and the like. All this was done manually. The second strategy was to collect intelligence by recruiting informers. In today's parlance, they are called moles. As a result Col Sleeman managed to collect a vast amount of intelligence. Actionable intelligence was acted upon with good results. The same technique was used in Bundelkhand. The collection of vast data enabled Col Sleeman to interrogate arrested dacoits for disclosure of full facts.

In Bundelkhand, the dacoits are called '*Bhagies*' or rebels. There is a past history behind this. The locals who rebelled against Delhi Mughal rulers were hiding in ravine areas for guerrilla warfare against them. This tradition continues. Bhagi is a respectable name given to a dacoit. Even when I was there, some of the gang leaders would give a long lecture on social injustice and inequality before commission of dacoity. Respectable gang leaders like Man Singh distributed money among the needy and poor. This provides a good image to such characters. This Robin Hood image enabled them to build up local support. The gang leaders deal with the informers harshly. Some are even executed on the suspicion of being police informers.

My experience was that a strong police leadership under a strong political will could achieve desired results. Inter-state dacoit gangs survive on the weakness of the political system. To win elections political parties should not garner the support of gangsters. In the eighties, the gangs were largely drawn from all castes. It came to my notice that individually members of the gangs were religious. Phoolan, I was told, used to perform pujas and rituals in the morning. She was a great devotee of Ma Durga. This probably she learnt by visiting temples in the ravine areas and met some sadhus.

Station House Officers, [SHOs], led the police force. Some of them rose to the occasion. One such person was Dhrub Lal Yadav of Kalpi police station in Jaulan district. The gangs used his jurisdiction for transit. He participated in almost all major encounters. In some cases, he would take with him a small well-motivated group of policemen. For exhibiting high level of leadership and courage, he was awarded a number of gallantry awards like of which were rare in police service. Because of his competence, he was posted in difficult police stations in several UP districts.

I soon found that the vast ravine area in Bundelkhand provides a safe zone for easy hiding. The best way to solve the problem is to create a network of roads. The movement of traffic means lesser opportunity of hiding and easier movement of police force. Where roads have been built the gang movements were reduced considerably. Both sides of the Jamuna bridges need to be built for easy movement of traffic. This connectivity would provide infrastructure for economic growth. Added to this, mobile telephone connections would enable the police to know the presence of gangs and their activities. On a given situation, time for the police to react will be reduced considerably.

Col Sleeman, after elimination of *Thuggies*, was asked to create a central agency for collection of criminal intelligence. The agency was called the Central Criminal Intelligence Bureau (CCIB). Subsequently, the Bureau was named the Central Intelligence Bureau, IB in short, and was entrusted the collection of political intelligence. The idea of a central authority for collection of criminal intelligence was given up. Now, the need is felt for creation of a central agency for gathering criminal intelligence of inter-state and transnational crimes. This is needed to tackle organized crime, terrorism, forged currency circulation racket and the like. The government in its wisdom has now created the National Investigation Agency. This is a step in the right direction. For tackling Naxalism some states like Andhra Pradesh have created special task forces.

When I took charge of the Jhansi Range, the gangs of dacoits were working in tandem. While committing dacoity or kidnapping for ransom, the total strength would exceed 150-armed men. The strategy adopted was simple. The easy movement of such big gangs had to be prevented. The Provincial Armed Constabulary, in platoon strengths, were positioned at strategic locations like hill tops. The local police station house officers of the rank of sub-inspectors were tasked to collect intelligence on such gangs. On receipt of first information, they were first to engage the gang as the first responder. In the event of receipt of specific information, the SP and DIG were to be informed by wireless and they were required to proceed to the scene of action with additional force. The neighbouring SHOs were also to proceed to the site and SP on arrival at the spot would take charge of the operation. Thus, senior officers were leading the force from the front. In Army this happens as attacks on enemy positions are led by a captain or a major. This motivates the force to attack the enemy positions without caring for safety of their lives. Just recall what happened in Kargil where young Indian Army officers laid down their lives for the country.

A story was in circulation in Bundelkhand that the decoit gangs were receiving local support. This was wrong. The local people were terrorized. Sometime the bandits killed innocent people by branding them as police informers. The terror was so overpowering that I found shopkeepers downing their shutters before sunset. The SP Jalaun, once visited a village in those days of dominance of the gangs; he found villagers were trying to please him and his men with plenty of milk and tea. He thought that the villagers were happy that the police had come to their help to fight the dacoits. When he announced his official position, the villagers who were entertaining him, fled the scene. Initially they thought that the police were dacoits. Dacoits of Bundelkhand used to wear police uniforms by way of prestige with badges of rank.

This myth of local support was reinforced by another experience worth recalling. I decided on a plan of capturing splinter group of Phoolan Devi gang that was ultimately reduced to a couple of members only. The plan was to plant a group of dedicated SHOs in the ravines as a new dacoit gang. Dhrub Lal Yadav was leading the group wearing village attire armed with ordinary firearms and pistols. This group could stay in the ravines for a fortnight or so. They too were welcomed by the villagers and told them in Hindi 'Ap Bhe Khoob Raj Kariae' that is 'you are welcomed to rule'. In Naxal affected areas, this seems to be true also. Naxals have managed to survive as administration has failed to deliver. Forest contractors have exploited the poor rural folks by paying them pittance as wages. There is no healthcare or schools for good education for bright boys of these regions. If proper care is taken, some of them may turn out to be outstanding athletes. Our democracy has failed to root out corruption which is the greatest threat to the Indian democracy and to the country's internal security.

Dharna encounter

My daily focus was on anti-dacoit operations. All my SPs were keen participants. SP Uma Shanker Bajpai's district Jalaun was most affected. He was always on the run. I distinctly remember a case of encounter happening during my visit to Jalaun district. It was 23 May 1981 when I was inspecting the office of the SP. In the midst of inspection in the morning, a message was received that a group of dacoits was seen in the Dharna village under Kuthond Police Station and the station officer plugged their escape routes. I asked Bajpai to proceed to the site and I too wanted to go along with him. SP Bajpai told me not to visit the spot, as, in the event of any controversy, the DIG range i.e. Jhansi would hold an enquiry. I returned to the Dak bungalow. I kept the wireless set on. At about midday I heard that we suffered casualties. This prompted me to proceed to the spot. On my way, I saw a police jeep with one casualty. I talked to him. In spite of bullet injuries, the constable was in high spirits and told me that the gang would be dealt with severely. When I reached the spot, I found bullets hit constable Viswanath dead as his head was pierced with bullets. Viswanath was to be married soon and perhaps he had already taken leave. In this encounter Meera Thakur, a lady member of the gang, along with others was killed. In those days, three women dacoits were famous. They were Phoolan Devi, Meera Thakur and Kusma Nain. They belonged to different gangs. Constable Viswanath was given a ceremonial cremation after holding a mass prayer meeting attended by a minister, IG police of UP, Commissioner of Jhansi and many others. My wife too attended the ceremony. For her it was a realization that all police officers were laying down their lives for restoration of peace in the troubled Bundelkhand region. She too became fearless.

Gulauli encounter

Dacoits of every gang would sleep during the day in a sheltered house or hut and operate at night or change their location taking advantage of darkness. Many of them could walk 30/40 km a night. Phoolan too could do the same. Their stamina was more than the policemen of a police station. On 31 March 1981 Dhrub Lal Yadav, SHO Kalpi, on receipt of specific information of Phoolan gang's presence in village Gulauli, rushed to the village with a small contingent of armed policemen. The village was in his jurisdiction. The gang seeing the police party started firing. Dhrub Lal and his party fired back in retaliation. Some dacoits were killed. There was no trace of Phoolan.

As per our standard operating procedure SP Jaulan, SP Hamirpur, DIG Jhansi[self], DIG Kanpur, Additional IG in charge of anti-dacoity, all SHOs of nearby police stations reached the village with additional police force. As evening was setting in, search for Phoolan was not given up, as Dhrub Lal was sure of correctness of his information, reinforced by the fact that some dacoits were spotted and killed in the encounter. The police dog brought from Lucknow was in position. The villagers of Gulauli were asked to come out with raised hands. Each one including women was checked to find out if Phoolan was one of them. One old lady refused to come out of the village. We all could hear her constantly shouting 'Hai Allah'. We could not make any sense of this peculiar behaviour of the old lady.

At midnight, there was gunfire from somewhere. The PAC positioned behind us started firing in panic. We were between the village and the PAC contingent and were occupying a high ground. Realizing the danger, all of us just lay flat on our stomach or else all would have been killed or injured. We shouted at the PAC to stop firing. They ultimately stopped firing. This was a panic reaction. I never, as said already, faced such a situation in East Pakistan frontier, as our boys were deployed into the trenches only after battle inoculation for a week or so. BP Singhal, additional IG in charge of anti-dacoity operation, kept on announcing on mike Phoolan and others to surrender as was the practice in all such cases.

Why did Phoolan and her gang members visit the village Gulauli? As said already, Mustaquim was killed in Kanpur dehat on 4 March 1981. Gulauli was the village of Mustaquim. His relatives were mourning his death. There was a tradition associated with bandits to visit the village of dacoits killed in encounters. Tradition demanded that Phoolan too should honour the tradition. Gulauli was a large village with a population of more than 1100 of which 90 per cent of them were Muslims. There was hardly any Mallah, the caste of Phoolan, in the village. All the dacoit gangs of Bundelkhand respected Mustaquim and out of that respect villagers and dacoits called him Baba. It was said that he was a devout Muslim. The village was relatively safe because of Mustaquim's reputation.

SP Hamirpur Vikram Singh and SP Jalaun Bajpai were right inside the village. Vikram sat almost on the top of a ditch covered with huge quantity of dry fodder. He was hitting the ground with the butt of his rifle. Just after the daybreak, we all entered the village in search of Phoolan. The house she was supposed to stay was searched, but there was no trace of her. At midday, we called off the operation. We all left the place, as we were tired without any sleep. As we left the 'Hai Allah' shouting stopped.

A villager of Gulauli months after the incident told me a strange story. Phoolan and Man Singh took refuge in the ditch covered with fodder. The 'Hai Allah' woman was just signalling Phoolan and Man Singh not to come out of their hiding place because of the presence of the police. When all clear signals were given, the duo emerged. They drank a bucket full of water as they suffered from nightlong dehydration. After that, the duo vanished into the ravines. If this were true, I would call it as a thrilling and interesting story. Our mistake was that we did not take the police dog during the morning search.

The second mistake was that we did not leave behind a small police force for collection of local gossips and the like. Dhrub Lal had reliable informers and they could not have betrayed him for giving wrong information. Phoolan was saved by the grace of Ma Durga, her deity of daily worship.

This encounter reduced the strength of Phoolan gang to two members only with Man Singh as her constant companion. She was always, thereafter, on the run. No other surviving gang like Ghanshyam was willing to take her into their fold out of fear of police.

Malkhan Singh was guru of all the dacoit gangs of Bundelkhand. All the gang leaders like Mustaquim, Balwan, Ram Autar, Phoolan and many others used to call him 'dadda' out of respect. Many of them were members of his gang. He was so powerful that he used to hold special parade of all the splinter gangs on 26 January. This was the story I heard from people. He was six feet plus with a long moustache and always had a deep red tilak on his forehead. His eyes as described by people were fierce. He fits with the popular image of any leader of a dreaded gang. Behamai changed the situation unfavourable to the gangs as the combined police force of UP and Madhya Pradesh launched a massive operation against all the listed gangs. It was Malkhan's strategy not to kill policemen as that would invite retaliation. In chance encounters with the police, he would fire in the air enabling his gang members to escape. He was a dreaded dacoit but earned respect, as he never allowed his gang members to molest or rape the women while committing dacoity. In fact, I was told he used to touch the feet of the women of the house before committing dacoity. He carried a reward of Rs 70,000 on his head. It was Malkhan's strategy to shift his location after taking meals. This was true of other gangs. When the situation became difficult, the SP of Bhind, Rajendra Chaturvedi, with a proposal to surrender reportedly approached him. He wisely utilized the opportunity by surrendering before the then chief minister Arjun Singh on 17 June 1982. He had seen the fate of Mustaquim and Balwan and many others who refused to surrender and ended their lives in challenging the police.

There is a small anecdote that at the time of surrender, Dipannita wife of Rajendra Chaturvedi tied Rakhi to Malkhan. Much later, after 25 years, Dipannita accused her husband Rajendra Chaturvedi of domestic violence, illicit relationship and attempting to grab her properties. This was announced by her in a press conference and reportedly sought Malkhan's help as her Rakhi brother. Malkhan responded, as per press report. In India Rakhi brother has the responsibility of helping his Rakhi sister.

The story of efforts made to deal with the Ghanshyam gang by Vijay Shanker who took over the charge of SP Jalaun after Bajpai's transfer needs to be recorded. Brij Lal was posted as Additional SP, a post created on our insistence. Young Brij Lal then 27 years only was a dynamic officer with new ideas. He received a letter from Ghanshyam Singh offering to surrender. He was a resident of village Hanuman of police station Rampura. In July 1976 he killed Uma Shanker Giri, not for money but for Giri's alleged atrocities like non-payment of wages. In this act of murder, Malkhan and Ram Sanehi Jatav joined him. Ghanshyam was a cousin of Malkhan. Ghanshyam, his brother Karan Singh and Jatav joined him to form his own gang. Subsequently, Bashir Khan and his wife Munni Bai joined the gang. Like Phoolan, Munni Bai too used to wear jeans. Every gang in Bundelkhand had a female member.

Brij Lal through a contact managed to open a communication channel with Ghanshyam Singh. Ghanahyam agreed to meet Brij Lal on one condition that he should come alone with no arms. Brij Lal agreed. The contact left him at a point from where a man of Ghanshyam took him to jungles of Gwalior. This happened on 15 August 1982 at around 1.30 pm. Ghanshyam was wearing a safari suit holding American grenade rifle 7.62, which he had acquired from a fauji who reportedly got it from Bangladesh war in 1971. Ghanshyam never believed that Brij Lal would come alone with no arms. He touched his feet by way of respect and put a tika on his forehead. We all knew about this daring initiative of this young officer. Brij Lal was supposed to return in the evening. As there was no news of his return, SP and I were worried for his safety. If I can recollect correctly he returned at midnight. On his return, he narrated the entire story. He did carry his camera and that Ghanshyam agreed to be photographed along with other members of the gang by Brij Lal by way of proof of his meeting with Ghanshyam. After Brij Lal visit, MP police had an encounter with Ghanshyam gang. Ghanshyam returned to UP in November 1982. At this crucial juncture SP was transferred. Hakim Singh took over as the new SP. After much bargaining Ghanshyam agreed to surrender before the DIG at a police station. I am told that SP too created a separate channel of contact with Ghanshyam for his surrender along with Phoolan. Ghanshyam did send a member of his gang to contact Phoolan. This contact was killed by perhaps in Etawah in an encounter with the local police. This infuriated Ghanshyam. The Madhya Pradesh too managed to establish contact with Ghanshyam and Phoolan with an attractive offer of surrendering before the chief minister of Madhya Pradesh that we had refused earlier. There was total lack of coordination between two police forces. Madhya Pradesh wanted to take credit when these two gangs were operating in UP. Ghanshyam and Phoolan surrendered before the chief minister of MP in January 1983. There was a lot of publicity and Phoolan got all the publicity. Ghanshyam was seen as a marginal actor, which he did not relish. He managed to escape from the police custody and was subsequently killed in Chitrakoot by MP police. As all this happened much after my transfer from Jhansi I have no idea why and how Ghanshyam escaped.

As said, already, the surrender drama happened in 1983 in Madhya Pradesh. It may be mentioned that decoits had earlier surrendered in 1972. They received royal treatment without deprivations of their ill-gotten money. Many of them engaged in profitable businesses like transport, owning big houses. Mohar Singh, who had surrendered in 1972, was rolling in wealth. This surrender drama does affect the police morale in a big way. Phoolan had no option but to surrender to save her life. She subsequently became an honourable member of Parliament. She was shot dead by a Thakur by way of revenge of Behamai massacre.

Vikram Singh SP Hamirpur was a brave officer who became the DG, UP police. Bhatia, SP Lalitpur, is now heading a paramilitary organization. All the major gangs were either liquidated in Jhansi range or surrendered in Madhya Pradesh. I found that many police officers, after a period of service, became spiritual. A police officer's life is full of challenges and faces threats on a daily basis. His survival largely depends on destiny. Later in his life, he starts introspection to know the real meaning of life.

I had the privilege to meet SP of Shivpuri, Handa of Madhya Pradesh. Handa came to call on me by way of courtesy. He was from Himachal Pradesh. During conversations, he told that he could read the mind of others. I requested him to demonstrate his ability. He asked me to write on a piece of paper a sentence and then fold the paper. Saying this he left the room. I wrote a sentence in his absence and folded the paper. I asked him to come. He then asked me to mentally utter the sentence and strangely enough, he repeated the sentence word for word. I got curious and wanted him to reveal the technique. He said that in Himachal Pradesh many people knew this. One had to undergo a course for forty-five days. He promised to teach me the technique, but I lost track of him. He said that it was nothing religious but can be acquired. If true, then why not train police officers in this science for interrogation. It can be a useful tool helpful in working out difficult cases.

I met two interesting personalities in Jhansi who were well known on their own rights. Tarun Bhaduri, father of Jaya Bhaduri, and his wife visited us for a brief period to share lunch with us. They were on their way to Bhopal from Lucknow. Tarun Bhaduri was a journalist of repute. He had covered anti-dacoity operations launched by Rustamji, then IG Madhya Pradesh. Rustamji was meticulous and had a ready list of top dacoits, and after each encounter, he would strike off the name of the dacoit liquidated. Tarun Bhaduri became so knowledgeable that he wrote a book in Bengali on Chambal Valley dacoits, which became popular in West Bengal.

Amitabh Bachchan, his son-in-law, had then just recovered from a near death situation, as he was severely injured while shooting a picture may be 'Coolie.' People from all over India prayed for his recovery. Tarun Bhaduri admitted that the prayers of people saved Amitabh Bachchan. Jaya Bachchan looked exactly like her mother. We had pleasant conversations on various subjects including his days with Rustamji. I have never met Amitabh or Jaya Bachchan. Amitabh's case, to my mind, proves the efficacy of mass prayers directed to a suffering person. Vibration of positive thoughts helps a person to tide over a crisis. Positive thought waves travel faster than sound and light. Thus, many pray that 'let me radiate thought waves of the kind which I wish to receive from others'.

Another interesting film personality I met in Jhansi was Ram Mukherjee, father of now famous film actress Rani Mukherjee. Sasadhar Mukherjee, the eldest of the Mukherjee clan in Mumbai, is originally from Jhansi. They had landed property in Jhansi which has a sizeable Bengali population of teachers, professors, doctors and even some lawyers. Shushital Banerjee, IAS, was a product of Jhansi. He became the defence secretary. Ram Mukherjee and his wife Krishna met us several times in Jhansi. We had several dinners and lunches together. He was very fond of his childhood days in Jhansi. We saw a film together. He was wearing a silken lungi. My wife and I met them in their Juhu residence in Mumbai, which was more like a small cottage. During our stay Rani, a small school-going girl returned from school. She was a lovely doll with a smiling face. We took her photograph that we still have as a prized possession. Little did I realize at that time that Rani would be a successful actress? My wife by chance met Ram's sister-in-law in Puttaparthy. She is also well known in Bengal as a singer and cine actress. She told my wife that her sister Krishna told her all about us. Healthy relationship is always enduring even if there is loss of contact.

My long stay in Jhansi for more than two and a half years was unusual as in UP, officers were transferred frequently because of political pressure exercised by dissatisfied politicians. One politician was against me as I removed one SHO of a particular police station, which fell in his constituency for adverse remarks in his character roll. The rule was that such officers were debarred from holding such posts for a specified period. Even then I survived, maybe because of our success in anti-dacoity operations without any adverse reports in the media. In 1983, I was posted as DIG Railways. With the surrender of major gang leaders and elimination of many others in fierce encounters, the Bundelkhand region became peaceful. The shops were open in late evenings and marriages were held during the night. I must record my deep appreciation of the dedicated services rendered by police officers of all ranks for bringing back peace in the five districts of my jurisdiction. I also saw a lot of oppression inflicted on lower castes like Mallahas, Gadarias, lower caste Muslims and Hindus. I have become a champion of social engineering for upward movement of the poor and the oppressed.

Manu, who is credited for caste classification, has been misunderstood for all the evils of caste system as is prevalent now. The character and conduct of each individual will determine his caste, not by the logic of hereditary. Intercaste immobility was the result of a few vested interests for social and economic domination. All the great sages, past and present, are and were not Brahmins. Now things are changing fast. The credit mainly goes to Mahatma Gandhi and Dr Ambedkar and Narayan Guru. The bandits of Bundelkhand were mainly from lower castes. They faced humiliation from upper castes. All our religious gurus must initiate a change in the mind of the people of the higher castes. Karma theory has been wrongly interpreted to justify caste system.

I cannot end this chapter without narrating the last act of extreme bravery exhibited by Inspector Dhrub Lal Yadav in rescuing four foreigners abducted by ISI operative Omar Sheikh. Four foreigners were abducted from Delhi from time to time and three of them were lodged in Saharanpur and one in Ghaziabad in 1994. The UP police was not aware of these developments. Omar Sheikh was born in UK on December 23, 1973. He was just a young man of 21 years. Being a son of wealthy father, he was a dropout of the London School of Economics. He became a jihadi after visiting Bosnia. His fluency in English was excellent. He came to Pakistan and joined Harkat-ul-Ansar, an ISI sponsored jihadi group. He was assigned the job to abduct foreigners in India for hostage negotitation for the release of Maulana Masood Azhar imprisoned in Indian jail. The three British hostages were Paul Benjamin Ridout, Chrishtopher Myles Croslon, Rhys Patridge and Bela Nuss, an American.

The events unfolded in a dramatic manner as often seen in a Bollyhood movies. A police party had reached village Massuri, some 14 km away from Ghaziabad to enquire about a stolen electric motor. They noticed one person was fleeing from the adjacent house. People of the locality could not provide any information about persons living there. This raised suspicion. The police broke open the door and found an American chained in a room. The police party could not understand his English. He was brought before the SP. The discovery of facts startled the SP. Bela Nuss revealed how Omar Sheikh befriended him and how he was abducted by a gang of six abductors and lodged in a house in Ghaziabad. From the talks of abductors, he came to know about three others who were lodged somewhere else. The SP soon realized that it was not an ordinary case. The immediate task for the police was to apprehend some of the accused, as they would normally visit the place for supply of food and mineral water.

The police took up position in the vicinity. At around 7 pm a Maruti van reached the house in question. After dropping the man, the van left the place. The police apprehended the man who did try to flee the place. The police fired on him and as a result, he was apprehended and sent to a local hospital for treatment. The man apprehended was Omar Sheikh, who had posed as Rohit Sharma. Two others were apprehended as they too arrived by the same van again. One was an Afghani Abdul Rahim and the other was Shahid, an Indian hailing from Meerut district of UP. All this happened on 30 October 1994. From their interrogation it was revealed that three others were kept in a house in Saharanpur district under the jurisdiction of the police station Mandi.

Dhrub Lal Yadav, station house officer of Sahibabad was called to lead the police team to Saharanpur. He had vast experience in dealing with such situations and many times dealing with dreaded criminals. The house was spotted by the arrested accused. It was debated whether the operation should be mounted in the midnight or early in the morning. The uppermost consideration was the safety of the hostages. In the early morning raid there would be no element of surprise. The terrorists might kill the hostages before they faced the bullets from the police. This clinched the issue.

Dhrub Lal knocked at the door at midnight. There was no response. He then decided to break open the door by hitting the door with the butts of rifles along with other four constables. The door soon collapsed and fell inside the house. With torchlight flashed by Head Constable Rajesh Yadav, Dhrub Lal spotted a bearded man and asked him to surrender. Other terrorists started firing from inside the house, which killed Dhrub Lal and Rajesh Yadav. Even injured Dhrub Lal fired back killing Mohammed Ali Khan. Others managed to escape by breaking the rear wall of the house. If the house was really surrounded by the police, there was no question of escape. Dhrub Lal laid down his life, the way MC Sharma laid down his life in the Batla House encounter.

On 1 November 1994, there was huge crowd of people to pay homage to brave Dhrub Lal and Rajesh. Prominent politicians and eminent citizens were there. I could not reach Ghaziabad as I had retired in July 1993. There was logistic problem. I did pray for the departed souls. The British Government paid tributes to Dhrub Lal. I am still in touch with Dhrub Lal's wife and Premlal Yadav, elder brother of Dhrub Lal. Dhrub Lal's daughter is a professor in the Miranda House and his son is in a private sector firm holding a good position. God has compensated the family. A park in Ghaziabad is renamed as Shaheed Dhrub Lal Park and his statue has been installed by way of perpetuating his memory. Many policemen and officers had laid down their lives in their youth fighting terrorists, dreaded dacoits and members of mafia gangs. It is sad and bad that there is no memorial for such brave men in the capital of our country. Every year some 1000 policemen and officers die while fighting dreaded criminals for the safety of people. They deserve to be honoured.

12

DIG Railways

I handed over charge of Jhansi Range on 1 June 1983. Thus, I stayed in Jhansi for more than two years and four months. This was the longest stay for a DIG in Jhansi. I was posted as DIG Railways in Allahabad. The state government and the Railways jointly finance the Government Railway Police [GRP]. The major crimes in those days were luggage lifting from stations and coaches of running trains. This is a highly professional crime committed by organized gangs. Each gang had its own area of operation. Often the allegation was that the Railway police earmarked the area of operation for a particular gang. UP became notorious for this type of crime.

As DIG Railways, I was once returning alone to UP from Mumbai by train. When the train entered UP from Madhya Pradesh, the passengers told each other to secure their luggage as they had entered UP. Such was the reputation of GRP, UP. I felt distressed and hanged my head in shame. The Railway police possibly have no other avenue to earn extra money except allowing gangs to operate freely on consideration. This was the perception of people. The GRP posting was considered a punishment posting for subordinate ranks.

Once I was on duty in Lucknow and decided to stay in railway station rest house. I just entered the Railway police station in the early morning and found a person in underwear and vest. This was a pathetic sight to see. When asked why he was so scantly dressed, his reply was that his entire luggage had been stolen from the compartment. I immediately ordered for kurta and pyjama for him. This gesture moved him into tears.

In my office everyday a large number of complaints pertaining to thefts in the compartments or from stations were recieved. Complaints were generally addressed to the PM, Railway Minister, zonal managers and a copy addressed to DIG Railways. I started replying to the complainants assuring them of investigation and conveyed to them our feelings for the loss and agony caused to them. This exercise yielded good response as many expressed their gratefulness for at least taking notice of their letters while complaining that their letters addressed to others did not even invite a formal reply.

Another case of theft of jewellery of a lady VIP is worth mentioning. The victim was VP Singh's wife who was travelling alone from Delhi to Lucknow in a coupe. At midnight she went to the toilet leaving behind her handbag, which contained jewellery. During her short absence, someone took away her bag. The doors of coach were locked from inside. On investigation, it was found that Railway thieves were adept in getting into the coaches through vestibule connecting two coaches. It was then decided to close the doors of vestibules at night.

13

DIG Police Headquarters

The DG, UP Sri JN Chaturvedi thought that I should take over as DIG Police Headquarters located in Allahabad. My basic work was to prepare budget proposals, and control budget allotted to units. Budget proposals are largely based on previous figures and proposal for new items of expenditure.

Previous allotments to various formations have tendency to overspending on items not required for utilization. This is done to obtain more money in the next year's budget. Once I asked a visiting Commandant of a battalion how much money was available before the end of the financial year under head contingency fund. He said fifty thousand rupees. I asked him if he would surrender the unspent money. His answer was no, reason being that in the next year his allotment would be reduced on the ground of previous expenditure. Since then I kept on toying with the idea of a system of an alternative formulation. I found that each unit, given the chance, could easily save 10 per cent each year. The fund so saved should be withdrawn from the treasury and credited into a bank in the name of the unit. This surplus fund so generated should remain under the control of DG of the police and police headquarters. Over ten years the fund so generated would be almost equal to the total budget of a year for that particular unit. After ten years, the budget allotment should be freezed at one constant level. A time would come when in the department there may be almost a situation of zero budgeting in the sense that no extra allotment would be made. I wonder if this concept will ever be implemented for want of a clear understanding and a long time view of a new method of raising funds for developmental work so needed for rapid economic development. Leaders, with vision, can perhaps give a concrete shape to this idea. In the current system, there is no incentive to save. Extravagant and useless expenditure can be targeted for saving. Can someone take the initiative to introduce an innovative scheme in the concept of zero budgeting? The current idea of zero budgeting is limited to elimination of estimates of surpluses, which no one would surrender or allow happening. The traditional concept of zero budgeting has no takers. I have been thinking on this after gaining vast experience of spending in government departments.

Every year the CID (Criminal Investigation Department) probe used to be ordered against PHQ in two areas, in purchases of vehicles for the entire police force of UP and purchase of books. The entire vehicle purchase was centralized from Allahabad. Only one dealer in Allahabad was given the authority to sell the vehicles to all the police formations. The dealer's margin of profit was huge. The allegation was that someone from the PHQ including officers shared a part of profit. I discussed the matter with my SP Ahmed Hussain. We decided to find out from the manufacturers whether dealership can be given to others in other major cities in UP. Prompt came the reply that they have no objection as the Allahabad dealer was one of them only. We started placing orders to various dealers in UP because of nearness of the requisitioning units. The babus objected to introduction of this new scheme based on past tradition, which was turned down. Thereafter, no complaints were received. My SP Ahmed Hussain was a capable officer. After retirement, he joined politics and became a minister.

The second area of CID probe was in respect of centralized purchase of books on behalf of all formations without seeking their requirements. This absurd system was going on for years. Again, Ahmed and I had a brainstorming session. We decided to allot money to all formations based on their strength. The units were free to purchase books of their choice. Babus again objected based on past practice, which we ruled out. After introduction of these transparent innovative schemes there were no further CID inquiries. The centralized system of purchase is prone to corruption. In UP the babus have strong grip on administration. They can interpret the rules the way these suited them. There are good babus also who work hard and are honest.

As said, the system of centralized purchase is always prone to corruption. The same is true of recruitment of constables. When I joined service, the local SP and the Commandant filled up the vacancies in districts and battalions. The vacancies were few in a year. Only suitable candidates were selected after a good deal of tests. There was no scope to make big money from recruitment of a few constables. This limited recruitment made it possible to select a few from the families of the retired or serving old policemen. Hardly, there were any complaints. Now the system is to recruit constables by a board of officers to fill up all the vacancies of constables in UP. Thousands are recruited by a central board. Massive scope has been created for obtaining bribe from the candidates. The going rate is quite high. Recruitment is a highly profitable industry flourishing in every state. There are allegations that in this scheme of things the politicians are also having a big pie. My idea is that we should revert to the old system of recruitment by SPs and commandants to curb corruption.

For transfer and promotion, heavy bribe is demanded and paid. For lucrative posts, the amount paid is said to be colossal. How do we expect a corruption free police service when the recruits have to raise money to pay back to those who had provided the bribe money by way of loan? The recruit's first task as constable is to take bribe from people who are at the cutting edge. Easy targets are the vendors, the street hawkers, the cobblers and even the shopkeepers. Once they taste blood, they carry on to thrive on corruption.

The UP PHQ maintains a couple of private funds. Some funds were donated by individuals before independence. The total money was nearly to the tune of Rs one crore. Some funds were meant for widows of constables and head constables by way of paltry pension. The money paid was a pittance. Some fund was available for village chowkidars, which was never utilized. The main fund was the benevolent fund for which each constable paid one rupee per year. That fetched nearly Rs. 1.5 lakh a year. Out of this fund, the newly bereaved families were paid some amount of money for funeral expenses. Now the pay scales of all ranks have been raised, contributions made by an individual can be raised to Rs 100 a year. The strength of UP police is now around 2,00,000, the total fund would be sufficient to open UP Police school as is being done by paramilitary forces. I believe one such police school has since started functioning near Lucknow. It is futile to expect the government to open such schools for paucity of funds.

The social life in Allahabad was limited to few persons. One such person was the wife of RK Nehru, a distinguished career diplomat of India. The widow of RK Nehru called on us rather unexpectedly. Meeting my wife was a surprise to her as she recalled her name as my father-in-law was posted in Cairo Embassy. My father-in-law was an IFS (B) officer. In embassy like Cairo all groups of officers, often used to get together for holding functions. My wife was a good singer of Rabindra Sangeet and sang on Radio Cairo.

Mrs RK Nehru was living alone in Allahabad and was a loner. She invited us on many occasions for high tea. She used to narrate how the Chinese used to relish snake dishes. Her sophistication and style of living was like an ICS officer. She never bragged of her family's closeness to Nehrus. The district police used to provide her security. She told us that her main door was never locked, as that was the safest way to call for help in case of emergency. Her son was well-settled in Delhi, but she preferred to stay alone. I used to ponder how best would we be able to tackle loneliness in security and the like in our old age. I started believing that each officer and his wife should start practising detachment from worldly pleasure while in service. I know an officer going mad after retirement. This happens to politicians who feel neglected after getting old. Old politicians should also practise detachment from the age of 65. They too must realize that the leadership must be passed on to the new generation. 'People will gather around you so long as you have pelf and power; you will be left severely alone. When you lose these. They are like swarms of frogs that infest a full lake, croaking flattery but disappearing when the lake is dry.'

There was not much of challenging work in PHQ. Two of my batchmates were promoted as IGP while two of us were left out for want of vacancy. I was itching for going out on deputation to the Centre. All my promotions were in the Centre. Again, destiny played its part. I was offered a post in the Central Economic Intelligence Bureau [CEIB], which is a part of the ministry of finance of Government of India; I joined the new post as deputy director general [DDG] equivalent to the post of IG.

14

Central Economic Intelligence Bureau

VP Singh, as finance minister, created the Central Economic Intelligence Bureau [CEIB]. He was interested in rooting out wrongdoings in the private sector. Much of the malaise was due to the quota, licence and Inspector Raj. A series of raids only generated fear to industrialists. The central idea behind the creation of this unit was to collect economic intelligence by obtaining inputs from the customs, excise, and income tax and then combine them and generate actionable intelligence for raids and searches unearthing big frauds for action against entities and generate more revenue for the government. There was no central agency for collection of economic intelligence.

I was one of three DDGs; two of them were drawn from customs and income tax. They were given charge of their respective work. I was given central excise. The job involved was to collect intelligence on excise duty evasion. This was something very new to me. The only evasion case that I had dealt with while I was in the CBI Kolkata was in respect of a very big income tax evasion committed by a reputed company for years together.

We were told by the Director CBI that a reputed company based in Kolkata allegedly did not deposit the tax money deducted from the salaries of its employees. This deduction was required to be deposited and reflected annually in the prescribed form to

TDS unit of the Income Tax Department. This unit dealing with tax deduction at source was not considered a good posting. It could have pinned down the defaulting company easily. The allegation was found to be true on enquiry. This information came from a Parliamentary debate. The CBI in those days used to scan Parliamentary discussions for lifting worthwhile information for preliminary probe. The company involved escaped from payment of income tax collected from its employees for several years, may be more than a decade. As we learnt the tricks, the CBI could locate a few more companies committing the same crime. There are leakages in the system, which are hardly detected for want of motivation or for lack of supervision and may be because of collusive corruption.

In another case, the Kolkata branch was asked to find out the reasons for scarcity and unprecedented rise in prices of mustard oil in Bengal. We checked the total holding of mustard oil by checking nationalized banks records as against such stocks loans which were obtained from the nationalized banks on hypothecated basis. The holding of stocks of mustard oil was found to be almost the same as compared to the previous years. Then we checked arrival of mustard seeds and oils by railways. The railway records indicated the name of parties receiving the huge stocks of mustard seeds or oil. When physically checked the traders were found to be non-existing or showing the same address. The bank records brought out the real names and addresses of the traders. Six important traders were located and Income Tax authorities were given all information collected by us. The Commissioner of Income Tax found that our information was true. He asked how CBI could locate income tax defaulters so easily. I told him that a little bit of cross-checking was required to catch tax evaders. He was impressed by the way we unearthed the tax evaders.

I took sometime to understand how the excise duties were collected. My boss did not feel it necessary to brief me about the task assigned to me. May be he himself was not conversant with excise duty matters as he had mostly worked in anti-smuggling operations. One has to understand the working of the system to spot the areas of leakages. The Central Economic Intelligence Bureau [CEIB] was a Delhi based organization with no field staff for collection of intelligence at the grassroots level. Not a single information or intelligence was passed on to CEIB by the customs, the income tax or by the central excise. The Director of the Bureau, Wadawan did try his best to obtain cooperation by issuance of a government order. The government order contained something unusual. It gave powers to the CEIB Director to add his own remarks on the character rolls of officers of the income tax, customs and excise officers. The respective departments vehemently objected this. In view of this strong opposition, the order was promptly withdrawn. In case of CBI this problem of interdepartment cooperation was solved long ago by issuance of a single directive for all government departments to extend cooperation to CBI whenever such cooperation is sought. In government, there is hardly interdepartmental discussion before issuance of such orders of vital importance.

In my area of work, I tried out an experiment on the assumption that against large orders placed on the manufacturers by public sector units there might be scope for evasion of excise duties. I, as a police officer, contacted vigilance officers of some public sector undertakings, who were mostly police officers on deputation to provide information on substantial purchases from private sector companies. As we had no field officers, such information was passed on to excise commissioners of respective jurisdictions for verification. I found the experiment a great success. There were many cases of total excise duty tax evasion. The initial success encouraged me to gather similar information from many more public sector undertakings. All these informations yielded substantial money for the government. My subordinate officers working with me received monetary rewards of substantial amount. Thus, I could justify my assignment for my own satisfaction. The director never wanted to know the way intelligence was collected nor did he ever congratulate me for good work done. For some personal reasons he did not like me. I do not wish to write about it, as it was not a pleasant experience. I deserved to be treated better as I came from a different background.

The extent of evasion of excise duty it appears to me was colossal. Let me give an example. In the newspaper, I found a proud declaration by a company showing turnover as seven crore for manufacturing mosquito repellent annually. This prompted me to find out the amount of excise duty paid by the company from the local office of the central excise. The reply was strange. It was claimed that the mosquito repellent was treated as a heater and heater was exempted from payment of excise duties. I did speak to senior officers of excise department and they too were amazed to know that repellent was being treated as heater. I am not aware if mosquito repellants are still being treated as heaters.

Products sold without payment of excise duty means that the production was not perhaps shown on paper. There was a standing joke that daytime productions were shown on record and night productions were off the record. If productions are not recorded it would mean that our gross domestic production i.e. GDP is not true. Therefore, when GDP figures are shown in the newspapers I always wonder if we are not projecting a lower figure. I always feel that Indian GDP is much higher than what is projected. When we eradicate total evasion of taxes and duties, perhaps, we may be able to arrive at the real growth rate. Let an expert body be set up to examine whether compilation of production figures is in tune with the realities on the ground. I am no expert on the subject but I feel strongly that something is amiss in our way of calculation.

I was also given the task to find out if foreign contributions received by some non-governmental organizations were being used properly. Foreign Contributions Regulation Act [FCRA] that comes under the department of the home ministry regulated the foreign contributions for such organizations. The enquiry, thus involved obtaining information from the banks and FCRA. While utilization was perfect on paper, but the donors had mostly issued Swiss bank cheques. The donor names and addresses could not be verified in the absence of facilities for enquiry abroad. Mostly money remittance route is hawala, which is the fastest way for transnational transfer of illegal money. There is no special law on Hawala transactions. Foreign contributions can also be another route for money laundering. Remittances received from abroad by individuals in India from relatives living abroad are not taxable. Only requirement is that the remitter has to declare that money sent to individuals is out of 'love and affection'. This route is susceptible to misuse and can be used for money laundering. There is no agency to verify the genuineness of such transactions. Only the income tax officer can look into it based on individual tax returns. Foreign contributions and individual remittances are called 'invisible' foreign exchange earnings. The total invisible foreign exchange earnings are quite substantial.

CEIB had to obtain an 'oral political clearance' for carrying out searches. I found this to be repulsive and detrimental to independent functioning of a vital organ for revenue collection. This was unusual for me. This was my first understanding of politicization of bureaucracy and threatening the big business. The political implication of a proposed search was assessed by another intelligence agency. Only the head of the agency perhaps kept to himself all that he conveyed to powers that be. I wonder if he ever obtained information or views from his subordinates. I often wonder why the bureaucracy was keen to align itself with regime in power. The reason I found was to obtain a position of authority after retirement. This post-retirement lure of office has now penetrated deep in the system. My advice to such worthies is to join active politics after retirement in case their convictions are strong. In CBI, this has been done in a most nuance way by barring the CBI to register cases against officers of and above the level of joint secretary unless there is clearance from the government. By implication, the CBI is thus barred from collecting intelligence against politicians. Only during investigation of security scam cases this provision was partially withdrawn for the bunch of cases.

In 1988, the Director EIB retired and the new incumbent was from Customs, an officer of my batch. It was not possible to continue to work in EIB, as it would embarrass both of us. Before retirement of Wadhawan, I made a representation to Government to post me elsewhere or repatriate me to my cadre UP. A proposal was made to post me to BSF Jodhpur. DG BSF was agreeable to take me on deputation. Finally, the file went to Shri Chidambaram, then a minister of state in home affairs. I had not known the minister. He read my ACR and found that I had more than ten years of experience in CBI with very good reports. He decided that I should be posted to CBI as a Joint Director, which is equivalent to the post of IG. I then realized that some of our ministers were impartial and could work without bias. I also realized that the minister had the capacity to scrutinize files with critical eyes. In many cases I had known bureaucracy's recommendations were invariably accepted as the minister was required to write 'yes' only to avoid reading the file critically. To say 'not accepted' the minister has to record reasons for the same, which is far more difficult. This reminds me of a joke that acquittal judgment is far easier to write than writing a punishment judgment. For acquittal, one has to cite some discrepancies in the prosecution case. My regard for Chidambaram went up. He was the architect of fencing of borders with Pakistan to prevent border crossing by terrorists and smugglers. This proved effective. He is a fluent speaker who can articulate his ideas. The face of the country will change if we have such competent ministers, independent of the party that rules the country.

15

My Last Tenure in CBI

I joined CBI in 1988. One day my Director late MG Katre called me to know if I had received President's Police Medal for distinguished services. I said no. He said that he would recommend my name to the Government. Thus, I got the most coveted medal. Late Katre, an officer of Maharashtra cadre, was professionally very sound. He was fair and impartial. He sent me to Paris in 1989 for an Interpol Conference on 'Assets Derived from Crime.' I had enough time to prepare a paper on Underground Banking (Hawala) focusing on Hawala network for transfer of money from one country to another without resorting to regular banking channels. Since this was my first exposure to international community, I was a bit nervous. I found European ministers addressing the gathering. When my turn came, I started speaking on Hawala. The chairman of the meeting, who was an American, intervened to say that this subject was not covered. I got strong support from some African and Asian delegates who argued that for the third world this was the problem. I also got support from the delegate from UK, who said that he had dealt with the problem in a similar case and deserved to be studied in-depth. Such strong reaction made it possible for me to explain the situation. The Americans were focusing on drug money not realizing that illegal drug money was also being transferred through Hawala route. I found that the Americans were dominating all Interpol conferences by putting pressure on European counterparts. They set the agenda. They would come in a group of at least 10 delegates. The Americans finally accepted my presentation when I showed them US papers advertising payment abroad through Hawala route. That convinced them of a problem. Ultimately, the Interpol decided to look into the matter by a study group. After 9/11, the USA found to its horror how terrorists were being funded through Hawala route mostly from the Middle East. If a safe world is to be secured Hawala has to be uprooted from all corners of the world.

Anti-Terrorist Coordination Cell

Terrorism in Punjab predates terrorism in Kashmir. The obvious reason was that until 1989, the ISI was involved in waging a proxy war in Afghanistan on behalf of the USA, European powers, China and Saudi Arabia against Soviet troops in Afghanistan since 1979. The Sikh diaspora settled in Canada, USA and UK mostly fuelled Punjab terrorism. They received support from Pakistan's ISI and its military intelligence. It is on record how prominent Sikhs living abroad were hosted by Pakistan and their images were seen on Pakistan TV. 'Raj Karega Khalsa' was even written on the walls in Delhi in the late sixties. Many were trained in Hekmetayar's training camps in Afghanistan-Pakistan border. The idea of inflicting thousand cuts to India was conceived after creation of Bangladesh.

There were killings of innocent people in Punjab. People travelling by buses were brought down and were killed selectively. There was enough stockpiling of arms and explosives in the sacred Golden Temple in Amritsar. All attempts to flush them out from the Golden Temple proved futile. The Army, as the last resort, launched the Operation Blue Star in 1984. Such Army operations resulted in damage of some portions of the Golden Temple. There was natural resentment and many sections of the Sikh society were outraged. I was then DIG Railways in Allahabad. I received a message through railway telephone that Jawans of a regiment in Danapur had deserted their camp with arms and trucks. They were intercepted in Benaras. There was no fuel left in their trucks to move ahead. The deserters then started moving on foot in small groups. When they reached Allahabad, they started enquiring about the route to Delhi. By that time people knew what was happening. They gave misleading information and that made them travel in the wrong direction, which was tiring for them.

In 1984, Indira Gandhi was assassinated by her own security men. There were many anti-Sikh riots and killing of innocent Sikhs for no rhyme or reason. Thereafter, terrorism escalated. Sometime in 1988 or early 1990 RK Pradhan, then Union home secretary, by an executive order, created an Anti-Terrorist Coordination Cell headed by DIG, CBI Chandigarh. All the affected states would send their officers for weekly meetings. They would share their information or intelligence in the meeting. Immediately after the meeting, the coordination cell would prepare report on action to be taken by each participant states. This method of close chasing of terrorists from any part in India proved highly productive. If a terrorist was caught by a state agency, previously other states would never know the brief contents of his interrogation.

The coordination cell did build up a huge data bank. If any suspected terrorist was caught and a call received from the state concerned, the cell would provide information it had on him. Because of such background information, the suspected terrorist would face a tough interrogation. As a result, the arrested terrorist would make more disclosures. In many cases, I recall recoveries of arms and arrest of terrorists. The cell would receive constant support from KPS Gill, who was then DG of the Punjab police. Several plans were made by terrorists to eliminate Gill. That did not disturb him at all. Like Rustomji, Gill too kept mental note of all the leading hardcore terrorists. For example, Devinder Pal Singh Bhullar, a leading figure of the Khalistan Liberation Force was on his list and he followed each lead for his apprehension. Bhullar eventually masterminded an attack on former youth Congress leader MS Bitta in front of Raisina Road office of Youth Congress on 11 September 1993. He was sentenced to death in 2001. His mercy petition is still pending with the President of India.

The credit for success of anti-terrorist operation in Punjab would definitely go to KPS Gill. BK Nehru, then Governor of Assam, recorded in his book 'Nice Guys Finish Second' his appreciation for Gill as an outstanding officer of Assam cadre of the Indian Police Service. In Assam, efforts made to evict illegal Bangladeshi immigrants were always frustrated by Delhi as per Governor's version. Once the task of eviction was entrusted to Gill. He would ask the villagers to produce the new illegal immigrants. The obvious answer was that there was none. 'He used to draw himself up to his full height [over six foot], stroke his moustache and say in a threatening voice, 'well, then shall I ask my men to search your homes?' They would then request Gill not to carry out the search. The illegal immigrants were deported back to Bangladesh. Of course, this operation of Gill was withdrawn as outcry was raised from Delhi. As rightly said by BK Nehru,' 'Gill had earned the gratitude of the people of Punjab and of India for ridding the state of terrorism from Punjab and India.'

The greatest lesson from Punjab terrorism was that there has to be an immediate exchange of intelligence by all the affected states and decisive police leadership leading from the front with no political interference. The Coordination Cell had huge data bank that can be profitable for any researcher on the subject of terrorism. We have now the National Investigation Agency [NIA] created by an Act of Parliament. This is a right step in the right direction. This could happen in our disturbing democracy because of 26/11 attack in Mumbai. The records of the Coordination Cell should be transferred to NIA or else they will be destroyed by some officer who has no knowledge of the great role played by the Coordination Cell during the peak of terrorism in Punjab and in some neighbouring states.

Attempt to kill Ribeiro in Romania

On August 20, 1991, expatriate Sikh extremists made a desperate attempt to kill Riberio in Bucharest, capital of Romania, where he was posted as India's ambassador to that country. Perhaps his posting as ambassador was to ensure his safety as he and many others were on hit list of terrorists. From time to time, the Romanian government was kept informed of conspiracies to kill Riberio. Information that was more specific was communicated by MEA in July 1991. On August 1, 1991 the Romanian agencies received from their own sources that some Indians had already arrived in Bucharest for executing the plot of killing Riberio.

I have strong reasons to believe that the country that provided this specific intelligence to Romania was West Germany. I had an occasion to visit Berne, then capital of West Germany. The Indian embassy arranged my visit to their intelligence outfit. Every officer of that unit met me individually. One of them told me a startling story of getting this specific information of the plot to kill Riberio from his source and he passed the information to all concerned European countries, and by oversight, this was not communicated to India. This officer, whose name I cannot recollect, was so informed of the Punjab terrorism that he told me that he might write a book on the subject. I have no idea if he has written the book. Maybe, this was the intelligence that was claimed by the Romanian as their own intelligence. The German officer also told me that he received the intelligence from a source from another country.

According to the version of Riberio, the conspiracy was hatched in Switzerland at the residence of Balls, Indians settled in Switzerland. Riberio was given two security men armed with revolvers concealed in their pockets and they too used to walk along with Riberio when he used to go out for evening walk keeping a distance of 30 metres. The security car driver, who was a commando, used to park the car near the residence of the ambassador. The driver was required to rush to the spot in case of emergency on receipt of call on walki-talki.

Five men were involved when they fired at Riberio by using AK-47 Rifle injured him. The security driver rushed to the spot and fired at two terrorists, one was killed and another injured. The third one was caught red handed with his weapon. The fourth and the fifth escaped by another gateway vehicle. They remained untraceable. These five were members of the Khalistan Liberation Force and were all expatriates from different countries.

Here, it must be mentioned that two activists of the Punjab Human Rights Organization based in London immediately reached Bucharest and met Romanian officials for organizing defence of the arrested terrorists. In Romania like many other European countries, investigation is carried out by the Public Prosecutors office. The role of police is limited to arrest of the culprits. To mount pressure on Romanian government for release of the arrested culprits, the drama shifted to Delhi. The terrorists kidnapped Livio Radu, who was then officiating as Romanian Ambassador to India. Their demand was to get the captured terrorists in Romania released. After 23 days, the police rescued Radu. The Western Governments stood firm by requesting the Romanian government not to yield. The arrested terrorists were convicted. What happened to Bal brothers in Switzerland is not known. MEA alone can confirm or deny if the Swiss government had sent any proposal to Government of India to offer monetary compensation in lieu of prosecution of Bal brothers. This was the rumour at that time.

London, as I have said elsewhere, was the magnet that drew terrorists from all countries to operate freely on the unwritten condition that no crime should be committed in UK. Thus, Islamic terrorists from Arab world take refuge in UK, some with even records of convictions, LTTE, the Sikh terrorists were allowed to operate without any restrictions. Once the UK Home Secretary [Home Minister] met all the heads of the enforcement agencies in India. While explaining that the Punjab terrorists were freely raising funds and issuing statements for escalation of terrorism in India, I read out the statement of a Sikh leader who fled to UK advising selective killings in India.The UK Home Secretary immediately told his staff to collect a copy of the interview. Thereafter, the said leader stopped giving interviews. Only after 9/11 and underground train bombing in London, things have changed significantly. Most of the Middle East terrorist sympathizers and those who had been convicted in courts of their respective countries were deported.

Before 9/11 the FBI too was the most reluctant to deal with expatriates with terrorist links. Even on specific information, they took months to report back that the person concerned had changed his location. Only agency that I found effective was Canada. Our intelligence sharing was structured. I still remember how the Canadian agency prevented hijacking of Air India plane on 26 January. Their reporting was so correct that we had no difficulty to pick them up at the right time.

Pilferage of stamp papers

Stamp papers are printed at Government of India's Nashik Security Press. In late eighties a number of pilferage of stamp papers in bundles were referred to CBI. It must be remembered that sale of stamp papers yields considerable revenue to state governments and storing and release of stamp papers is regulated by the states.

The stamp papers thus pilfered were sold clandestinely. All bundles of stamp papers used to be dispatched by Nashik press to various states by trains. There was huge scope for pilferage of stamp papers from the point of dispatch to point of destination stations. Money involved in such thefts was in crores of rupees.

Since the cases were old, nothing much could be done by way of arrests of the culprits. We had a meeting with Nashik authorities and found that the entire system of printing, dispatch, and receipt were defective. Stamp papers are like currency and should have been transported by plane only, which was not at all a costly proposition.

Stamp papers could be sold anywhere in India. There was no system of guarding the bundles of stamp papers during transit. I wonder if the system has been changed to secure them from pilferage. The stamp papers did not bear the name of the states. As a result, stamp papers received and released by a state can be used in another state.

A small crime has a tendency to escalate into a bigger crime if there is enough profitability. Telgi stamp paper fraud is the manifestation of aggravated crime of printing forged stamp papers like printing fake currencies. Such fake stamp papers should look genuine and sold to bulk purchasing customers. For this to happen a good printing press is required. It was reported that an old printing press was acquired by Telgi from Nashik, perhaps in connivance with officials. No organized crime can operate without a big support system. It seems to me that Telgi alone could not have been in this crime. The press reported that amount involved was to the tune of thirty thousand crores of rupees.

ISI Operative Mohd Sharif

In the early nineties a most wanted Pakistani ISI operative was caught. He perhaps called himself Mohd Sharif or Mohd Hanif. He had visited India several times and stayed at different places by different names. His task was mainly to create cells in different parts of India. He created modules in western UP, Hyderabad and many other places. He even visited Madras stock exchange for a trial run along with an Indian accomplice for blasting the same. He did try to get into the Bhaba Atomic Research Centre for some nefarious activities. All these plans for serial blasts happened much before the demolition of Babri Masjid. Thus, it would not be entirely correct to say that idea of organizing serial blasts happened only after demolition of Babri Masjid. He revealed many facts that were not known to agencies.

His previous visits were unknown as we lacked in designing a system for verification of suspicious persons staying in hotels, rest houses etc. Every such stay is recorded and sent to police. There is no system in place for sample checking of such entries. A mere computer analysis of such entries will provide scope for sample checking. Checking is possible as our intelligence agencies have vast network all over the country. Based on this experience I put up a note on "retrieval and analysis of open documents" to Home Secretary and the Cabinet Secretary. Only the Cabinet Secretary responded positively. He agreed that the system could be given a fair trial. A unit was created in CBI but nothing much could be done, as none could understand how to generate data for sample checking of people staying in hotels. This data was only available with Delhi police. There was lack of computerization of such data during those days. Mohd Sharif was convicted by the court of law. There are hundreds of Sharifs in India, many as sleeping agents to be activated at proper time. All these persons who came to light as recruited agents of ISI are required to be brought on permanent record for discreet surveillance. State agencies have more information as they have good network. If their headcounts are available, the number of such elements may run into thousands.

Diamond merchant kidnapping case

I was in London when five rich diamond merchants of Mumbai were invited to Delhi for a big deal and were kidnapped from Delhi in September 1991and kept in a newly constructed house in Sukhdev Vihar belonging to a DDA employee. My feeling while in London was that it was planned and executed by ISI of Pakistan. They were released after a week or so. The case was handed over to CBI from Delhi police, which I still believe was a wrong decision. Such cases should continue to be investigated by the local police, Delhi. The momentum of investigation is lost in the process. In case of inter-state ramification, CBI help is always available. The kidnapper assumed the name Ravi Choudhry. He was found to be a Pakistani with complete knowledge of the topography of Delhi and Bombay. This indicated that he had visited Bombay and Delhi many a time previously. This was found to be true as he used a rental car without a driver. So-called Ravi Choudhry left behind a vital clue. He met another prominent politician of Pakistan at Marina Hotel where a prominent Pakistani politician was staying. The politician was Ghulam Mustafa Khar of 'My Feudal Lord' fame, this book was authored by his previous wife Tehmina Durrani. Ravi Choudhry organized Khar's trip to Ajmer Sharif by providing transport and Ravi Choudhry paid the fare. The diamond merchants were invited to Delhi by Ravi Choudhry from Mumbai for a big deal. The diamond merchants after release were perhaps keen for closure of the case. With great deal of persuasion, the Pakistani authorities agreed to allow Indian investigators to speak to Mustafa Khar in Karachi. Police or ISI always surrounded Khar so that he did not speak the truth. At one point of time Khar, for a brief period, was alone and told that Ravi lived in Defence Colony, Karachi. Indian intelligence agencies could not provide any information on Ravi Choudhry, in spite of availability of Khar, who often visited India for pilgrimage to Ajmer.

The case is still open, as CBI has declared him a proclaimed offender. The case can still to be solved with the help of US as Ravi Choudhry had good contacts in the USA and might have also visited the US perhaps several times and might be involved in financing the 1993 WTC attack in New York. Our intelligence agencies can even now locate him and I would even go to the extent of advising the agencies taking Mustafa Khar into confidence when he visits India. I believe Mumbai serial blasts and WTC attack 1993 might have been financed by Ravi Choudhry's massive fund collection in Diamond Merchant kidnapping case. However, payment of ransom money by diamond merchants was denied by them, which was not believable.

I have reasons to believe that ransom was paid abroad and the same was used for ISI's nefarious activities. The network of ISI operates in a big way in India. A press correspondent was assigned for a posting in Pakistan. He told me that before issue of visa his antecedents were checked even from his ancestral village. India specific terrorist groups operate in tandem with the ISI now well established by documentary and oral evidence.

In mid - 1992 Raja Vijay Karan, my boss, was to retire from service. As the replacement became a problem, he was given a month's extension. He was reluctant to continue on moral grounds. All officers who never worked in CBI jumped into the fray. They allegedly pushed their cases. Some favoured me too. The home secretary reportedly was not in favour of me. The panel of officers did include my name as third in the list of three. Much later I learnt that the Cabinet Secretary reversed the position bringing my name on the top. In this flux situation I decided that I would tender my papers in case of denial of promotion as I had served the CBI in all capacities like SP, DIG, Joint Director and lastly as Additional Director the last in the ladder then. I remained in CBI for nearly 15 years. However, I became the Director of the CBI.

16

Syed Modi Murder Case and Anti-Sikh Riots

Syed Modi was a famous badminton player winning eight times national badminton champion; won the Austrian International in 1983 and 1984; won singles bronze in 1982 Asian Games; received the Arjuna Award in 1981. Syed Modi was born in 1962 in a lower middle class Muslim family of a small town Sarsarnagar in Gorakhpur district. He worked with North East Railway in Gorakhpur and subsequently transferred to Lucknow. He was ranked number one in the country at the time of his tragic death. He married another badminton player Ameeta Kulkarni. Modi was deeply attached to his wife. Being a Muslim, he even went to Pasupathinath to bring *prasad* for his wife.

Modi was shot dead by a group of persons around 7.45 pm near the exit gate of KD Singh Babu Badminton Stadium, Lucknow on July 23, 1988 as he was on his way to his residence on scooter after his regular practice. One of the assailants fired five bullets into his body. The culprits escaped in a white Maruti van bearing No HYG 1959. The case was initially investigated by the CID with no progress. After a good deal of outcry, the case was handed over to CBI on 2 August 1988 at the request of the state government. The CID briefed the CBI officers and the point they were making was that murder might have been committed by a don of the eastern UP without any iota of evidence. They even did not have the gateway vehicle number. They were not even sure about the colour of the vehicle. Thus, initially it was a blind case.

We decided to induct two DIGs and a team of good Investigating Officers [IOs]. It was decided that the CBI would investigate the case afresh from crime to criminal principle. Thus, the IOs were firstly engaged to record the statements of people who were in the vicinity of the scene of crime. One witness surfaced who had recorded the vehicle number only. He along with others used to gamble on correct number of incoming vehicles. The gambler recording the correct number used to get the prize money. This was the first partial breakthrough of the case, partial because the state or district alphabets of the vehicle were not available. The same number could be of any district or state.

A sub-Inspector of a local police station attached with the CBI team spotted a vehicle bearing the same number parked in Hazratganj. He took the driver and occupants of the vehicle to CBI. The name of the real user of the vehicle Akhilesh Singh surfaced. Senior officers interrogated him. Because of sustained interrogation, the full story of the case came out. Based on his disclosure statement, searches were conducted with recovery of documentary evidence against the suspects. Akhilesh had got the Maruti van from one Abdul Khaliq known to him on the pretext of some important work. Akhilesh Singh was a rich person of Rae Bareilly having a number of cars. This was significant evidence against Akhilesh Singh and his intentions to carry out some important assignment by using some other's vehicle. He provided the crime weapon and ammunition to Amar Bahadur Singh and Bhagwati Singh who was a bodyguard of Akhilesh Singh. All the accused persons mainly the killer group were linked with Akhilesh Singh as evident from previous FIRs registered against them. The weapon used in the murder was recovered and matched with the bullets used in the crime as reported by forensic expert. Akhilesh Singh and Sanjay Singh were very close to each other as proved by documentary and oral evidence.

Sanjay Singh as the sports minister of UP was the chief guest in a badminton tournament in Lucknow held in 1983 when he came in contact with Modi and Ameeta. From here, the story of relationship developed between the two. In 1984, Ameeta came to Lucknow for her B.A. exam, stayed with Subroto Roy's family for sometime, and subsequently shifted to A-8 Park Road, Lucknow in May 1984, the house was in unauthorized possession of Sanjay Singh. Sanjay Singh arranged the marriage between Modi and Ameeta on 14 May 1984 and the certificate of marriage was issued by Ram under pressure when he was not the authorized officer for the purpose.

Ameeta who was working as a clerk in Bombay tendered her resignation and Sanjay Singh created a post of manager of Pradeshik Cooperative Dairy Federation and Ameeta got the job. Gradually the duo developed illicit relationship. Much of this was found from oral statements and diary entries and letters written by Ameeta. Modi was averse to this relationship and even doubted the pregnancy of Ameeta. The girl child was born on 4 February 1988 at the Army Command Hospital through the influence of Sanjay Singh. At the time of birth, Modi was nowhere because of obvious reasons.

As most of the suspects were political, there was a huge debate on the 'holes' in the investigation of the case in the press and in organized press conferences. CBI engaged the Samant a prominent lawyer from Mumbai as its special prosecutor for obvious reasons. The CBI filed a chargesheet against former minister Sanjay Singh of Amethi, Ameeta Modi, Akhilesh Singh, Bhagwati Singh, Jitender Singh, Amar Bahadur Singh and Balai Singh on November 7, 1988. Against the conspirators namely Sanjay Singh, Ameeta Modi and Akhilesh, the case was based on their conduct before and after the murder, the conspirators were in touch with each other on phone and Akhilesh Singh returned to Lucknow after the murder after visiting Hardwar and stayed in a Lucknow hotel with a fictitious name. Evidence of intimate relationship between Sanjay Singh and Ameeta was found recorded in Ameeta's diary and letters exchanged between the mother of Ameeta and Ameeta.

Something happened on 20 July 1988 at the residence of Modi which was seen by Gyan Prakash Jaiswal when he visited his old friend Modi. He found Modi sitting in the drawing room alone while Sanjay Singh and Ameeta were in the bedroom watching a video film. Modi wanted to play cards with his friend and went inside the bedroom to fetch cards. Modi returned with anguished face, told his friend that he was in no mood to play cards, and gave clear indication to leave him alone. There was other evidence to prove that Modi was getting averse to Sanjay Singh. Modi had no enmity with any one except Sanjay Singh because of reasons already explained in the chargesheet.

In support of the chargesheet, the prosecution cited 296 prosecution witnesses and 146 documentary evidence. As stated already the CBI appointed Advocate Samant from Mumbai who had handled Gen Vaidya's murder case as PP of this case also. The chargesheet was filed on 7 November 1988.

As there was change of government, there was change of Director who took charge of the CBI on 11 January 1990. The new Director Rajender Shekhar was perhaps asked to study the case again. He did not find anything wrong in the investigation of the case. One day I received a telephone call from an officer close to Cabinet Secretary that hearing for framing of the charge in the case was being preponed from the day already fixed for hearing and I should agree to it and not oppose the move. I said that it was not possible as our special counsel was in Mumbai and it was not possible for him to come earlier as there was no time for that. He expressed his surprise. Moreover I told him to contact the Director who was abroad.

Next thing that came to my notice was that the Director was told to change our special counsel. The Director asked me to meet him at his North Block office. He told me that the government wanted to know whether the Director would change the counsel. He wanted my views. I told him it was not possible in principle. He agreed with me. He asked me if I was prepared to put in my papers if the counsel was changed. I said 'yes'. He felt happy, as he too had decided to do so. I do not know whom did he communicate our decision.

Next thing that happened was something unheard of. All of a sudden, in the name of economy, the government issued an order cancelling the appointments of all special counsels engaged by various departments to deal with their court cases. Therefore, our special counsel's appointment was automatically terminated. All were surprised, but did not know the real reason. A Mumbai newspaper published a story on the subject hinting at the Modi murder case as the reason behind such an unusual step of the government. There was a panic reaction as a result of which our counsel's appointment was restored. The appointment of other counsels stood terminated. The CBI used to resist any interference in the investigation or during the trial of cases. As Director I was called to meet the Principal Secretary to the Prime Minister. He was almost furious and wanted to know why the CBI was proceeding against Anderson, an accused of the Bhopal Gas leak case. He said that by doing so we were preventing foreign investment. I argued that the case was in court and we can do nothing. I was not sure whether he was acting on his own or due to political pressure. On return to office I did nothing as I was not hankering after post retirement assignments or violating rule and law.

The trial court dropped charges against Sanjay Singh and Ameeta on September 17, 1990, at the time of framing of the charge, while the high court dropped the case against Akhilesh Singh on August 29, 1996. Accused Balai Singh died during the trial, while accused Amar Bahadur Singh was later murdered. I wonder if the local police solved this murder of Amar Bahadur Singh. What was the need to murder one accused during the trial will remain a mystery.

The high court and the Supreme Court upheld the discharge of Sanjay Singh, Ameeta, and Akhilesh Singh. It may be mentioned here that charges were framed against Akhilesh Singh and four others. Akhilesh Singh moved the high court that as the alleged two conspirators were discharged for conspiracy, he being shown as a conspirator also deserved to be discharged.

Here, I wish to elaborate deficiency in the Indian judicial system where confessions or statements of the accused as recorded by the police officer of any rank are not admissible in court. Only in TADA and POTA, such statements are admissible.

Statements recorded by custom officers of the rank of inspectors are admissible in court. The Supreme Court while dealing with the case has observed that 'the learned Additional Solicitor General has frankly admitted to the query from the court that an attempt on the side of the prosecution to record a statement under section 164 of the Code of Criminal Procedure from any of the accused, was not fruitful.' The fact was that Akhilesh Singh had spelt out the entire conspiracy not only before the investigating officers but also before very senior officers of the CBI. He knew that such statements are inadmissible evidence in the courts. Every effort to change the law failed so far. Our special counsel had opined before filing the charge-sheet that the CBI case was strong on four specific grounds like identification of assailants, evidence of Abdul Khaliq who gave his car, evidence of the man in Haridwar who said on hearing Modi's death, face of Akhilesh had gone pale and made attempts several time to contact Sanjay Singh on 29, 30 July 1988. He further observed that 'approver or no approver, the chances are bright'.

In August 2009, the trial court sentenced Bhagwati Singh for life imprisonment. The other surviving accused was acquitted for lack of evidence. It was argued on behalf of accused Bhagwati Singh that he had no motive to commit the crime. In the judgment the trial judge observed that since Sanjay, Ameeta and Akhilesh had already been discharged, there was no need to reexamine the evidence against them. This is a significant observation.

There were no candle light gatherings and processions for justice for Modi. The saddest part was that nobody took up the case for showing public anger against the ghastly murder of a young badminton player of international repute. It became a case of motiveless murder by a solitary man who had no enmity with Modi or had even known him. Sanjay married Ameeta, may be just after their discharge from the trial court. The CBI charge-sheet had mentioned that the main motive to murder Modi was to eliminate Modi as he was proving an obstacle between Ameeta and Sanjay. Let Modi's soul rest in peace. As one commentator had written that Bhagwati Singh was mere a scapegoat and the case history of this case does leave a bad taste in the mouth of justice.

Anti-Sikh Riots

The anti-Sikh riots happened in 1984 after the assassination of Indira Gandhi. I was then posted in Allahabad. Most of the killings happened in Delhi. Many innocents were targets of the carnage. I know many Hindu families even saved Sikh families. There were attempts to divide the Hindus and the Sikhs on communal lines. The reality is that Sikhs and Hindus are intertwined. As a student of university I happened to visit the home of a Hindu friend living in Karol Bagh. He introduced a turban wearing Sikh as his blood brother. I was amazed how a Sikh could be his real brother. He told me that his family or for that matter many families in Punjab had the tradition to have a Sikh in the family. This was the reality of the Punjab society.

The ISI had a gameplan to divide India into several independent states. Before launching full scale terrorism in Kashmir in 1989, the ISI was working on this plan and did succeed in creating a rift between the communities by training and sheltering Sikh youths in Pakistan with the help of Sikh expatriates.

The anti-Sikh riots was a blot on India's image as a law abiding country. A number of commissions and committees were instituted to find out the culprits of this carnage. Sajjan Kumar was indicted by a commission. The case was referred to CBI for investigation in 1990 during VP Singh's regime. The DIG heading the unit was a mona Sikh from Andhra Pradesh cadre. He along with his officers reached the residence of Sajjan Kumar in the early morning for search and arrest of Sajjan Kumar. The Delhi police was informed of the proposed raid in advance. From nowhere hundreds of supporters of Sajjan Kumar surrounded the residence of Sajjan Kumar and the DIG was under threat to his life. He could have been lynched. The DIG was ultimately rescued by the local police.

As usual the case was investigated professionally with the recommendation for prosecution of Sajjan Kumar and others. The case was referred to the Home Ministry for sanction as there was one section of IPC for which sanction was required. The ministry sent the file to Delhi government in 1991 as Lt

Governor was required to issue the sanction. The CBI kept on reminding the MHA for issuance of sanction almost on monthly basis. The sanction was received in 1994 after change of regime in Delhi government. By then I had retired in 1993.

Julio Ribeiro has since provided the reason for lukewarm response of the government in his book *Bullet for Bullet*. He has written in his book that he had raised this issue before Rajiv Gandhi several times and on one occasion Rajiv Gandhi 'lost his temper' and bluntly told him not to raise this issue again. According to Ribeiro, Sajjan Kumar was 'a loyalist committed to Gandhi family'. This would perhaps explain why the Lt Governor was not issuing the sanction for years together.

17

Rajiv Gandhi Murder Case

I was Additional Director, CBI, when the brutal assassination of Rajiv Gandhi took place. The year was 1991 and Rajiv Gandhi was fully involved in election campaign for forthcoming general election. The prime minister was Chandrashekar. Rajiv had hardly any security cover. He was provided with a sub-inspector of Delhi police armed with a revolver. The state government under the President's rule however did provide police bandobast at election meetings and campaigns. For political reasons many in this country and abroad were opposed to his leadership.

On May 21, 1991 at about 10.30 pm, I got a call from S Ramani, DIG CBI, Madras, now called Chennai that Rajiv had been killed in a blast in Sriperambudur where he was to address an election meeting. I told him that the case would definitely come to CBI for investigation. Therefore, he should be ready with a selected group of officers and keep himself abreast with all possible information. The government of Tamil Nadu, as expected, handed over the case to CBI on 24 May 1991. We collected Tamil knowing officers to form the core team. DR Karthikeyan, then serving in CRPF as IG in Hyderabad, was inducted to head the Special Task Force [SIT] in the team. He had been to Sri Lanka earlier for assessing IPKF's role. His one condition was that he would hold the dual charge of Joint Director CBI and IG CRPF. This was agreed to. This was a wise decision on the part of Karthikeyan as the CBI lacked manpower even to guard its own temporary headquarters at Malligai. Radhavinod Raju, an IPS officer from J&K, was drawn into the team as DIG. Raju had proved his mettle in operational matters in the anti-insurgency operations in J&K. Sri Kumar, already serving in CBI, was also drawn, as was Amod Kanth, who was posted in the CBI Delhi as DIG. DIG Ramani was very clear about the way the teams to function. He formulated the idea that three teams would be required. One team would be called operational group to hunt for all the suspected persons on the basis of leads. The second team was called interrogation team to interrogate all the possible persons. If the interrogations were fruitful, the persons concerned would be handed over to investigation team. All the teams were headed by officers of the rank of DIGs. The fourth team, if I can call it, was to provide logistic support to all the teams. This team was headed by Ramani, in addition to his duties as DIG of CBI Chennai. We anticipated that the case would require huge manpower as initially it was a blind case.

We reached Madras by a special BSF plane. We visited the scene of occurrence where Raghavan, then IG forest Tamil Nadu, was present. He was made in charge of police arrangements at Sriperambudur where the killing occurred. It was a blind case as there was no clue to start a vigorous investigation. The identity of the lady who acted as a human bomb could not be established. Her body was found blown up in several parts. The parts of the body were recovered form different areas. Some parts of her body were recovered from far off places. I had some knowledge of DNA testing facility available in Hyderabad under the guidance of Dr Lalji Singh. Singh was the pioneer in establishing DNA centre in Hyderabad, India. He was to establish if the parts of the body recovered of a lady were of one person. Lalji Singh gave a report that confirmed that the parts of the body belonged to same person, the woman suicide bomber.

The bespectacled woman, who acted as suicide bomber, was wearing green and orange salwar-kameez. She was not frisked, as women were not frisked or bodily checked by metal detector. This would perhaps explain why a woman was selected as a bomber and not a man. Some thought that woman suicide bomber was a Punjabi as she was wearing salwar-kameez. Haribabu, a photographer from Chennai, clicked ten pictures including the last picture of the blast by using a borrowed Chinon camera. He too died in the blast. The blast was so powerful that the fire rose up to 20 feet high. Eighteen were killed, forty-four others were injured, some with grievous injuries including Mohd. Iqbal, the SP of the district. I had known Iqbal during my previous visit to Kachipuram to meet the world famous Swami. Paul Burton had written about him in the thirties in his famous book 'Search in Secret India'. I felt very sad when I heard about his death.

There was total chaos and utter panic. Many including policemen fled the scene of dastardly crime. However, the IG Raghavan and few other police officers remained present to secure evidence. By instinct Raghavan got the camera of Haribabu seized and helped the injured to hospital. He believed in presence of his body and not absence of body. He secured the scene of occurrence for collection of evidence.

The Tamil Nadu Forensic Science Laboratory in short TNFSL headed by its Director P Chandrasekharan had visited the scene of occurrence. He and his team gathered evidence to prove that a jacket was used for the blast. Director CBI directed that the blast site and area beyond be searched again by what he called a 'sweeping' exercise and that proved useful by way of collection of metallic pellets, parts of battery, detonators, switches and other material objects relevant to the case. It was proved beyond doubt that RDX was used. The *Hindu* published an edited photograph of the first picture of salwar-kameez woman holding the sandalwood garland flanked with Latha and her daughter Kokila. The photograph of the kurta-payjama man with a notebook in his hand was also in the frame of the first picture but not shown in the published picture in the *Hindu*. I still wonder whether the partial publication of the edited picture of salwar-kameez woman helped or hindered the investigation.

For nearly 10 days, the CBI did not benefit from briefings from intelligence agencies as either they had no intelligence or there was attempt to conceal facts. Some stories were published in some newspapers that a breakaway group called Black LTTE might have carried out the killing and acted on its own on some old previous instructions of the LTTE. It was decided to work out the case on the well-established crime detection theory of crime to criminal basis. As nothing was immediately available by way a good clue, Vijay Karan, Director CBI, decided to move to Colombo to interact with their agencies. On May 30, 1991 the Director, and Additional Director [self] and SIT Chief Karthikeyan reached Colombo. We found Shekher Gupta an eminent journalist travelling in the same flight. He stayed with us in the same hotel Taj Samudra. Often he used to interact with me. He appreciated why we were not in a position to disclose the briefing we had from the agencies.

The most effective agency in Colombo was their military intelligence agency, which had apparently moles in Madras. They, I must admit, gave a lot of information to us. We more or less concluded that the role of LTTE would require deeper probe. The Director and SIT Chief returned to Chennai and I was told to remain in Colombo for a good length of time for further collection of intelligence. It was fairly clear that LTTE operatives and their sympathizers had vast network in Tamil Nadu. All their places were searched with good results. It may be mentioned that while staying in Colombo we learnt that there was a telephone call to Indian High Commission at about 4 pm on 21 May seeking to know whether Rajiv Gandhi was still alive. The caller's name or his telephone number were not noted as that was not asked or the caller hung-up the telephone. To us this was significant as the call was made some six hours before the assassination of Rajiv Gandhi. This information was not passed on to Indian agencies as it was perhaps thought to be a prank or a hoax call.

I could obtain valuable information from an agency in Colombo that there was regular clandestine wireless communication between Jaffna and Chennai by LTTE. I got the code numbers of both the stations. I wanted their transcripts but the Colombo authorities who evaded the issue by saying that those would be available with the Indian agencies. This I consider was a big breakthrough during my long stay in Colombo.

The members of other Tamil militant groups like Tamil Eelam Liberation Organization, Eelam People's Revolutionary Liberation Front and Eelam People's Democratic Party met me and all of them blamed LTTE for the murder of Rajiv Gandhi. They failed to provide specific information on the identity of woman suicide bomber or man in kurta-pyjama captured in the camera of Haribabu as they did not have much presence in Tamil majority areas of Sri Lanka. These groups were mostly functioning from Colombo.

The SIT on May 29 issued an appeal to identify the photograph of the woman suicide bomber and the man in kurta-pyjama, which had already appeared in the press. The dedicated telephone numbers of SIT were published to communicate any information and the caller's identity would be kept secret. The SIT was flooded with informations and most of them were bogus or untrue. However, one information was leading us somewhere. A man living in Villivakkam in Chennai disclosed that his wife had seen their neighbour called Nalini along with the suicide bomber and the kurta-pyjama man and another female going out together on 21 May, the day Rajiv was killed. He also provided additional information that one Das used to visit Nalini's house very frequently. Nalini vacated her house on May 26 and left for an unknown destination. She worked somewhere in Adyan. This was indeed a big development. In the second picture of Haribabu, Nalini and another girl were seen sitting in public ground. The duo did not match with the crowd of local people by dress and appearance. Why Haribabu did capture their photograph in his camera?

On my return to Delhi via Chennai, I contacted the Indian agency to provide us with the transcripts of LTTE messages between Jaffna and Chennai. The initial response was evasive. I then provided the station codes of both the stations. Finally, they provided the transcripted messages before and after the Rajiv Gandhi's death. The culture of intelligence agencies is to keep such messages secret. Instead, all over the world such vital messages are converted into source information. Recall, when conversation between Gen Musharraf and Gen Aziz were released to the press in India during the Kargil War, many of my friends who had worked with such agencies, felt that India had snapped a vital link built up with great effort.

However, in our case the messages were important from the point of view of evidence. We did receive the decoded messages, which indicated a plan to do something big. These messages were decoded only after the assassination of Rajiv Gandhi. The delay was for various reasons. The messages were clear to show how the planning to assassinate Rajiv was meticulously planned and executed. There was mentioning of an Indian girl being a part of the conspiracy.

In the first week of June a bunch of papers was received from Tamil Nadu police. They had received them from unknown source, may be by post. The papers related to the photographer Haribabu. A scrutiny of these papers revealed close links of Haribabu with LTTE. A letter written by Haribabu's fiancé was found to be clinching as she had warned Haribabu from venturing into a dangerous path. That Haribabu purchased a sandalwood garland from an emporium could be found from a receipt of the emporium on the date of assassination. Haribabu did emerge as a suspect and not a mere photographer.

Why Haribabu was engaged with the task to capture all the relevant photographs leading to the final act of assassination of Rajiv Gandhi? We learnt that LTTE supremo was always doing that for every major operation by way of record and for training the LTTE cadres. Some even said that he used to get sadistic pleasure by seeing these pictures. Haribabu made a mistake by not positioning himself at a safe distance. He knew about the blast as he clicked the last picture of the terrific blast with a fireball rising to a great height. IG Raghavan realizing the importance of snapshots in camera was a vital piece of evidence. Many efforts were made by interested persons for retrieval of the camera and requested the same to be given to them on one ground or other. He did not yield to such pressures.

There was perfect coordination between the Tamil Nadu police and SIT. The local police picked up one Shanker because of his suspicious movements near Thanjavur, the route to seaside to escape to Jaffna. From his possession, two pieces of paper were recovered, containing a telephone number and names of Nalini and Das. The other paper contained the telephone number and address of a store in Porur. This was another significant breakthrough as Nalini was found to be working with a company.

A smuggler from a coastal village was questioned by local police on the basis of information furnished by Shanker. He identified kurta-pyjama man captured in the first picture of Haribabu as Sivarasan with one false eye. Soon he was called 'one-eyed jack'. When Bhagyanathan was interrogated, he confessed that Nalini was his sister. Realizing the developing situation Nalini ran for her life after putting in her resignation letter to her office. On the basis of Bhagyanathan's interrogation the identities of Nalini, Subha, Sivarasan, Das alias Murugan and Dhanu, the suicide bomber, were firmly established corroborated by bits of information/papers received independently from various suspects and witnesses. The task was to arrest the gang of four. Their blown up photographs were pasted on the walls all over Tamil Nadu. Murugan became very close to Nalini as a result she was in the family way.

To cut the long story short, it may be of interest to readers to know that a dry run was organized by the conspirators to cover VP Singh's public address on 7th May 1991 and the drill included garlanding by Dhanu. All the main conspirators were present as found out from a video recording. This was a good piece of admissible evidence.

Raju's tracking team chased Nalini and Murugan on the basis of each lead. On 14 Junre 1991, the tracking team informed SIT Chennai that the duo had left for Chennai from Villuppuram by bus. Several teams were sent to several bus stands at night in Chennai and kept watch on other hiding places. Before midnight the duo was caught at Saidapet bus stand. Their interrogations led to various discoveries of facts all relevant to prove the conspiracy.

The main task was to apprehend Sivarasan and Subha. Subha, Dhanu and Sivarasan had arrived in Chennai on 2 May 1991 just 19 days before the assassination of Rajiv Gandhi. Out of two ladies, one was to act as the suicide bomber. I heard a story that the two were so inspired that Dhanu was given the privilege to kill Rajiv Gandhi. Sivarasan, the one-eyed jack as he was called, was always in wireless communication with Pottu Amman, the intelligence chief of the LTTE and a confidant of Prabhakaran. I was taken into confidence by the wireless tracking agency in Chennai to show how the system worked. At fixed hours both the stations would send coded messages. The agency's set would show a clear line between Jafna and Tamil Nadu. I enquired if it was possible to pinpoint the exact location of the clandestine station in Tamil Nadu. A very senior officer manning our interception set told me that it was possible if we had two direction finders to be located outside Chennai. I asked why this was not being done. His reply was that extra sets were not available. I then said why not procure them. He said such procurement would be time-consuming. Three monitoring stations would give us only the area location of LTTE clandestine station in Tamil Nadu.

On return to Delhi, I approached the defence ministry for providing two mobile stations. My own school batchmate was heading the Army Signals. He told me that they had truck driven mobile facility and parking them in remote parts of Tamil Nadu would create suspicion and disrupt the stations in Chennai and Jafna. I did understand his logic as the LTTE intelligence setup was very active in Tamil Nadu. Added to this was press reports of SIT's efforts to locate Sivarasan's mobile wireless station.

Clandestine operation of wireless communication is an offence. I approached minister Rajesh Pilot for two more mobile sets. He tried his best, but failed to locate two spare sets. All this was required to locate the area from where Sivarasan was running his mobile wireless set. Evidence had already surfaced that he was always carrying his mobile wireless set with him. Once the area location is found, the hand held signal detection device would lead us to the exact place of operation of Sivarasan's mobile wireless station on the basis signal strength and catch Sivarasan alive by a commando action. This I learnt from a retired communication expert who had experience in catching smugglers in this way.

We knew that all LTTE operatives of Sri Lankan origin or Indian origin carried cyanide capsules to be consumed in the event of arrest and therefore we arranged procurement of cyanide antidote from a foreign country. I at least never knew that there was antidote for cyanide. I do not recall a case of survival of any LTTE operatives in our case even after the administration of antidote.

The SIT was working on each lead and managed to arrest many suspects. Huge quantities of documents were recovered. The interrogation and the investigation teams were acting in tandem. Each one feeding the tracking team with new leads. I am only narrating such events where I did my best to assist the SIT. Delhi was informed that an old man called Kanakasabapathy with a young girl called Athirai had left for Delhi sometime in May 1991 by the Grand Trunk Express. I told the CBI Jabalpur branch to board the train and keep a secret watch on them. At Delhi station they proceeded to their destination and were arrested. The girl's real name was Chanralekhea. If my memory is correct, they had already hired a flat in Shantineketan near Moti Bagh. The possible reason for safe house in Delhi was to provide a safe passage to Sivarasan to escape through the Nepal route as no visa is required by an Indian to visit Nepal. All his efforts to escape through sea route were blocked.

This happened, as there was heightened surveillance on sea routes by the customs, local police, coast guard, Indian Navy, Sri Lankan Navy to plug all the routes of escape. The SIT was always issuing alert notices to all concerned almost on daily basis.

We introduced the telephone call analysis in Modi murder case and in the case of murder of a custom officer Arora in Allahabad. There is a tendency among criminals to keep each other informed of a major crime. In both the cases, the results were fruitful. We inducted one Inspector from the Cochin branch who was highly qualified in retrieval of telephone call records and making a sense out of several calls. Use of telephone by Sivarasan led to an analysis of various telephones in India and abroad. Immediately after the killing of Rajiv Gandhi, Kittu, an

LTTE leader based in London received a call from Madras around 10.30 pm [Indian time] and Kittu in turn spoke with his counterpart in Paris immediately thereafter. It may be recalled Kittu was the first LTTE leader to issue a press statement that LTTE was not involved in the killing of Rajiv Gandhi.

London was the base available for all terrorist groups including Khalistani groups. The UK was equally non-cooperative in putting a stop to these terrorist groups. We decided to approach the UK authorities for search and questioning of Kittu. I personally met the agencies for this in London. Meanwhile, Kittu had already left UK for an unknown destination in Europe. How did Kittu know about the scheme of Indian investigators? Someone must have alerted him in advance. The LTTE's known office in London was not searched on the ground of one agency not agreeing with the other. Only after 9/11 under pressure from the USA, the UK authorities started repatriating wanted terrorists of Middle East countries, many of whom were convicted in their respective countries.

Sivarasan and the killer group could have escaped to Jaffna the same way they came to Tamil Nadu by a speedboat as they did in a previous case of a similar murder of a prominent Sri Lankan Tamil leader in Madras. The most possible reason was to kill Perumal Vardarajan, who was the chief minister of the Tamil dominated area in Sri Lanka. He was kept in some location which was known to LTTE. Such evidence did emerge during the investigation. If he had gone back immediately after the murder of Rajiv Gandhi, the investigation of the case would have ended in capturing small fries. The Indian Navy, Coast Guards, and Sri Lankan Navy were alerted on the basis of intelligence inputs almost daily on the basis of intercepts on wireless between the LTTE under the command of Pottu Aman, LTTE's Intelligence chief and Sivarasan. The LTTE continued to use the same code and with the same station numbers. This indicated that they were not aware of our interceptions.

Raju, our operational chief continued to follow each piece of information to its logical conclusion. Eventually, Sivarasan's hideout was located by the combined efforts of officers of Bangalore

Police and SIT which was on outskirts of Bangalore city. The place is called Konankunte. I received a message of this location at midnight from Ramani. I left for Bangalore in the morning. The Director CBI was in Delhi. Karthyeikan was already in Bangalore. Police secured the area. It was decided to storm the hideout by a contingent of commandoes of NSG who were already in Bangalore. In the evening, of 19 August the Director and all of us were discussing how to apprehend them alive. We knew that each of them was carrying cyanide capsule to consume in the event of their apprehension of arrest.

In the midst of discussion in a police station, we were told that Sivarasan group had started firing. On reaching the spot, we were almost in a war zone. The firing was relentless from the side of LTTE. Vijay Karan, Director of CBI, ordered the NSG commandos to storm the building. Vijay Karan was a pragmatic officer with tremendous common sense. His leadership qualities were worth following. The NSG wanted the attack to be mounted under the command of Col Datta who arrived in late night with a box of cyanide antidote. By the time he arrived the firing had stopped. There was a drama in the whole situation. Before firing started from nowhere a truck arrived near the building and got stuck may be because of mechanical failure. Someone came out of the building shouted 'pedo' in Tamil that is to get out from there. The Sivarasan group wrongly thought that under the cover of a stuck up truck the forces would mount an attack by storming the building. Instead of waiting for the attack, they thought it would be wise to start firing knowing fully well that there was no escape route available. At midnight, there was sound of a firing inside the house and there was sound of crying also. This indicated suicide by a prominent leader in the group. Thereafter, perhaps there was blasting of a grenade and complete silence. All these happened before arrival of Col Dutta. In the early morning, the NSG stormed the building from the roof and blasted the doors by using explosives. Reaching the ground floor, many dead bodies were found in a row. There was a heap of ashes that indicated burning of documents. Surprisingly, there was not much of blame game in the entire episode as capturing the group of LTTE members alive was already a remote possibility. They were highly indoctrinated to lay down their lives in the event of such a situation. After this major event, the main task of the investigation was over. Even the SIT could unearth much evidence the way Sivarasan escaped from Tamil Nadu to Karnataka by a tanker, changing houses frequently in Karnataka, moving around the city in two vehicles purchased in the name of other persons and examining people sheltering them.

The CBI and SIT's principal challenge was to work out a blind case into an open case of deep conspiracy hatched by a dangerous terrorist organization led by a ruthless leader who had eliminated all other Tamil Eelam groups to emerge as the only leader for the Tamil cause in Sri Lanka. In his scheme of things, there was a dream to create a Tamil National Retrieval Troops in Tamil Nadu. A small number of local Tamils were trained in Jaffna. This was a dangerous game that would have created a situation like ULFA in Assam. In fact, there was indication of LTTE's effort to contact Paresh Barua, the prominent leader of ULFA.

The dangerous game of LTTE was exposed when the CBI sent pointers to many countries giving them evidence of contact of Sri Lankan Tamils living abroad who were giving LTTE monetary help and organizing dispatch of arms from international markets. Even Japan came to know about their sophisticated wireless equipment were being purchased by the LTTE. The recovery of wireless sets of Japan in India could not be proved as in Japan the retailers did not keep records of sale of such items to purchasers. I personally checked this in Japan when I went there to attend a conference on organized crime.

Political murder cases abroad like Kennedy, Liaquat Ali murder case, Benazir murder case remained unsolved. Many more such cases can be in the list of unresolved cases in the world. However, India's track record is impressive as almost all political murder cases were solved. It is my firm conviction that such cases deserve to be treated differently as these cases affect the democratic framework of the country.

The IG headed the SIT; we had drawn four competent DIGs, eight SPs, 14 Deputy Superintendants of police, and 44 Inspectors.

In addition, there was a big contingent of sub-inspectors, head constables and constables. The state police also deputed their best officers. The entire police force of the country was working whenever they had leads to follow.

Imagine the scale of investigation of this case where accused identified were 41, witnesses numbering 1,044, 500 video cassettes, 1, 00,000 photographs, 1,477 documents and 1180 material exhibits. These were culled out from massive collection of statements, documents and exhibits.

The entire SIT under the able dynamic leadership of IG Karthkeyan and his group of dedicated officers deserve praise for working out the case quickly. The SP, under the provision TADA, can record the statements of the accused. Such statements were admissible in a court of law under the provisions of TADA. A great deal of care was taken to select the SP to record such statements from another jurisdiction, not connected with SIT in any way, so as to raise the confidence of the judge during the trial. This extra precaution was not required under TADA.

Interrogation is a difficult ball game. An experienced IO has to have an extra qualification that comes out of long experience. The psychology and mental frame of mind of the suspects need to be understood. Initially, there is normal resistance to speak out the truth. This is understandable. The idea of getting pardon granted to the accused under the law does not work. At times the suspect develops liking for some interrogators for some reason. He becomes friendly to the suspect. For this to happen, some so-called unfriendly interrogators initially put questions that perhaps could irritate the suspect. In police parlance, this is called friend or foe approach.

In CBI third degree method is not used. This method is used when the suspects remain in police custody for a short period, as is the case in ordinary crime. Under TADA, the period of detention in police custody was 90 days, enough to engage the suspect in long conversations. Success was very commendable to unearth the story of the conspiracy, who all had hatched the conspiracy, who all were tasked with specific duties, how logistics were organized and help obtained from the locals. The team leader Sivarasan was required to keep Pottu Aman informed of developments on a daily basis by wireless communication. We learnt of this mode of communication from Sri Lankan agencies. As said already a good deal of information came from arrested suspects and that added knowledge was good enough for further interrogation of suspects. It becomes easy if the suspects know that the investigating agency already has all the facts. In that situation, they open up and disclose many more facts.

I as an Additional Director decided to reinterrogate Nalini and another arrested suspect only to find out if some additional information could be obtained. Nalini was in the family way. She was deeply in love with suspect Murugan. She was more concerned with the fate of Murugan. I merely sympathized with her and that was enough for her to reveal more facts. She said that to divert the attention from LTTE she was made to write two misleading letters to Commissioner of Police, Madras and one to CBI. The letter addressed to Commissioner could not be retrieved, but one addressed to CBI could be retrieved. Her handwriting was established and that helped the prosecution case further. The other suspect was apprehended at night and he could not consume cyanide capsule, as he could not find his spectacles? Then the next question was how it happened. His answer was amazing. He said that he had no *bibhuti* of Sai Baba for application. I asked him whether he would like to have a bit of Sai *bibhuti*. He jumped with joy. I had a packet of *Sai bibhuti* with me and I just gave a pinch of it. It worked and he told many more facts not known before. Every police officer has fair idea and his own technique of questioning a suspect. For this time is required. That is one of the reasons why a special act is required to deal with terrorist and organized crime cases.

The investigation of the case could be completed within one year along with filing of chargesheet 20 May 1992. There was no interference from political side. The state government of Tamil Nadu provided all possible facilities including its dedicated telephone network that could reach any police station at any time day and night. On one occasion, the local police because of telephonic instructions could promptly bring out recoveries of wireless equipment, concealed under the earth. Help came from other states also.

The case ended in conviction by the trial court on 28 January 1998. All the 26 accused were awarded death sentence. The Supreme Court's final verdict was delivered on 5 May 1999 confirming death sentence of Nalini, Santhan, Murugan and Perarivalan alias Arivu. Three others received life sentence. One accused was charged only under TADA and he was not found guilty. Eighteen remaining were found guilty of lesser offences. Karthkeyan., Chief of SIT, did make a special presentation of the case in an Interpol conference before the trial court judgment. This was highly appreciated.

All the accused were acquitted of TADA charges even after the Supreme Court accepting the role of LTTE and its leadership in shaping and executing the conspiracy. The Supreme Court judgment of non-application of TADA in the murder of Rajiv Gandhi is likely to raise questions on interpretation of Section 3[1] of TADA. A Terrorist act is carried out 'with intent to overawe the Government as by law established or strike terror in people or any section of the people or to alienate any section of the people or to adversely affect the harmony amongst different sections of the people'. Rajiv Gandhi was killed because LTTE apprehended that in the event of his becoming the prime minister again, he may reinduct IPKF in Sri Lanka in terms of Indo-Sri Lanka accord and this would harm the LTTE's role for Eelam. This is why the LTTE decided to kill Rajiv in 1991 when the general election campaigning was on. Why he was not killed earlier? The intention was to overawe the present government and the government that would be formed after the general election. I as an ordinary citizen look at the definition of terrorism this way.

Now LTTE leadership structure does not exist on ground. Sri Lankan Army eliminated all of them in 2009. Other Eelam groups are still functioning. The Tamils in Sri Lanka have suffered a lot. They need healing touch. They need rehabilitation with dignity. Provincial autonomy is required to be introduced by amendment of the constitution. Unitary government is no solution. Diverse elements can be bonded togther by a federal structure.

In the end, I would recommend to all the police officers to read the book authored by DR Karthikeyan and Radhavinod Raju dealing with the assassination of Rajiv Gandhi. The book really unfolds the most gripping story of a world famous murder case. The chargesheet or judgment never provide how a difficult case is solved.

18

The Security Scam Case

While the CBI was at the completion stage of Rajiv Gandhi case, from nowhere a big security scam case surfaced in a big way. The case was handed over to CBI for investigation. From one challenging case to another was like galloping a horse without respite. This happens too often in CBI.

This was a unique fraud like of which had never seen before. This fraud was totally different from normal bank fraud cases with which we were fairly conversant. A journalist Sucheta Dalal smelt a rat in SBI by not accounting for a big shortfall in the area of recoveries in some big transactions carried out by Stock Market brokers.

Harshad Mehta had already earned the reputation of a financial wizard. His lifestory was that of a young man from an ordinary family hailing from a small town of Raipur to Mumbai where he built up the reputation of a Sultan of Dalal Street owning a fabulous house, Lexus car, all the trappings of a rich man graduating from rags to riches. He said that 'dream creation is not a crime'. The stock market hit the ceiling. Share prices went up to a new height. ACC shares were selling at Rs10,000 a share. Shares of a Modi Nagar nonfunctional manufacturing unit attracted the attention of investors. From a zero share price, it soon attracted much higher price. The bulls were dominating the market in a reckless manner. There was no system in place to find out the reasons for such unusual behaviour of the stock market.

Sucheta Dala, a lady journalist, broke the story of the contours of a big scam. She smelt a rat in SBI security dealings where there was shortfall in realizations from a broker. The news was picked up by other media persons. The matter rocked the Parliament. There was demand for a probe by CBI. There was also a demand for a Joint Parliamentary Committee to probe the matter in the national interest. Soon the fraud earned the name of a security scam.

Let me explain what security is. The securities are Government Securities which every bank is required to purchase as per statutory liquidity ratio [SLR] fixed by the Reserve Bank. If the holding of a bank has fewer securities than the statutory limit, then the bank would purchase securities from another bank holding excess securities. By sale of securities, the government generates money for its use. Thus, each bank is compelled to purchase Government securities earning low rate of interest.

Because of SLR requirement, a bank holding excess government securities would like to dispose of that excess to another bank holding less. It could be a direct deal with two banks. A broker who was doing this business for a commission could do the deals.

The selling bank of such securities to the purchasing bank will receive payment from the purchasing bank. In addition, the selling bank is required to intimate the Public Debt Office of the Reserve Bank of India of the sale of security to the purchasing bank. This is required for payment of interest to holders of such securities.

Brokers acted as intermediaries for sale and purchase of securities between the two banks. Harshad became the major broker for SBI. How did Harshad exploit this system for his own benefit? Harshad targeted two major banks like the SBI and UCO by cultivating officers dealing with this type of operations. Some of them behaved as if they were slaves of Harshad. They behaved the way Harshad wanted them to behave.

Let me, by way of examples; explain how the brokers subverted the system. Even in genuine sale and purchase of securities, the sale proceeds were deposited into the personal account of the broker. This money was thus made available to the broker for purchase of stocks or for diversion to other business purposes. This was in complete violation of RBI and Bank's own instructions.

There were cases of banks like cooperative banks to sell securities even to foreign banks, when the selling banks had no securities to sell. The selling bank even issued bogus Bank Receipts and Transfer Intimation to the Public Debt Office. Money, thus, obtained was again diverted to accounts of the fraudsters.

Greed became so powerful factor that brokers devised new methods to obtain money from the banks. One that came to notice was inducing the Public Sector Units like Maruti to park their surplus money as fixed deposits in some public sector banks. This too proved successful. Money so obtained was diverted into the personal or business account of the broker.

The other method was equally unique. Banks sold scripts of UTI to another bank. As the physical delivery of such huge quantity of Units was not feasible, the purchasing banks received Bank Receipts as a legal guarantee of holding such stocks. The fact was that the selling bank had no UTI units with them. Again, in such fraudulent transactions, the only beneficiaries were the brokers, who were playing with that kind of money in the stock market.

The security transactions were more complicated than what I have stated. It may only be stated that such transactions were for a brief period by adopting various technical terms like switch, buy back and the like. In this manner, there was enough scope to hide fraudulent transactions. In the SBI, for example, any security transaction of and above Rs 1,00,000 would require MD and Board's approval. This instructions were violated. The internal audit system, to the best of my knowledge, failed to detect such cases.

Harshad Mehta soon acquired the image of a great financial wizard. He had access to officers of the finance ministry for his high reputation. Some even suggested that he be appointed as a finance minister to change the face of India. Mehta and Dalal groups were found to be mostly involved. As these cases were complicated and new to CBI, it took time for CBI to understand the complexities of each case.

As usual, several groups of officers of the rank of Joint Directors, DIGs, SPs, Deputy SPs and a number of inspectors were drawn to investigate 40 odd cases. It was also found that some middle level officers of the nationalized banks were deeply involved. Some such officers were taken on world tour at the expense of the brokers. Searches revealed that bank cheques were issued by the broker to some persons holding high positions. The beneficiaries took the plea of having obtained loans from brokers. Interestingly, the payers and payees were not known to each other. Loan documents can be manufactured easily at any point of time.

In the course of searches by Income Tax, one or two Swiss bank account numbers were found. The Swiss authorities were approached. They claimed that the account holders were not connected with Harshad Mehta. They were, however, Indians. An Indian account holder told the Swiss authorities that he had deposited the money because of stringent fiscal laws in India. The Indian account holder's name was never revealed in the name of bank secrecy. The Swiss authorities did not bother to find out whether the money was illegally obtained. Mere assertion that he was not connected to Harshad Mehta was readily believed. What prevented the Swiss authorities to get that person examined by the Indian investigators? This is the usual route to attract foreign money into Switzerland. Swiss prospers on illegitimately obtained dirty and black money from other jurisdictions. In every Interpol conference, India has been asserting that such secrecy laws are depriving developing countries of their money and creating a worldwide financial disorder. Now the US and G20 countries have taken the view on tax haven countries that they must show transparency. This is the best time to retrieve Harshad Mehta documents showing operation of a Swiss bank account by an Indian. The concerned account holder may now to be questioned with reference to bank documents available with the Swiss authorities. Perhaps, we are not serious about initiating such action, as many heads are likely to roll in the event of disclosure of hidden accounts in seventeen odd tax haven countries. There is now a great deal of public awareness and government in power may adopt dilatory tactics in the absence of dual offence treaty with such countries. In future, a day will come when the whole world would demand lifting of bank secrecy laws to deal with organized crime money, terrorist funding, tax evasions and tax avoidance and clandestine political funding.

Here, I must admire the way the then Finance Minister Dr Manmohan Singh handled the security scam situation. He, in his wisdom, got an ordinance issued for attachment of property of the accused scam fraudsters and appointed a custodian for such properties, thus depriving the fraudsters of illegally earned money and property. The second step was that he lifted the restriction on investigation of officers of the level of joint secretary and above. Under the Single Directive of the Government of India, permission is required for investigation against such officers. This enabled the CBI to speed up the process of investigation. I feel the attachment ordinance should be applicable to all fraudsters and should not have remained security scam specific. I also feel that for bank frauds of serious kind there should a separate law treating it as a serious crime and punishment should be for 20 years imprisonment. I, now, find that my views are supported by the recommendation of the Law Commission, which has treated this type of offences as serious to be punished with life imprisonment. A separate Bank Fraud law exists in the USA treating it as an aggravated offence. I have not seen any such demand emanating from the political class so far. In no way can we allow subversion of our financial system by big fraudsters. The bail applications of the accused were rejected on this ground of serious subversion of the financial system.

The Finance Minister Dr Manmohan Singh was a class apart. His personal integrity was beyond doubt. His behaviour with public servants was unique. Personally, I have few sweet recollections worth recording. He never interfered with the investigation. He called me for discussion many times to update his knowledge of progress of investigation required by a minister to answer parliamentary questions and the like. He as minister would personally ring me up and ask me if I had time to have 'a cup of coffee' with him. Whenever I reached his office, he would greet me and both of us would sit on a sofa. At the time of departure, he himself would open the door, an unusual courtesy extended to an ordinary officer like me. His humility impressed me the way I was impressed by Lal Bahadur Shastri. I will carry these sweet experiences forever. I have never met him after retirement and in fact avoided meeting him in police functions, as I have nothing to seek from the government.

19

1993 Bombay Serial Blast Cases

On a single day i.e. on 12 March 1993, thirteen well-coordinated blasts occurred in the city which is the financial capital of India. Nothing like this had ever happened before. These thirteen blasts killed 250 innocent people and injured 700 others.

The seriousness of these attacks created a shock wave in the country. These attacks, many believed, were carried out in retaliation of communal riots in Mumbai after demolition of Babri/ Lord Rama temple structure in Ayodhya. I have already said that Mohd Hanif, an ISI agent toured India to select targets for future attacks. He along with some locals had a dry run of Madras Stock Exchange for a future blast. ISI was working on a plan for attacks on prominent installations, including the demolition of Babri/ temple structure. Attacks of the nature witnessed in Mumbai would require planning for a good length of time, may be a year or more. Mumbai riots in 1992 December or after may have provided a cause for a massive attacks showing the same as a retaliatory attack.

The Union home minister along with some IB officers rushed to Mumbai to assess the situation. I received a call from the home minister from Mumbai to know if February 1993 New York World Trade Centre bombing was similar to Mumbai attacks. I said it would depend on the result of investigation. In the New York World Trade Centre, some local radicals organized blast with the expert assistance of Ramzi Yousef. His uncle Sheikh Khalid Mohammed [SKM] had partly financed the blast in New York. It may be mentioned here that SKM was the principal architect of 9/11 attack by using civilian planes as flying rockets to hit the World Trade Centre and other buildings.

The explosives used in Twin Tower blasts in New York in 1993 were locally procured. In this urea, nitrate-hydrogen gases were used to enhance the impact of the intended blast. The chemicals in all weighing 680 kg of explosives were put in a rental van and placed in the garage beneath the World Trade Centre at around noon.

In Mumbai serial blasts, the Dawood gang under the training and instructions of the ISI used more powerful explosive called RDX. It was not possible for Yousef to smuggle RDX in USA. Our system of border management is porous made possible by massive corruption at all levels. Our borders can easily be penetrated by greasing the palms of managers of the system. The trial judge has convicted many such public servants.

In the US case, only one rental van was used. In Mumbai several Ambassador and Maruti cars were used for organizing 13 blasts in one go. The experts of the Central Forensic Science Laboratory, which functions under the CBI, were sent to Mumbai for forensic examination of the scene of occurrences. The head of the forensic team reported on phone that they had completed their examination and possibly the explosives were RDX. I asked him to provide the engine and chassis number of each vehicle used for the blasts. He provided the details after checking the engines and the chassis of each vehicle. I promptly told DIGs Kolkata and Delhi to approach the manufacturers of these vehicles and report back as quickly as possible. The officers obtained the details from the manufacturer, as they understood the importance of the matter. The names of dealers and purchasers were also given. Next day I dictated a note to DIG CBI Mumbai for immediate transmission of this information personally to the Commissioner of Police, Mumbai without signing the note.

The above exercise was done by the police in New York too that helped them to catch the person who had taken the van on rent. The World Trade Centre blast case was solved in no time. Similar thing happened in Mumbai blast cases also. Samra, then Police Commissioner, was gracious enough to say that he had received useful inputs from the CBI. This initiative did not come on the request of Mumbai Police. We did it on our own as we thought that we could render little help to the overstressed Mumbai Police.

The case was professionally investigated by the Mumbai Police under the leadership of Samra and assisted by his able deputy NN Singh, who subsequently became the Commissioner of Police, Mumbai. He was a very competent officer who knew everything about every gang that operated in Mumbai. I rate him a very high professional police officer. Every difficult case can be solved if we police officers learn how to help each other without seeking credit and press publicity.

20

After Retirement

The residence allotted to Director at 22, Tuglaq Road New Delhi is a dedicated residence to CBI. Normally, any officer is entitled to remain in his allotted residence for eight months after retirement. I requested the government for an alternative accommodation for six months. On this argument, I was allotted a residence in Pandara Park. The house was just opposite to LK Advani's house. I never had a chance to meet him, as I remained non-attached to politicians. Our maid's sister perhaps was working with Advanis. My wife was getting information from our maid on Advani's household and their lifestyle. Advani's family lifestyle was very simple. He preferred South Indian food. He maintains good health by being a small eater and never indulges in excesses. Sabarwal was called Netaji in our college days and his daughter got married to Advani's son. Sabarwal too was staying in the vicinity and met me at my new residence. He offered me to be introduced to LK Advani. I politely refused as my service hangover was still there.

Thereafter we shifted to my bachelor eldest brother's house in Tagore Park, adjacent to Model Town. The CBI Cooperative Group Housing Society Colony was still under construction. The flats could be allotted only in 1998. There is a history behind my being a member of the CBI Group Housing Society. Sometime in late seventies my SP GOW Kolkata Santanu Sen came to meet me in my office to know if I had become a member of the

CBI Cooperative Housing Society. I said no. He was surprised. He said that I should be practical in life and should not depend on family house in the name of my mother. Situation would change after her demise. It really happened that way. Sen forced me to sign the application form and carried the same to Delhi as he was proceeding to Delhi in any case for official work. I said I had no money to pay for the registration fee. It was hundred rupees only. He said not to worry on that score. He would collect the money on his return. I now realize that some cosmic power was behind this initiative of Sen. It was impossible to purchase a flat after retirement with the limited money that I had at the time of retirement. I was never worldly-wise and paid no attention to future planning for family and myself.

There was a pay commission report that raised our pay in the seventies. My wife spent money in purchasing curtains and the like. The CVO of the State Bank of India, Kolkata, asked me what I did with my arrears. Nothing, I said. He compelled me to open a Public Provident Fund Account in the SBI, Park Street branch, Kolkata, where Chunni Goswami, the famous football player, was the branch manager. I opened an account with an initial deposit of Rs 1700 only. That was the surplus I had out of the arrears I had received. This was again a decision of the cosmic power. I maintained this account for 25 years. This helped me to tide over my financial crisis after the retirement. Now I force youngsters who are especially in private sector to open PPF account by way of their future pension plan.

I knew that one has to pay *karmic* debts. There is no escape from that. Even Sai Baba had said that one has to suffer for *karmic* debts and he seldom interferes, as that would amount to interference with the law of nature. Baba had intervened in rare cases and as a result, he at times had to suffer himself.

We shifted to a three small room apartment in Vikaspuri, Delhi in 1998. Providence, as I always believe, plays its own game. My wife had been teaching throughout her life before and after marriage. We were in Delhi and she got a teaching job in a school called Magic Years run by Madhavan Kutti's wife and Suresh Mathur's wife. Kutti was a well known Malayalam writer and Suresh Mathur was an IAS officer who held an important position in the Government of India. When I became director, my wife gave up her teaching job.

Providence shapes our destiny as I have said many times. Soon Mrs. Kutti contacted my wife to rejoin the school and decided to pay even for transport charges. Using taxi daily was impossible, as the cost was prohibitive. I volunteered to drop her to school and bring her back home. My problem was how to spend my time during the intervening period. Kalyan Mitra, an IPS officer of Orissa cadre, who had made me a member of the United Services Institute (USI) years ago, solved that by his company.

China-India War 1962

I started visiting USI library which was very close to my wife's school. The library has very good collection of books especially on Indian security. First few days, I read journals and newspapers. Then I decided to read Gen Palit's book on 1962 War with China. There are some details, which are not known to public. China had reportedly given advance notice to Communist Party of India about the impending attack and sought CPI's help in moulding public opinion in favour of China. Palit claimed to have seen the IB report on the subject. There are plenty of other books on the same subject. The fact of the matter was perhaps that India had no intelligence of the impending attack or ignored such intelligence inputs. According to a Russian military expert consulted by Purnendu Kumar Banerjee, then our Ambassador in China, such an attack would require at least six years of preparation. All slogans of *Hindi-Chini Bhai Bhai* were farce. Nehru was shocked by the behaviour of the Chinese. The American military aid to India unnerved the Chinese as that was not expected by them as India was championing the third block of non-aligned countries. In no uncertain terms, this was told to Indian Ambassador Banerjee by Zhou Enlai. Altaf Gauhar who was very friendly to Gen Ayub had recorded that the America threatened China with missile attack if they did not withdraw immediately. This may or may not be true, but the fact remains the Chinese forces retreated to their original position as fast as they could.

The Chinese mounted attack on the morning of 20 October 1962 at about 5 am and before that vicious and false propaganda in Chinese newspapers and radio were raised to a new height. To prepare grounds of attack Chinese gave 'prominence to the alleged treacherous and large-scale attacks by the Indian troops on the Chinese border guards'. The Indian officers captured by the Chinese were humiliated by taking them to various places openly as trophy of the war. Brigadier JP Dalvi's book (*Himalayan Blunder*) gives such details. The Chinese are known for deception. They kept on denying that Chinese maps showing Arunachal as a part of China was not true as they were prepared by the previous Kuomintang Government. Thus, the Indians were under the impression that the Chinese were reasonable and would agree to a final boundary settlement between the two countries. The 1954 treaty with China contained in the preamble five principles or Panchsheel were mutual respect for each other's territorial integrity and sovereignty, mutual non-aggression and peaceful co-existence. The treaty was valid for eight years. The attack by China was mounted just after the completion of eight years. They took the intervening period for organizing the war.

Their deception became evident when they signed a border agreement with Pakistan in 1963. Pakistan gave a large part of Kashmir to China. China is a part of Kashmir problem. China is not likely to give back the territory they hold now in Kashmir, although the Pakistan-China Agreement was provisional. China-Pakistan all weather friendship is India-centric. By way of digression let me narrate an interesting incident that happened in Beijing at the time of signing of the agreement by Bhutto and his Chinese counterpart. As the purpose of the visit was known, our Ambassador Banerjee suggested to Delhi that he should not accept any invitation for receptions or banquets associated with the signing ceremony by way of protest as is the normal practice of lodging protest. He was told to attend the reception by telegram not disclosing the sender's name. When he sent another telegram for reconsideration, he was told 'Instruction stands'. Again, sender's name was kept blank. Ambassador Banerjee had to face agony and insult as he heard attacks on India in the speeches of Pakistani and Chinese. 'Tin gods' of MEA did behave in a manner unbecoming of a country of India's size and national honour.

Much of utter humiliation of this war was due to Krishna Menon who became India's defence minister by courtesy of Nehru. Most of the cabinet ministers were hostile to him. Menon's hold on Nehru remained a puzzle to many. He frequently visited America only to abuse them as a result the American leadership never liked him. He targeted those who were independent and suspected having some influence with Nehru. The concocted story of a possible Army coup by Gen. Thimayya was to politicize army by replacing him. This, however, did not happen, as there was a strong public outcry. Menon succeeded after retirement of Gen Thimayya by placing pliable officer who raised no objection to favouritism being practised. This led to polarization of the army and demoralization of the force at all levels.

China and Pakistan in tandem have positioned their missiles with nuclear arms targeted at India. There is a great potential threat to India from both the countries. Altaf Gauhar had written that during 1962 War China even suggested Pakistan to attack India to capture Kashmir. Gen Ayub lost his nerves in view of American aids, which sustained its army, and civilian aids to sustain its economy. America came in support of India by providing all types of military help. Nehru's two telegrams of 22 November to Kennedy seeking military help made BK Nehru weep. To quote BK Nehru 'the last telegram was so pathetic that as I read it I could hardly contain my sorrow and my shame'. The last telegram 'was so humiliating that I found it difficult to prevent myself from weeping.' (Nice Guys Finish Second). It was sealed and kept in the Kennedy Library. I wonder if our foreign office has a copy of the telegram as BK Nehru claimed that the embassy had no copy of it. Roedad Khan a retired Pakistani bureaucrat of eminence earlier had visited the Kennedy library to look for the document. The telegram to Kennedy which I believe has since been made public.

The strategy of China has to be understood by Mao's doctrines one of which was that 'in war battles can only be fought one by one and enemy can be annihilated bit by bit. Strategically, we can finish a meal but when actually eating we do it a mouthful at a time. It would be impossible to swallow the entire feast in a single mouthful.' In 1950, China, ate up Tibet by attacking it on 7 October 1950. Indian reaction was tested by China. Then came Dalai Lama's flight to India to escape torture or death in 1959, which the Chinese viewed as an act of defiance. By 'one mouthful at a time' strategy the Chinese took over political sovereignty over Tibet which India did not oppose. Aksai Chin of J&K state was taken over scrumptiously and a road was constructed. If it was a part of India, Zhou Enlai argued, why then India did not prevent it. Nehru's famous utterance that not a blade of grass grew there in Aksai Chin prompted a famous parliamentarian Mahavir Tyagi to comment that his head should be chopped off as he too was bald.

Lashkar-e-Toiba

I started reading books on 1965 War with Pakistan. According to Pakistani versions it was Bhutto's war to defame Gen Ayub. Bhutto convinced Gen Ayub that leadership in India was shaky after Nehru's death in May 1964. It was also argued that the situation in Kashmir was in turmoil arising out of loss of holy hair of Prophet Mohammed. The operation was named Operation Gibraltar, which enabled the Muslims to capture Spain. Bhutto also argued that war would be limited to Kashmir only. Ayub was not in favour of a regular war with India, although he became Field Marshall by his own declaration, which became a joke in Pakistan and in the world.

I soon started reading Pakistani newspapers like *The Friday Times*. In December1998, I read a full report on Lashker-e-Toiba's annual convention held in the first week of November 1998. Nobody in India knew about this dangerous organization and operations they carried out in Kashmir, Myanmar and other areas of the world. The parent body of Lashker-e-Toiba was then called Dawa-wal-Irshad. It was founded by three professors of an engineering college in Lahore in the late eighties funded allegedly by Arabs. It was headed by Hafiz Mohammad Saeed and he continues to head the organization in another name called Jamaud-Dawa after 9/11. He is a Gujjar from India who migrated during creation of Pakistan. He fires breath against India as he claims that a number of his relatives were killed during the partition riots. Many Hindus and Sikhs were too killed during that time. He openly declares 'that revenge is our religion'. In 1998 convention, he openly declared jehad against India. The parents of jehadis killed in action in Kashmir, Myanmar, the Philippines were honoured with the intention to urge many more to join jihad worldwide. The retired ISI officers like Gen Hamid Gul used to participate in such annual conventions. The reality is that it was a creation of ISI as Tariq Ali said who is now settled in Britain.

Its headquarters are located in Muridke with landholding of nearly 200 acres. Muridke is just 30 km away from Lahore. It had more than 2000 recruiting centres in Pakistan. Its main aim is for disintegration of India and works in tandem with the infamous ISI. I was so shocked by the proceedings of this 1998 convention that I wrote an article in December 1998, which was published in the *Statesman* in January 1999. I thought it was my national duty to alert all concerned to an emerging dangerous situation, which would play havoc with India's security and communal harmony. Now we all know the dangerous character of Lashker especially in Mumbai attack on November 26, 2008.

The coup in Pakistan

The coup in Pakistan in 1999 by Musharraf was on expected lines. A close study of press reports of that period in Pakistan did indicate that possibility. That Nawaz Sharif would remove Gen Musharraf was in the air. A contingency plan was in place in Rawalpindi Army HQs. When Musharraf was sacked while he was in plane returning from Sri Lanka, Gen Ziauddin was appointed the COAS of the Pakistan Army. Gen Aziz incharge of the HQs issued orders not to comply with his orders, it was clear that the contingency plan was being implemented. The appointment of Ziauddin was announced on television. A Brigade from infamous called 111 reached the TV Centre to stop the announcement. Gen Zia had used this brigade too in his coup. One brigade of Pakistan Army is enough for a successful bloodless coup. Bhutto in his book had said that Pakistan should be called 'Coupistan'. He praised chaotic Indian democracy as far better.

My understanding of dynamics of Pakistan politics enabled me to write nearly 20 articles in the *Pioneer*. I almost defended the stand of Nawaz Sharif saying that coup was preplanned and Nawaz Sharif was not in power when he was arrested by the army at about 6.30 pm. Musharraf charging Nawaz Sharif for hijacking the plane was a drama as the Army had taken over the country by arresting all leaders. The question that remained an unanswered mystery was that the Corp Commander of Karachi did not reach Karachi airport when it was known that Musharraf was due to arrive at about 7.30 pm. The instructions issued by Gen Aziz were not revealed or brought on court record. In fact, under Article 6 of the Pakistan Constitution Musharraf was liable to be charged for the coup, punishment for that was death penalty.

The other flaws in the prosecution case were that the statements of all the prosecution witnesses were recoded under section 164 of Pakistan Criminal Code, which is similar to Indian law. Normally, such statements of the accused are recorded by way of confession to make iron cast case against other accused. I have not seen any case in India where all the witnesses were bound under oath before the magistrate to depose in a particular way. This amount to coercion in a sense. This is indicative of the weakness of the prosecution case.

I also indicated how Musharraf would resort to a sort of referendum in the way Ayub and Zia did to justify their illegal coups. I also explained the Judiciary would give justification by invoking the 'doctrine of necessity'. The power of judiciary was crippled by threat of removal and surveillance. All the events happened on the predicted lines barring hanging of Nawaz Sharif. The trial judge was bold enough to write that the act of Nawaz was impulsive. This means that Nawaz was under the physical control of the army and he had no other choice but to divert the plane elsewhere.

Rajeev Sharma, a senior journalist known to me during my service, took notice of my articles and contacted me on phone.

He used his contacts to find out my phone number. He met me and urged me to write a chapter on 'Pakistan: Unstable History, Precarious Future.' I told him that my writings were limited to articles published. He insisted that I had enough material to write a chapter. It was true that I had read books on Pakistan mainly written by Pakistani writers. The chapter with 23 pages did come out to my satisfaction. Other chapters were contributed by prominent persons like JN Dixit, Gen Sharma, K Subramanyam and eight others. I ended the a chapter with a quote from Gen Ayub delivered in his farewell address on March 26, 1969. He said; 'I don't know if in our political life we will have a good man for a long time… If nothing else I have held the country together for ten years. It was like keeping a number of frogs in one basket … The East (Pakistan) will last a few years and the West (Pakistan) will drag on – just drag on.' This is what Pakistan is today. The book called '*The Pakistan Trap*' was finally published in the year 2001.

My interest on Pakistan study increased rapidly. I, on the request of Rajeev Sharma, started on the project of writing history of Pakistan. This involved reading of all available books and articles on Pakistan. I decided to concentrate on Pakistani books mainly to know how they view the creation of Pakistan. This became very interesting as many new facts surfaced which our historians ignored. Historians basically project their own view-points by twisting facts and events. For example, how many people know that the Communist Party of India did pass a resolution in support of creation of Pakistan by passing a resolution on the subject in 1942? CPI had many Muslims and being nonbelievers how then they could promote the cause of Pakistan in the name of Islam. All these were found from Pakistani authors who had written several books on the creation of Pakistan.

Pakistan at the Crossroads

In the year 2001 Vice Admiral KK Nayyar, who headed the Forum for Strategic and Security Studies, decided to carry out a study of Pakistan. He invited me to become a member of the study group. The group included Arvind Deo, a retired IFS officer,

Prof. IN Mukherjee from JNU, Prof. Martin Zuberi, Lt Gen (retd) YM Bammi, Vice Admiral (retd) RB Suri, Air Marshal (retd) Bharat Kumar, and Maj Gen (retd) Afsir Karim. The study was completed in one year under the close supervision of Vice Admiral Nayyar. Nayyar has excellent understanding of the topics given to each of us and periodically he used to hold review meetings which I found quite rewarding. The results of the study in the form of essays were published between January and September 2002 in their *Agani* magazines. This evoked good response and a suggestion was floated that these write-ups were good enough for compilation in the form of a book to provide a part of history of Pakistan for wider readership and long shelf life. The book titled *Pakistan at the Crossroads* was finally published in 2003 by Rupa and Company. My subject was 'The Internal Political Dynamics of Pakistan'.

The theme of my chapter was that 'Muslim India' movement was vague in concept. The word Pakistan was the brainchild of Chaudhury Rehmat Ali, who was a student in Britain. He wrote a pamphlet called 'Now or Never' for creation of Pakistan as homeland for Muslims of India. Vagueness of the concept was deliberate to keep all the frogs in one basket as said by Ayub in his farewell address before his handing over charge to Gen Yahya Khan. People with divergent background joined the movement. They had their own visions and perceptions. The Direct Action in Bengal in 1946 resulted in series of riots and killings in Bengal, Bihar and elsewhere. In 1947 our leaders capitulated and accepted the division of the country on communal lines. Jinnah got his 'moth eaten' Pakistan. He told his ADC just before entering residence as Governor General that he had never expected creation of Pakistan during his lifetime. The movement would have collapsed if the Congress accepted Jinnah's proposal in 1946 for exchange of population, which majority of Muslims would have rejected Jinnah's 'two nation' theory. Till Jinnah was alive the Objective Resolution for framing the constitution was not adopted as Jinnah had delivered a secular speech in Constituent Assembly on 11 August 1947 saying 'you are free, you are free to go to your temples, you are free to go to your mosques or to any other place of worship in this state of Pakistan

...that we are all citizens and equal citizens...Hindus would cease to be Hindus and Muslims would cease to be Muslims, not in the religious sense, because that is the personal faith of each individual, but in the political sense as citizens of the state'. In his mind there was no question of an Islamic state of Pakistan.

Destruction of democracy was happening in Pakistan from the very beginning. It started with Jinnah who assumed the role of the Governor General and Prime Minister rolled into one. He was authorized to preside over the cabinet meetings and in the event of differences between the two, his decision was final. After Jinnah's death, it was the view of Maulana Maududi that Pakistan was led by a powerful agitation for 'Hamara Mutalaba: Islami Dastur' that is creation of an Islamic Constitution. Liaqat Ali Khan and his party just capitulated. The Objective Resolution is based on Jaamat-e-Islam's formulation that 'Sovereignty over the entire universe belongs to Allah Almighty alone, and the authority which He has delegated to the state of Pakistan through its people for being exercised within the limits prescribed by Him as a sacred trust.' This has converted the state into Islamic state which was never the intention of Jinnah. Pakistan experimented with several constitutions but the Objective Resolution remained unaltered. Even Bhutto's Constitution of 1973 did not deviate from this basic framework of the Constitution, when personally he never believed in such concepts. This is the reason why Pakistan has become over the years a state full of jihadis and a prominent role played by Mullahs and clerics with their chain of madrasas. History books have been rewritten with falsehood.

At one point of time in year 2000 there were 2,50,000 fully armed jihadis floating in Pakistan for worldwide jihad. In this process the role of Army and the ISI played a significant part to isolate the moderate political parties or breaking them whenever necessary.

Bengalis in East Pakistan were treated as half Muslims. The seats in the National Assembly were manipulated so that East Pakistan seats were never more than their due. Gen Yahya introduced one person one vote in 1970 which enabled Mujib to obtain majority in the Assembly. He was not called upon to become the prime minster as is the practice in all democracies. The creation of Bangladesh was inevitable and is a history now.

In the chapter there is comprehensive study of the reasons for drifting of Pakistan into the lap of extremism. History of Pakistan provides certain lessons. Religion based state is the greatest danger to all. Even after creation of Pakistan, *Dawn* newspaper continued to abuse India and Hindus without reason. BK Nehru asked Mohammad Ali, then cabinet secretary of Pakistan why this was so. His reply was that it was necessary to keep Pakistan together. Nehru then asked if Hindus float the theory that 'Hinduism is in danger', his answer was that Hindu religion 'was incapable of fanaticism.' My conclusion was that the silent majority in Pakistan would prefer a moderate Muslim state.

Pakistan: From Jinnah to Jihad

All these studies gave me confidence to write the book as suggested by Rajeev Sharma. He was looking after editing and dealing with the publishers as I had no previous experience in this area of work. He rightly became my co-author of the book titled: *Pakistan: From Jinnah to Jehad.* Seventy-six pages are devoted to Jinnah alone. I had to read a lot on Jinnah as he was a hate figure in India for dividing India into two. Jinnah was a great legal luminary but no scholar of repute. He regarded Tilak as his guru. He was a Gujarati and knew the language well, but never spoke Gujarati with Gandhiji. He had a number of Hindu friends. He did not observe any of the tenets of Islam. During Ramzan he used to smoke. He was fond of Ham which is a prohibited food item for Muslims. He had no knowledge of Hindi or Urdu. His public speeches were in English and ignorant audience clapped him without understanding a word. The Indian Muslims were in search of iconic figure to address their real or imaginary grievances. They found Jinnah to fit in that category. He married Ruttie, a Parsi girl of exceptional beauty, twenty years younger to him. He allowed Ruttie all the freedom and she embraced Islam to secure Muslim seat for Jinnah. Jinnah never changed her name into a Muslim name. Eventually they got separated. She died early and her body was buried in the Shia graveyard in Mumbai. Jinnah attended her last rites with tears in his eyes. He never married again nor did he indulge in romantic life ever.

The history of Pakistan after Jinnah was shaped initially by bureaucrats and later by Pakistani Army generals. It became a fertile ground for successive military coups. Isakander Mirza ruled Pakistan from 1955 to 1958. Initially, after army training he joined the Indian Political Service created by drawing officers from Army and ICS. During his rule he made Gen. Ayub as his minister of defence while allowing to retain the post of C-in-C of the Pak Army, a mistake for which he had to repent. Ayub had his own ambitions. He developed friendship with CIA chief Allen Dulles and played golf with him during his visits to USA. On 7 October 1956 Mirza dissolved the Parliament, state assemblies and abrogated the Constitution on the grounds of saving the 'country from a catastrophe'. There was no public reaction at all, a feature noticed after every coup in Pakistan. Mirza announced the new government on 27 October 1958 and appointed Ayub as prime minister. On 27/28 at midnight four loyal officers of Ayub stormed Mirza's residence forcing him to resign which he did. Ayub took over as President on the same night. Mirza was forced out of his residence at gunpoint with two bags only. Subsequently he was exiled to the UK.

Gen Ayub was rescued by Chief Justice Munir by declaring the coup as a sign of 'successful revolution' and gave legitimacy to Ayub's regime. Thus, the judiciary became pliable and justified every coup on the basis of 'doctrine of state necessity.' Thus judiciary became a 'new law creating organ' for the Army. Ayub appointed Zulfiqar Ali Bhutto as his foreign minister. Bhutto was very young, highly educated and had high ambitions in his political life. He convinced Ayub that time was suitable for annexation of Kashmir by launching a covert 'Operation Gibraltar' failing which to launch overt operation 'Grand Slam'. Bhutto's arguments were based on three assumptions: That Kashmir was in turmoil because of 1963 case of loss of hair of Hazarat Mohammad which was recovered by IB chief BN Mullick in a smart intelligence operation, the Indian leadership was weak under Lal Bahadur Shastri and the war would remain confined to J&K only. The expected support from USA was missing as Pak-US treaty of 1994 was confined to aggression by a communist regime. China did make a lot of noise by threatening India by accusing India for border crossing to ensure Indian troops remained confined to China border. The China factor really complicated the world view. All the three assumptions were proved wrong as the Indian army waged a full attack on Pakistan under the able leadership of Lal Bahadur Shastri. This war and subsequent Tashkent Agreement brought disgrace to Ayub, Bhutto cleverly distanced himself from Ayub and managed to give a view that Tashkent Agreement as a 'Sell Out' by Pakistanis. It was widely believed that Bhutto made a secret pact with Gen Yahya Khan to ensure the downfall of Ayub. Because of intense agitation against diverse forces Ayub abdicated in favour of Gen. Yahya Khan disregarding the constitutional provision that he ought to have transferred power to the Speaker of the Assembly who was a Bengali.

Ayub faced the same treatment as his predecessor Iskander Mirza. He too was forced to vacate his official residence immediately and no official send-off was accorded to him. He moved to Swat which was his favourite retreat. Subsequently, he moved to Islamabad and lived in oblivion. His controlled democracy was a total failure. The only credit that he could claim was that he could conclude the water sharing agreement with India. His anti-Indian doctrine was peculiar. He equated Indians as Hindus and developed a theory that 'Hindus had no stomach to fight' and they 'hide in bunkers'. He believed in creating the fear of Hindus in the minds of people in Pakistan so as to unite Pakistanis against India. This was not expected of a Sandhurst trained officer of the Indian Army. He knew the character and ethos of the Indian Army. Islamization of the Pakistan army was really started by him.

Gen Yahya after taking over as President of Pakistan ordered a general election and Mujib's party emerged as the absolute majority party. He should have been called upon to take over as the elected prime minister of Pakistan which was prevented by

Bhutto announcing 'Hum Idhar Tum Udhar' a clear indication for division of the country. The 1971 war was again a Bhutto's war. But he managed to escape from being blamed. Ayub did not order for any enquiry into 1965 war and took the blame on himself. The Justice Hamidur Rehaman enquiry report avoided commenting anything against Bhutto as the Commission was appointed by him. In Pakistan the established practice is to favour the power in control of the state. Yahya Khan had to abdicate in favour of Bhutto by compulsions of the prevalent situation of the country as junior army officers were not in favour of another army rule. Like sell-out theory Bhutto in 1972 made scathing remarks against the armed forces insisting the power hungry junta despite his warnings Pakistan plunged into a war leading to intolerable surrender causing grievous harm to the country and blamed Yahya Khan for separation of East Pakistan. He removed top most defence service officers including the chiefs of the three services only to avoid a coup. In Simla Agreement he got the captured Pakistani officers and soldiers released without solving the Kashmir issue. He was a skilled negotiator who only agreed to make the line of actual control into line of control which amounted to de-facto recognition of division of Kashmir. This was the reason why President Clinton told to withdraw forces to the respective line of control. Thus, there is virtually no point in debating the issue of plebiscite which is dead and gone. Thus, Bhutto gave a solution without admitting publicly. Privately, it is said that he pleaded that he would require time to create a favourable public opinion to accept this as a permanent solution. This truth must be recognized in totality. Bhutto rose to power by 'taking away eggs one by one without the bird realizing it'. This is what he had said to a foreign journalist. He played this trick on Ayub and Yahya Khan and they realized this after being thrown out of power by his clever manipulation. Yahya was silenced by the Hamidur Commission Report, release of which would have resulted in Court Martial. In that situation the officers would have exposed the role of Bhutto damaging his reputation and possibly removal from office.

Gen. Zia-ul-Haq trapped him in his own game. He started cultivating Bhutto when he came in contact with Bhutto in an army conspiracy case. He proved too loyal and trustworthy. Zia like Bhutto pretended to be stupid and docile. He absorbed Bhutto's statement made to a foreign journalist that in politics one had to pretend to be stupid so as to take away one egg at a time. Bhutto allegedly rigged the results of the general election in March 1977 to secure 155 seats and the opposition could secure only 36 seats. This huge majority became a liability to Bhutto. The opposition started an agitation leading to violence and total chaos. He initially was not prepared to concede the opposition demand for holding re-election as that would prove that he was a manipulator. He always believed that he had a place in history.

Bhutto had a meeting with Gen. Zia to discuss the political situation, which in a democracy was uncalled for. Not only that he had dinner with top generals on 19th April. As the situation did not improve he arranged to arrest top political leaders that paved the way for Army takeover. He after consulting defence service chiefs imposed martial law in Karachi and Lahore which was against his own declaration in 1973 that in future no martial law would be imposed in Pakistan. Some officers were retired for opposing such a move. Zia was not sleeping idle. He cultivated the second level politicians to take on Bhutto. Bhutto managed to work out a solution with the opposition parties and on the same night Zia took over the reign of the country by a coup. Bhutto who was a bitter critic of India, praised Indian democracy when his fate was sealed.

Bhuto's murder trial was a farce. Confessions were obtained from arrested officers of Federal Security Service who found safety for self and family to confess. The judges were asked to take a fresh oath of allegiance to martial law regime. Some judges like the chief justice of the Supreme Court refused and these judges were promptly removed. All this happened as wife of Bhutto challenged the validity of martial law before the Supreme Court and the petition was admitted. Zia soon realized that either of them should survive on the basis of 'two corpses and one grave'. As expected Bhutto was awarded death sentence on untenable evidence and the Supreme Court decided the appeal by a split decision, four in favour and three against. In a case where a decision is divided by a narrow margin, capital punishment is most uncommon. Roedad Khan, as secretary in interior ministry, did not muster courage to highlight this for lighter punishment for Bhutto in his note to Zia.

The last days of Bhutto in a condemned cell was of inhuman torture like of which has not been heard of before. Zia had declared Bhutto a murderer much before conviction. Zia knew that under Article 6 of 1973 of Pakistan Constitution he was liable for death sentence if Bhutto came out of jail after serving jail sentence. Two corpses and one grave really haunted him. On 3rd April 1979 daughter Benazir and wife Nusrat met him for the last time. Bhutto shaved himself as he did not wish to die like a Mullah. A paper and a pen were provided to Bhutto in the evening by a Brigadier to write his confession as there was a desperate attempt to prove Zia's innocence in the farcical trial. Bhutto reportedly tore up the papers which provoked the Brigadier to kick Bhutto hard in the stomach. Bhutto just collapsed. This explains why Bhutto was carried on a stretcher at midnight to the gallows and hanged. For hanging at midnight the Governor of Punjab issued a special order in relaxation of the jail rules where hanging is allowed only in the early morning as is the practice in India also. Brigadier Rahat Latif who reportedly kicked Bhutto to death accompanied the body to Larkana. As was expected he was promoted as Major General without anybody's recommendation. Gen Chisti deliberately left Rawalpindi to escape the blame of torture on Bhutto. On the day of hanging on 4 April he was elsewhere. Even then stories were floated that torture was inflicted on Chisti's instructions. This false story was not killed by Zia's publicity organ. The legend of Bhutto still lives on and Zia is hardly remembered.

Pakistani Army officers are all potential snipers. It is an irony of fact that Generals wait in ambush to forcibly remove their civilian benefactors. Zia is no exception and by manipulation remained in power till his tragic death on 17 August 1988 in an air-crash. He was called a Julandhari as he was born in that part of India. Muslims who migrated from Punjab are not considered Muhajirs in Pakistan as this is reserved for those who migrated from UP or Bihar. The tragedy was that Muhajirs were responsible for creation of Pakistan. They are the worst sufferers of this new state. Realizing their present plight they no longer demand for creation of Jinnahpur by way of their tribute to Jinnah.

Zia's grandfather was a Maulavi and he inherited the religious bug of his grandfather. He was a devout Muslim who observed all the five pillars of Islam. At a young age and only after13 years of service he became a Brigadier because of vacancies. Three years later he became a Major General and a General in 1975. His career graph was unimpressive and never fought a war. He had prepared in advance a contingency plan for coup on the ground that in a turmoil situation 'Pakistan might become a part of confederated India'. This is the typical mindset of Pakistani Army. General Arif and General Chisti who helped Zia in the coup and consolidated Zia's position were all from Punjab part of India. They revealed these facts only after Zia's death.

Afghan Jihad 1979 – 1989

After hanging Bhutto in April 1979 Gen Zia became a pariah in Pakistan and abroad. His luck was good that the Soviet Union sent its troops to Afghanistan to save the leftist regime in December 1979 which became a rallying ground for international community to aid liberally Pakistan to fight a proxy war in Afghanistan. It was like a Christmas gift from Brezhnev to Zia. The war was in the name of Jihad. Muslims all over the world were mobilized by the US and its allies in the name of jihad. The US even invited jihadist leaders to visit US for fund raising and preaching jihad. This is all history now as admitted by Hillary Clinton later on. What was not realized then was that there would be blowback effect of this jihad in several countries of the world. The jihadis soon realized that it was the might of jihad that ended in withdrawal of Soviet troops, a wrong analysis of the reality of the facts of the situation. Without US, Western powers, China, Egypt and Saudi Arabia the war could not have been ended.

The credit for waging covert war in Afghanistan goes to Gen. Akhtar Abdur Rehman, then chief of the ISI. ISI had no experience in fighting a covert war as their job was to collect intelligence as is the case of other intelligence agencies. Its covert capability was the outcome of the US-Pakistan cooperation. The US imparted 60 skilled officers to ISI for covert operations. The CIA chief frequently visited Pakistan for effective cooperation. Many ISI officers were sent to USA for advance training including Gen. Hamid Gul who later on became a jihadi supporter. This infrastructure remains intact even now. The infrastructure, after the end of Afghan jihad, was diverted to India for waging a similar proxy war from 1989 in Kashmir. Like Afghan war jihadis' different parties were created by ISI to support jihad in Kashmir. The locals were not favoured, instead Pakistanis and foreign jihadis were inducted to fight in Kashmir. The ISI-controlled jihadi groups like Lashker-e-Toiba, Harkat-ul-Mujahideen, Al Badar and Huji were largely created during the Afghan Jihad.They were diverted to India. There is no dismantling of these infrastructure facilities despite world opinion and UN resolution. When Benazir Bhutto attempted to reform the ISI, Gen Afzal Beg announced that the ISI would not be restructured. That ended the story of reforming the ISI.

Zia never gave up the post of COAS even being the president of Pakistan as he never trusted anyone. He gave extensions to several generals loyal to him. Another reason for support from the Army was that he built up marriage alliances with Army families. His son was married to a daughter of Gen. Rahimuddin's daughter and Gen. Akhtar's son was married to daughter of Gen Zahid Ali Akbar forming a gang of four powerful generals who always supported Zia. For promotion of officers he discarded the promotion board system of selection. After hanging he could not sleep at night as literally the ghost of Bhutto haunted him. He was equally afraid of his own assassination. He was a master manipulator promising general election and postponing them with variety of excuses.

Zia was called a Mullah in uniform and introduced a series of measures like establishment of Directorate of Religious Teaching in the Army Headquarters to provide guidance in case of any doubt. One chief of the ISI who was the only chief, who never made money, asked the Directorate whether it was Islamic to gather intelligence by all kinds of deception. The Directorate quoted Koran in support of deception. An Islamic law of evidence was introduced as Hudood. Under this the testimony of a woman is half that of a man. In case of rape there should be four pious witnesses which is impossible. As a result the victims of rape were to be prosecuted for adultery or false allegations. Thus, there is gender bias in Pakistan.

Most of current generals of Pakistan Army were juniors and are now holding high positions. They are still under the spell of Zia's Islamic vision. Zia was a diehard fanatic Sunni. This has created a rift in the Army and general public at large. We now witness sectarian clashes in Pakistan. Ahmedias have been declared as non-Muslims. Demands are often made to declare Shias as non-Muslims. The bonding factor of Islam is losing ground and the reason for Pakistan creation was Islam only. Zia died in a plane crash on 17 August 1989. There is still no answer to the plane crash mystery. The result of enquiry was never released. The bodies of the victims were not subjected to postmortem which would have yielded a wealth of information. The well established route to crime investigation is from crime to criminal as was done meticulously in Rajiv Gandhi murder case. No police case was registered either. In Pakistan almost all political murder cases were never solved including killing of Benazir Bhutto.

After Zia's tragic death Pakistan Army leadership decided not to impose another army rule. This was because the people were fed up with the army rule. From 1989 to 1999 there was a semblance of democratic rule under the tight grip of the Army and the ISI. The ISI is a unique institution like CIA and FBI rolled into one. The CIA has no role inside USA. The ISI plays a big internal role in political dynamics of Pakistan. Each district in Pakistan has presence of the ISI in substantial strength. All political parties and leaders are under watch of the ISI. Najm Sethi, a prominent journalist was detained in Pakistan for some utterances he made in India. When his detention was challenged in the Lahore High Court, the stand of ISI was that since it was an extension of Pakistan Army, hence the Court was not competent to hear the case as the army functions under the Army Act. As expected the docile court under the regime of Gen. Musharraf ruled that it was not competent to deal with the case. No political leader has the courage to stand up to ISI. In Pakistan no civilian democracy can function. Even Benazir after winning the general election after the death of Gen. Zia was made to wait for a long time till she agreed to abide by the wishes of the Army.

In a decade of so-called democratic system, the prime ministers were thrown out four times because of the Army and ISI manipulations. The last Prime Minister Nawaz Sharif was humiliated when defence chiefs refused to receive the Indian Prime Minister Vajpayee at Wagha border. Sharif knew that his chosen Army Chief Parvez Musharraf was in for a game. Musharraf's Kargil war was an attempt to discredit Nawaz Sharif by implicating him for being 'on board'. The contingency plan for the coup was in place as would be evident from the way the army acted when Musharraf was sacked. Gen Aziz refused to obey the orders of the newly appointed chief and sent messages to all formations. The famous Rawalpindi Brigade 111 took charge of Islamabad TV station and entered into the house of Nawaz Sharif at about 6.30 p.m., which amounts to arrest of the prime minister. The Corps Commander of Karachi could have taken over the Karachi Airport for safe landing of Gen. Musharraf from Sri Lanka. There was no need to build up a drama to stage a coup. The messages sent out by Gen. Aziz were not brought on record before the trial court to prove that Nawaz Sharif was ousted from power much before Musharraf's landing at Karachi airport.

By temperament Musharraf was considered rash and had taken the risk of launching an operation with a success rate of 20 per cent. He presented a paper on the arms race in the subcontinent arguing that Kashmir issue must have been settled in the Royal College of Defence Studies in the sixties. His Kashmir-centric mindset never changed. In 1988, he under the orders of Zia crushed the Shias of Gilgit and Baltistan ruthlessly what the people of that region have never forgotten. Since he was a Muhajir, Sharif thought it would be safe to promote him as chief of the army staff, an error Sharif must have regretted later. Like Bhutto, Musharraf convinced Sharif that a local and limited war in Kashmir by giving the colour of Mujahideen war in Kargil was inevitable. The Indian forces gave a befitting reply and the world demanded withdrawal of Pakistani forces from the Indian side i.e. the line of control as enunciated by Bhutto and Indira Gandhi in Simla Agreement. Musharraf to save his skin and reputation kept harping that the Kargil war was the joint decision of the Army and Nawaz Sharif. During trial of Nawaz Sharif, he demanded an enquiry into Kargil misadventure. The American interference on 4 July 1999 saved the situation by demanding withdrawal of troops from Indian part of Kashmir. Like Bhutto, Musharraf did try to make out a case of 'sell out' to India but that did not click.

Musharraf's strategic vision fully came out when he addressed a select gathering in Karachi in April 1999. He formulated low intensity war with India because of argument that India was determined to splinter Pakistan. He claimed Afghanistan as a success story for Pakistan. Moreover, most importantly, he argued that even after resolution of Kashmir issue, Indo-Pakistan conflicts would continue on. Musharraf's pet theory that Muslims in India would require Pakistan's protection. This was the mindset of a Pakistani Gen. Thus the Army in Pakistan alone determines the foreign policy and not by a civilian politician. Even the government was singing the same song out of a fear of Army backlash. The Army always manages to draw support from Jamat-e-Islami, who organized a violent protest in Lahore when Vajpayee was there for Lahore Declaration in February 1999.

Musharraf, on record, pleaded, with the world community to recognize the Taliban regime in Afghanistan as a reality. Pakistan Army and ISI were helping the Taliban regime for capture of the Northern Area under the command of legendary leader Masood. The annual assaults on the northern region by the combined forces of Taliban, Al-Qaeda, and ISI were known to all. All military supplies were supplied by Pakistan.

Al-Qaeda

Osama bin Laden became a hero to majority of Muslims of the world. His network was built up all over the world. Osama's political agenda became clear when some clerics issued a fatwa in 1998. He wanted a regime change in Saudi Arabia and Egypt as they were seen as stooges of America. A series of attacks were mounted on US interests. In January 2000, he openly declared attack on US soil. This happened on 9 September 2001. It was an attack well planned in advance. The aerial attack by hijacking four US domestic airline planes was beyond the imagination of the FBI and CIA.

Gen Nambiar then Director of the United Service Institute (USI) asked me if I could deliver a talk on the subject on al-Qaeda. I readily agreed. The talk was well attended. People like Rasgotra and many other distinguished retired generals were there. Finding such a distinguished gathering made me little nervous.

The political philosophy of al-Qaeda was explained in terms of the world view of Islam as projected by Islamic scholars. Majid Khadurri was the one who said that Islam views the world in terms of two divisions i.e. Dar-ul-Islam which is under the Islamic jurisdiction and Dar-ul-Herb that is under the non-Islamic regimes. This jurisdiction is the area of conflict. The Dar-ul-Islam is the area of peace. Jihad is the instrument for subjection of Dar-ul-Herb. Al-Qaeda agenda has been to conquer the area where Islamic rule prevailed earlier. Osama bin Laden had announced Jihad in 1998 against the crusaders and Jews and included a large part of Myanmar, Thailand, and the Philippines as part of jihadi struggle. Often Andulasia is mentioned. Bin Laden calls Spain Andulasia. Spain was conquered by Muslims and remained under their control for nearly 400 years. It was reconverted into Christianity and churches which were converted into mosques were again converted into churches.

America has been considered as the greatest threat to Muslim world as it has been protecting Israel and deviant Muslim countries like Egypt and Saudi Arabia. Therefore, attacks were mounted against these for effecting regime change. Most of 9/11 hijackers were Egyptians and Saudis. Many details were given of attacks mounted by al-Qaeda in different parts of the world in the name of jihad. The idea of worldwide jihad came out of a belief that the Soviet troops were forced to withdraw because of jihad. It was erroneous as the decade long jihad in Afghanistan from 1979–1989 was the result of US led unofficial coalition which provided arms, training and financial aid. In this coalition, China played a big role by sending Ughirs Muslims from Zinjiang province to Afghanistan. The US provided logistic help to Muslim clerics to draw jihadis from all over the world. The US printed copies of Koran for distribution in Central Asian Republics which were then a part of Soviet Union. For the US the game was to disintegrate the Soviet Union. For China, the game was to teach a lession to its communist rival. For Egypt, the game was to throw out extremist elements to Afghanistan and the logic was applicable to Saudi Arabia. Saudi Arabia provided one dollar against one-dollar contribution of US. The ISI was used to fight the proxy war on behalf of the US-alliance. The ISI, which was spy agency, learnt the technique of waging a proxy war and it built up a huge infrastructure, which was never dismantled. The end of Afghan jihad was in the months of 1989 and Gen. Zia conceived a proxy war against India.

The blowback effect of the Afghan jihad was felt all over the world. A nation of Islam with no boundaries was the final concept of al-Qaeda to be imposed in the world in accordance with the concept of Dar-ul-Islam. The 9/11 was the final attempt to drive out the US influence in the Middle East. The Taliban which was the back up regime of al-Qaeda was attacked by the US for not agreeing to hand over Osama bin Laden for trial in USA. Taliban regime was only recognized by three countries like Pakistan, Saudi Arabia and UAE which they withdrew only after 9/11.

My presentation was well received and many clarifications were sought. Someone asked if shrinking of Islamic power was the cause of the present conflict, then surely the Indians too could provide a concept of shrinkage of India over the years. I had to confess that such a view was considered during the partition days. Even Suhrawardy who championed the cause of creation of Pakistan said that 'isthan' is a Sanskrit word and all places, which carry the word 'isthan', were part of Indian influence like Afghanistan, Baluchistan, and Kazakistan and the like, but Bharat never attacked any country for domination.

Some questions were asked on the definition of jihad as many had read that jihad means internal purification i.e greater jihad. There is no mention of greater jihad in the Koran, but find mention in the sayings of prophet Mohammed. After a final war, Prophet's wife Aiyasha asked what the Muslims would do now. Prophet's advice was to wage a greater jihad i.e. purification of mind within. I felt satisfied with the presentation as I have no pretension of being a scholar of political Islam. My previous presentations, while in service, in international fora were mostly on money laundering, underground banking i.e. Hawala, stashing of illegal money in tax haven countries and the like.

21

Spiritual Quest

My spiritual quest started with Anandamayee Ma at a very young age when I was a school-going kid. That quest has not ended, as the subject is limitless. India has been endowed with rich spiritual heritage, much of it is hidden or much has not been explored by researchers. I thought that I might record a bit of our spiritual heritage to inspire many beginners to explore the limitless horizon of Indian spiritual science. In the '*Mysterious Universe*', Sir James Jeans writes: 'The universe begins to look more like a great thought than a great machine'. The day is not far off when science will prove the supremacy of cosmic power. This is what Sathya Sai Baba had also said long ago.

Those who believe in ethical values of life or are God-fearing are not usually tempted by corruption. They will suffer but will not yield. Poor people are more honest than the rich, which should be otherwise. I have seen many cases of prompt bank loan repayment by the poor than by the rich. This may be the reason why spiritualism survives in India by a strong belief system in other dimension of life. This also explains why India has produced spiritual giants from times immemorial.

Strangely, many north Indians have virtually no knowledge of 18 *Siddhas* of south India like Nandi Dever, Agastyar Muni, Thirumoolar, Boganthar, Konkanavar, Sattamuni, Sundaranandar, Rama Devar, Kudambai [lady saint] Karuvoorar, Idai Kadar,

Kamalamuni, Dhanvanthri, Paambatti. Many consider Machamuni, Gorakhnath, Valmiki, Patanjali, Mahavatar Babaji and his sister Annai Nagalaksimi were from south India. Many are not perhaps aware that various ancient treatises on treatment of diseases are still available in south India.

As a child, I used to accompany my mother to visit Anandmayee Ma whenever she visited Delhi. She used to stay in the compound of Dr JK Sen's. Hanuman Road house in Delhi that was near our residence. I often found her in a state of trance whenever *kirtan* was performed with ecstasy. At that time, I had no knowledge of *Samadhi* or communion with cosmic power. Ma was a lady saint with charming divine beauty with a smile of bliss in her face. I recollect an incident when a stranger came and started abusing her for not covering her head with her sari. Ma as usual remained in her blissful state. Finding no response the stranger hurled a pebble at her that did hit her. The devotees were in a violent mood. Ma told them to remain quiet. The stranger, all of a sudden, fell at the mother's feet and begged for mercy. He said that he was fortunate enough to see Ma as incarnation of a Devi.

Judge Sadhu

In my first posting as ASP Mathura, Vrindavan was in my jurisdiction. In Vrindavan I noticed a middle–aged man wandering around with a loin cloth but never entered a temple and slept under a tree. I was told that he was a district sessions judge in a neighbouring district. Once he was in Vrindavan and remained in a state of ecstasy, forgetting that his office would be inspected by a judge from the Allahabad High Court during that period. When he came to his senses, he rushed back to his district and pleaded mercy for not being present. The visiting judge was taken aback as he was very much in attendance. He was told that something was wrong with his mental capacity. The district judge was in his full senses. He understood how God came to his rescue by appearing as him. He then decided to live in Vrindavan as a recluse. In 1993 I was in Jaipur. SP CBI arranged a dinner where only two sadhus were present. I narrated the story of the district judge. One of them said the judge was alive and lived in Pushkar. I soon visited Pushkar where I could locate his hut. He was then living with a family in Ajmer and met him there. He was nearly 100 years old wearing a dhoti and speaking only Bengali. I was destined to meet this highly evolved soul as I had a longing to meet him in person. The scriptures say that if one's desire is strong, it is always fulfilled. This I found to be true on various occasions in my subsequent journey in life.

A similar case has been mentioned by Swami Rama in his book '*Himalayan Masters*'. Once Gopinath a treasury officer of the Reserve Bank of India at Kanpur along with few others got in ecstasy in a *kirtan* held in the makeshift ashram of Swami Rama. At about 9 pm he came out of frenzy and said something terrible had happened. He said that his niece marriage was to be solemnized that day at about 8 pm. He had the key of the almirah with him. The jewellery items were in the almirah. He rushed back home and found everything was intact. He enquired about the jewellery. His wife said that he himself had opened the almirah and handed over the jewellery. He said how that could be when he was in a *kirtan*. This amused everybody. Gopinath wondered who came as his duplicate. He lost his mental balance and ultimately took premature retirement. I did try my best to locate Gopinath but failed.

As ASP Mathura, I happened to camp in Barsana for some festival associated with Lord Krishna. Barsana and Nandgaon are associated with *Krishna leelas*. Barsana was the place of Gopis and Nandgaon was of Krishna. Local people told me that boys and girls from these two places never married each other. Not only this a Barsana boy can stay in any house in Nandgaon and vice versa. There is no incident of lust in this relationship. The legacy of Krishna era has thus lasted more than 5000 years. I have not known any case in history where a tradition has been kept alive for that long period. Recently, I met a driver-cum-owner of a private taxi car who hails from Nandgaon. He confirmed what I had heard as a young ASP in early sixties.

Krishna Prem

My SP Satish Dutt Pandey, as mentioned earlier, took premature retirement after holding the post of DG CRPF to join his *guru's ashram* at Mitrola in Almora district. He was a disciple of Ronald Nikson, who was a pilot in French Air Force during the World War I. As a pilot he took his plane to German army positions. His plane was hit and went into flames.

Nikson was a non-believer, but in that critical situation of a burning plane, death was inevitable. Losing height, he murmured 'if there is God save me'. When the plane crashed in French area, he remained in coma for two months. All other co-pilots were dead. He started visiting Churches and priests to seek God and speak to him. He found no answer. On the advice of friends, he came to India in search of God. To earn his livelihood he joined the Lucknow University as a professor of English. Under the able guidance of his *guru*, he read the Gita, the Upanishads, the Vedas and Shrimad Bhagavaatnam. He realized the Supreme Lord and used to talk to him like Ramakrishna. Out of deep devotion he called himself Krishna Prem and this is how he was known in India.

The other foreigner who joined him was Alexander. Realization for ordinary mortals is a slow process. For many it is a fast process because of their past good *karmas*. Many past and present sages have stated this truth many a time, but argumentative people wish to have instant results like instant coffee. Everybody has a turning point in life and that window of opportunity comes once or twice in life. Nikson's case illustrates how the window of opportunity was fully used by him to see God and talk to him. When God is all-powerful it is but natural that he would appear in the form of the devotee's desire. This fundamental truth has to be assimilated by all seekers of all religions. God is formless but can take any shape to satisfy the yearning of a seeker.

A Yogi Prince-Tapaswaiji Maharaj

My greatest regret is that while posted in Mathura I did not seek to find out great souls who resided in the district of Mathura.

After retirement, I came to know about Tapaswaiji Maharaj, who at the end of his life on Sri Krishna's instruction started living in Kotban forest, which is very near to Kosi Kalan, which I had visited many times. Tapaswaiji Maharaj lived for 185 years. He was the crown prince of Patiala. I heard about him from a German lady in Nainital where she had gone to meet her *guru*. She just enquired if we had heard about the prince of Patiala, the way she pronounced. She had read the German version of the book. Col Dalmeer Singh, who is spiritually inclined since his childhood found out from a German publisher the name of the Indian publisher. After a year or so Col Dalmeer Singh could procure the Indian version of the book from Bangalore.

The story goes that the prince was fed up fighting with the Muslim invaders and ultimately decided to plead his case before Bahadur Shah Zaffar in Delhi. Bahadur Shah Zaffar told the prince that writ of his authority was not beyond Delhi. Instead, he advised him to devote his time to Godliness. This proved to be the turning point in his life. He went to Haridwar alone discarding his royal dress and lived almost naked.

He was initiated by a *guru* from Ayodhya in '*Hata Yoga*' and constant practice of *pranayam*. By doing so, he reached the Samadhi stage. Under instructions of his *guru*, he started visiting holy places. Many things happened during this long journey. While roaming around Himalayas he happened to meet a very old yogi living alone in a cave. The old yogi explained that the secret of his long life was due to consumption of herbs including somolata creepers juice with milk. About this creeper, mention has been made in a book on Narayan Gufa in the Himalayas where Sathya Sai Baba had sent some highly spiritual people for sadhana.

In Kamakhya Tapaswiji had darshan of *Kamakhya Devi*. At Parasuram Kund Tapaswaiji found a mahatma in a cave. Parasuram Kund is in Assam. Tapaswaiji Maharaj was then 100-year old and told the mahatma that being old he would like to cast off his body. He knew the *yogic kriya* to do so. This prompted the mahatma to suggest *kaya kalpa* treatment for rejuvenation which he could perform with herbal treatment, a highly guarded secret not known to many yogis. After *kaya kalpa* treatment, his body became youthful. In all he had undertaken thrice *kaya kalpa* treatment and lived up to 185 years. He too learnt the *kaya kalpa* treatment from the mahatma.

On the request of the Ayurvedic doctor of Pandit Madan Mohan Malviya, Tapaswaiji Maharaj gave *kaya kalpa* treatment to Malviya when he was 70 years old. After the treatment, Malviya was looking mid-fifty. All the foreign and Indian newspapers carried this news and Tapaswaiji Maharaj became widely known. The photographs of Malviya before and after *kaya kalpa* are on record. I wonder why this ancient method of rejuvenation should not be a subject of study and research. In the internet, a lot of publicity is given to *kaya kalpa*, but my impression is that these claims may not be true at all. I posed this question to Arun Kumar Sharma, who is very knowledgeable and has written spiritual books based on his own experiences. He confirmed only few are still available who have this knowledge. Col Dalmer Singh tried his best to obtain knowledge from a disciple of Tapaswaiji Maharaj but failed.

On 12 October 1955 Tapaswaiji Maharaj asked his followers to read Gita. He opened his eyes at 5 pm and asked to be lifted from the cot and placed on the floor, a clear indication of casting off his mortal body. Soon he sat in *padmasan* and eyes were fixed between the eyebrows. After a minute or so, he uttered the word OM in a long drawn tone loudly. This was the real story of eternal Samadhi of a great yogi in the 21st century. Because of the German lady who called him prince of Patiala we could locate his biography written by his disciple Anantha Murthy.

Deoraha Baba

As ADC to the Governor of Uttar Pradesh BN Das in early sixties (1962–64) I had an opportunity of meeting Deohara Baba when the Governor met him in Allahabad. Baba was looking like a 70-year-old saint. His real age was not known, as saints never reveal their past. Dr Sharma, former vice chancellor of Bundelkhand University, had written a book on Deoraha Baba where he had calculated his age to be around 350 years. Swami Rama had stated in his book (*Living with Himalayan Masters*) that as a child Dr Rajendra Prasad met Deohara Baba when he was looking 70 years old. Indeed, he was a great saint who lived long on his own volition.

In Indian yogic science, a man generally breathes 21,600 times per day. With this pattern of breathing, one can live for 120 years or so. Faster breathing reduces the life span as more *pranic* energy is lost by way of exhalation. While inhaling the intake of oxygen is said to be 20 per cent only and at exhaling 16 per cent goes out and oxygen retained in the body is 4 per cent only. By this reasoning life span can be increased by reducing respirations. Theoretically, if the respiration is five times per minute, the life span may go up to 360 years. Thus, Indian yogis formulated the theory that the man's span of life is intimately related to the rate of breathing which is one of the ways of absorbing *pranic* energy through breathing. Same is true of animals like frogs, bears, mice that go in hibernation during the winter months when they breath less.

In the ancient temple of Chidrambram where the presiding deity is Shiva as Nataraja, the cosmic dancer, is located in Tamil Nadu. Shiva in a dancing pose stands under a roof. The roof has 21,600 gold tiles representing 21,600 times of breathing of a human being a day. The 21,600 tiles are fixed with 72,000 golden nails representing 72,000 nadis of a human being. Thus, our ancient temple builders were aware of the breathing and nadis of a human being. Does it not indicate that our heritage is unique and needs to be told and retold to generations after generations?

Another way of storing pranic energy is by absorbing *prana* from the sun, the earth and the space. *Pranayama* is one such method of storing *pranic* energy. Those who practice *pranayama* and yogic asanas radiate glow in their faces and vitality in activities. The real secret is that advanced yogis have the knowledge of diverting the breathing to awaken the seven *chakras*, which are also called psychic centres. An adept can taste ambrosial nectar that further strengthens the human system. *Khecheri mudra* is one such technique. All these are highly difficult and are to be learnt from adepts. Otherwise, one may land up in a difficult situation. Unfortunately, books are not much of help.

I knew nothing about Deohara Baba in the sixties as a very young officer. During my first visit to Baba as ADC to Governor, Deohara Baba took notice of my presence. He gave me plenty of cashew nuts on my request. All my four pockets were full. I was wearing khaki bushshirt, which was a prescribed dress at that time. My relationship with Baba continued for several years and on each occasion even at late night, he would give me cashew nuts. I learnt that Baba never stored any offering that he used to receive from devotees. He used to distribute these then and there. For a saint of his stature materializing any object was possible. Subsequently, I learnt that energy could be transformed into matter and matter into energy. I have seen many saints doing so effortlessly. His mantra was '*paro-upokar*' that is guiding people to the path of God. Many Christians and Arab Muslims used to visit him. He used to say that a saint had no religion. This is the message of India to the world. Baba had special leanings for police officers and was not favourably inclined to politicians.

I had heard from a monk of the Ramakrishna order in his Sunday discourses in Lucknow that a great master of realization leaves his body by his own volition and the soul leaves from the top of the head with a crack with blood oozing out. This was the way Deoraha Baba left his body in late eighties in Vrindavan. Baba was an adept in '*khecheri' mudra* wherein the tip of the tongue touches the top of the head through the throat cavity. In this position, one tastes the nectar that flows from the top of his head to the tongue. I had met many who could perform this *mudra*. One such yogi is Jaidev still living in Haridwar and often goes to deep Himalayan region. He demonstrated how he could suck in his tongue into the cavity of the throat. He is around 100 year but looks like a yogi of 50 year only. The importance of this *mudra* has been mentioned in many books. This yogi told me that he could go into trance and deep meditation for hours together in this *mudra*. Rana who works in Haridwar Development Authority introduced me to this yogi.

Bharater Sadhak

In Kolkata, I happened to purchase one book on Saints of India called in Bengali '*Bharater Sadhak*'. The stories of great saints of not distant past are amazing. The life story of Trailanga Swami was unique. He took *sanyas* when he was nearly 80 years. He reportedly lived for more than 300 years. Finally, he settled down in Varanasi. He wore no clothes. Prominent great saints like Ramkrishna Paramhans, Lahari Mahasaya and many others, visited him. Such accounts are well documented. When Lahari Mahasaya met him, Trailanga Swami embraced Lahari Mahasaya who was wearing *dhoti* and *kurta*. After Lahari Mahasaya left, people asked Trailanga Swami why did he embrace an ordinary man. Swami said that the dhoti-clad man he embraced had reached the spiritual status like him. He was not an ordinary soul. *Kriya Yogis* like Lahiri Mahasaya never sought publicity. Lahiri Mahasaya, because of this unique incident, became known to many *sadhaks*. One of his disciples was Brinda Bhagat, a peon in the postal service who attained success in *Kriya sadhana*. Once a *Kriya Yogi* wanted more advanced training in *Kriya*, Lahiri Mahasaya asked Brinda Bhagat whether he would like to be initiated into advanced *Kriya*, Brinda said he was in bliss from what he had already obtained from his *Guru*. That satisfied the seeking *sadhak*, as he had not reached the stage of bliss of Brinda. Trailanga Swami, one day, took out a huge *Shiva Ling*a from the bed of river *Ganga* and placed it in the compound of a house where occasionally he used to stay. I have seen the *Shiva Linga* in Varanasi house. It was with great difficulty the house could be located, as the present generation hardly knows anything about such a great soul who lived in Varanasi and left his mortal body in his pre-announced *samadhi*. He was named Trailanga Swami as he hailed from Telengana region of Andhra Pradesh.

Trailanga Swami's weight was more than 300 pounds. He seldom ate his meals. Being a naked sadhu, the police would put him behind the police lockup. He would soon be found on the rooftop of the lockup smiling all the way. How did he escape from the lockup with his huge body is still a mystery. Some mischievous person once offered him limewater as milk. He consumed the bucketful limewater, which did not harm him. Instead, the person who did this mischief on him was burning from within. He begged for his life. Trialanga Swami cured him immediately with the advice not to do so with saints. These are well documented by contemporary writers on Trailanga Swami.

During the same period Bengal and Banaras had the unique distinction of witnessing great spiritual personalities like Sri Ramakrishna Paramhans, Sri Lokenath Brahmachari, Bama Khapa, Bijoy Krishna Goswami, Lahiri Mahasay, Trailanga Swami and many others with the message of India's great spiritual truth of oneness of God and all paths were relevant to reach the stage of communion with the supreme power. Sri Bijoy Krishna Goswami was so impressed with the Sri Guru Granth Sahib that he asked one of his disciples to translate the same into Bengali. It is said that many Bengalis are not aware of Bengali version of Sri Guru Granth Sahib. It is a rare book now.

My interest to know more about *sadhakas* increased. Each book of *Bharater Sadhak* was available for Rs 10, a big amount in those days. It became clear that people are born with a purpose. There is a spiritual science, which requires study. India is the only country in the world, which had produced and continues to produce great spiritual giants. I became proud of our spiritual heritage as I continued to purchase and read all books of the Saints of India i.e. *Bharater Sadhak*. The author never revealed his real name. Reading such books provided clues to locate *sadhaks* who follow their own traditional line of *sadhana*. Thus, spiritual search becomes fruitful. There is a danger also. There are fake *sadhus* who are interested in milking money. All miracle stories are to be verified by scientific proof. In addition, one should have his own experience. One need not be guided by agents who create superman out of ordinary man.

The basic requirement in spiritual science is to have a clear understanding of human nature. As Ananadmayee Ma often used to say, the first requirement is to do *Chita Shuddhi* i.e purity of soul. It is not simple. Purity of mind and soul comes out of love we generate for all beings. One has to cross the letter I i.e. like the cross of Christ. Ego has to be buried. Ma always said 'this body'. Many *sadhaks* never tell their names. Instead, they refer this body. Ego destruction means destruction of lust, jealousy, hatred, that is, destruction of all negative tendencies that kill all positive tendencies like love, sympathy for all. After *Chita Shuddhi* comes *Nadi Shuddhi*. People who try *Nadi shuddhi* first hardly succeed. They are likely to fail miserably and are likely to develop neurotic problems.

An old Yogi visits my residence in Kolkata

I was staying in the first floor of a flat in Belvedere near Alipore in Kolkata. One day I was standing in the verandah overlooking the main road. I found an old *Sadhu* walking towards our block of six houses. The *Sadhu* with a young *chela* came to our bloc. I thought that they might visit the ground floor flat of a South Indian family who were very religious. After sometime my doorbell rang. When I opened the door, I found the old *Sadhu* with the young *chela*. I asked if they were searching for another flat. The old *Sadhu* said, "No". He wanted to meet me. I invited them inside and requested the *Sadhu* to take his seat. The young *chela* introduced the old *Sadhu*. He said that I was a blessed person to be visited by a *Sadhu* whose age was not even known to him. Then out of curiosity, I asked him if there was specific purpose for such a visit. The *Sadhu* said that he was under instruction to meet me. I asked if he would like to reveal his permanent place of stay. He said he lived in *gufa* number 8 of Girnar Parbat in Saurashtra in Gujarat. After sometime he left the place. Immediately, I came back to the verandah to find out if he was visiting some other flat. I just failed to locate him as if he had just vanished. Here, I must admit that during that period I was facing some serious personal problems. The cosmic power does help in case of distress. After retirement, I happen to read Dr Brian's monumental book '*Many Lives, Many Masters*'. That reinforced my belief in *karma* and theory of rebirth. Those who wish to know about rebirth and *lokas* where souls rest for a period before rebirth should read this book.

Two Faces of Indian Communists

A communist in theory does not believe in God or cosmic power. Most prominent communist ministers in West Bengal would be elsewhere during Durga puja. However, I was surprised to learn from a lady who was a great devotee of Sri Lokenath Brahmachari that Jyoti Basu's wife was a great devotee of Sri Lokenath Brahmachari. Jyoti Basu's father was a direct disciple of a great saint and he selected Basu's wife for initiation. She used to organize *kirtan* at her residence. The lady told me that Jyoti Babu would sit in another room and accept prosad from his wife. When Jyoti Basu visited Dhaka, he made a trip to Baradi village where Sri Lokenanth spent last days of his life. Jyoti Basu had said that Sri Lokenath Baba used to bless him. A reason for his success in political career and long life may perhaps be due to the blessings of Sri Lokenath. Sri Lokenath lived for nearly 180 years without *kaya kalpa* for rejuvenation. He was a great saint visited by persons of eminence and saints of India. He gave a promise to his devotees that, he even after leaving his mortal body, would respond to the distress calls of his devotees. The calls should be sincere and earnest.

I read in some Bengali newspapers that late Prof Hiren Mukherjee, a prominent CPI leader and a most vocal MP in the Indian Parliament, was a believer. He was found counting beads of his 'japa mala' accidentally noticed by a member of a Parliamentary delegation abroad. When asked why he was doing 'japa', he reportedly told that he was an Indian communist. Our spiritual past is too strong to be ignored. After all our great spiritual masters like Swami Vivekananda and Rishi Aurobindo were highly educated and their preaching's cannot just be brushed away.

My introduction to Sathya Sai Baba in Jhansi

One evening while working in my camp office in Jhansi, some prominent citizens wanted to meet me. I did not know them. I told my orderly to tell them to wait in the sitting room and started disposing of the files. For a good length of time, I forgot about the visitors. I asked the orderly to find out if they were still there. I thought they must have gone back cursing me as an insensitive person. The orderly on return told me that they were still there. I asked him to usher them in immediately. When they entered, they did not exhibit any annoyance or bitterness. I apologized for my delay in calling them. They were a group of Sai devotees who wanted me to join a Sai function. which I readily agreed. I had no knowledge about Sai Baba. I borrowed from them some books on Sathya Sai Baba and read them. The group wanted to hold monthly *bhajans* at my residence. I agreed on the condition that *bhajans* must be held even if I remained out of town on reasons of official assignments. However, that never happened.

Uma Shanker Bajpai was SP Jalaun who was fully involved in anti-dacoity operations as his district was badly affected. He had participated in major operations even risking his own life. Gradually, Uma Shanker Bajpai became spiritual. Years after he decided to meet P Rajagopalachari to get initiation into Sahaj Marg by Rajagopalachari. Sahaj Marg is a spiritual service organization. Sri Ram Chandra Maharaj of Shahjahanpur founded the Sahaj Marg, UP in 1945. Rajagopalachari was nominated head of the organization in 1983 after his *guru* left his mortal body. He operates from Chennai. Bajpai is now the secretary of Sahaj Yog Mission operating from Allahabad, UP. Rajagopalachari has since nominated his successor Ajay Kumar Bhattar who is said to be living in Kolkata. Sahaj Yog in essence is Raj Yog with emphasis on the region of heart i.e. *anahat chakra*.

Sai *Bhajans* were well attended and I never invited police officers to involve in such activities to avoid criticism. I started enjoying *bhajans*. I was always seeking 'descent of grace divine'. This is what I had learned after reading a couple of books of Sri Aurobindo. Nothing happens without the grace of the Divine, which one has to seek earnestly. I must confess that I had an unusual experience of a flow of powerful current from head to toe after the *bhajan* only on one occasion. The current was so powerful that I had to pray for termination of this experience. So far I have not shared this experience with anyone. I never got this unique experience again.

Introduction to Sai Baba in Kolkata

Under head office instructions we were asked to find out another building for CBI office in Kolkata. We visited many places. One building needs to be mentioned as something unusual was observed there. One Roy a rich man owned a multistoried building. After our visit of the building, someone, not from CBI, suggested us to visit the top floor, which we call 'barsati' in Delhi, to witness an unusual happening there. We reached the top floor by lift and found that 'barsati' room was occupied by a South Indian woman of middle age. When we entered her room, we found to our surprise mounds of *bibhuti* on the large photos of Sai Baba. We sat down to see if there was something unusual. I observed that size of *bibhuti* was growing. We received some quantity of *bibhuti*. Years after I got the real story from books written by Sai devotees. Roy visited Baba and was blessed with an interview. Roy insisted that he should do something for Sai by way of service. Sai Baba said he did not require any help. Roy kept on insisting that he should do something for Sai. Sai then told him that an *amma* lived in his neighbourhood in a bustee and is poor. Roy should accommodate her in the barsati. *Amma* had never met Baba or had *darshan* of Baba. As a maid working in several houses she found Sai photo in the *puja* room of a house. She liked the photo and *amma* requested the lady of the house to give her a photo of Baba. After receiving the photo, she started putting *dhoop* sticks in little corner of her hut room. This worshipping of Baba by an illiterate lady never went unnoticed by Baba. That is why Baba is called *antaryami*, who knows his genuine devotees. This was my first introduction to Sai miracles in Kolkata.

The second introduction to Sai was equally interesting. I took my mother for a heart check-up in Kolkata. The doctor was a well-known cardiac specialist. I was sitting with him alone when mother was taken to the ECG room. I saw a big picture of Sathya Sai Baba on the wall behind the doctor's chair. I became curious to know how a doctor could keep openly a big picture of Baba. The learned doctor told me without any hesitation, that Baba was the real doctor and whatever he did was really the work of Baba. I did not ask further questions as that might irritate him or he may snub me for being ignorant. This was my second introduction to Sai Baba who never physically visited Bengal for reasons best known to him.

My boss Lahiri, who was my DIG Kolkata branch, narrated the third Sai miracle. He was a disciplinarian and knew how to work out a case. He was a thorough professional and I derived pleasure in working with him. He was always sweet to me knowing that I was from a different cadre [UP] and deserved to be treated with due respect. One day he told me about a strange thing happening in the house of a doctor whom he knew. His wife was a Sai devotee and in her *puja* room everyday two *laddus* would come from nowhere. The doctor husband did not believe the story. He wanted to expose the hoax being played by his wife or by someone else. He decided to stay in the room for 24 hours after checking every nook and corner. He locked the room from inside. In the morning he found two *laddus* in the *puja* corner. He was surprised and could not deny this unusual happening. This he heard from the doctor himself. Thus, slowly I was being introduced to Sai Baba. At that time, I had no time or opportunity to get in touch with Sai devotees in Kolkata. I was more interested in Mahavatar Babaji. I read about Mahavatar Babaji in the book titled *An Autobiography of a Yogi* written by Sri Yogananda. I purchased the book from a bookstall at the Bhopal railway station where I had gone for a police sports meet in 1964. The book was so interesting that I read it throughout the night. Mahavatar Babaji initiated Lahiri Mahasaya into *Kriya Yoga*.

My first meeting with a *Kriya Yogi* in Kolkata

In Kolkata, I came in contact with a Swami Satyeshwarananda Giri who remained in Dronagiri hills for years in search of Mahavatar Babaji. He was a *Kriya Yogi* in the tradition of Sri Lahiri Mahasaya, who was a direct disciple of Mahavatar Babaji. Swami Yogananda has made public all about Babaji known to the world in his famous book *An Autobiography of a Yogi*. Swami Satyeshwarananda initiated me and my wife in preliminary *kriya yog* in the late seventies. There is a story behind it. Bipin Babu, a Dy SP (Deputy Supertendent of Police) of CBI, visited him in Dronagiri hills. He told me about Sri Satyeshwarananda and told me to post a letter to him for more information. I did post a letter and the reply came that in due course he would visit Kolkata and I could meet him.

Here, I must record my impressions about Bipin Babu. He never married and was spiritually inclined from his very childhood. He did a lot of *sadhana* and met many *sadhaks* in his life. He used to tell me about *sadhaks* living in and around Kolkata. He told me about a lady *sadhak* living near Daksineswar. I met her and was impressed by her radiant look especially during her meditation posture in lotus position. Once she called me to know why CBI officers like me were interested in her. I did not know how she knew my background when I never revealed my identity. Such visits were always secret without any company.

Many respected people used to meet Bipin Babu in office. I used to wonder how a *sadhak* could be in the midst of us. After his retirement, he built an ashram often visited by scientists, scholars of repute. He has adopted many orphans and needy children for higher education. All of them call him 'Dadu' or grandfather. I am told that he has had out-of-body experience. He is humble and believes in *Bhakti sadhana*. He is now 79-years old and lives happily with his group of devotees. He told me that this was his last birth.

In *kriya yoga*, the technique of meditation is to interiorize all the five senses as a result one sees light and sound within, taste and touch again within. When that happens, the mind is free of thoughts, which is in a state of bliss. Sri Satyeshwarananda initiated me and my wife to the first stage of *kriya yoga*. I must admit that because of constraints, I could not pursue the practices. I lost contact with Swami Satyeshwarananda and found from internet that he has settled down in the USA.

Peter Harkos

In seventies, I read about the amazing extrasensory powers of many ordinary people. The case of Peter Harkos is an extraordinary one. He was a wall painter and once fell down from a ladder. After this fall, he could clearly see the events that had happened before and those that would take place later. He could identify murderers by looking at the victims. As a result, he was in great demand by the American police. He could solve many of the difficult cases not only by identifying the suspects but also helped the police in the recovery of weapons used in such cases. He became rich but ultimately decided to establish Harkos Foundation to explore the hidden talents of people.

The mental power is hidden in each man. The western psychologists are researching how to harness the mental power for conversation between two individuals by telepathy. A day may come when mind can be trained to move objects or drive a vehicle without fuel. Indian Yogis can do it. For Indian *yogis* these are *siddhis* not to be used or exhibited.

Edgar Cayce

There is another recorded case of ESP of Edgar Cayce who was born in 1887 in the US. He was the son of an uneducated farmer who became an amazingly accurate clairvoyant. He could prescribe medicine for those living thousands of miles away from him. From letters and conversations with the concerned persons, he could form a clear picture of the ailing person and his illness. He had no idea of medical science, but the records of Cayce Foundation at Virginia Beach are there for everyone to go through.

How did Cayce acquire this extraordinary power? This was also accidental. At the age of twenty-one he was afflicted with laryngitis and lost his voice. No medicine could cure him. Hypnosis conducted by an expert called Hart could cure him during the period he remained in hypnotic spell, but on awakening, he lost his voice again. Another hypnotist called John Layne offered to take over. Layne suggested Cayce that he should describe his disease while he remained in hypnotic spell. He described his problem, as he was unable to speak because of partial paralysis of his vocal cords. It can be cured by increasing the circulation by autosuggestion in hypnotic spell. Layne then suggested that let him imagine that affected parts were receiving greater circulation.

Soon Cayce got up and he was cured of voicelessness. Layne realized that his subject could also be used for curing others. Cayce did as proposed by his hypnotist with amazing results. Soon he became a well-known figure for curing difficult cases. As it was draining his energy, he died at the age of 67 on January 3, 1945. He became a legend.

In Reiki also the same principle is applied by touch therapy. The affected parts are touched for at least three minutes for greater circulation and activation of psychic centres. In distant Reiki, the same principle is applied by holding the image of the affected man in the mind and signs are drawn in the mind for transmission of energy to the concerned man. The important point to remember is that self-healing is a possibility that should be explored.

A Fakir turning a pebble into candy

I came to Allahabad from Jhansi to witness Kumbh or Ardh Kumbh mela in early eighties. I was in the police camp in the mela area and made it a point to visit camps of many sadhus all alone. All sadhus of importance stay in the mela area. In his *Autography of a Yogi*, Yogananda described that mela had a holy tradition and high spiritual personalities invariably attend the mela to bless the devotees. Even Mahavatar Babaji, the *Guru* of Lahiri Mahasaya, visits the mela and such spiritual persons hide their identities to avoid attraction of ordinary people. The origin of Kumbh is not known, but lakhs of people plunge into the Ganga for a holy dip with the belief that they will be blessed with salvation. This belief is strong and there must be reasons for the belief. It is like Muslims visiting Kaba for Haj with the belief of divine dispensation.

I met many sadhus and woman saints in the mela area. I found some of them were like ordinary human beings. One of them started criticizing other sadhus for display of their wealth. He himself became famous subsequently and built up big ashrams in the Himalayas. I did not like his attitude. Acquiring *siddhis* is no proof of enlightenment. Once I was roaming in mela ground alone. A fakir was sitting alone and he called me to sit near him.

I had no objection to do that. He just ordered me to take out a pebble from the ground. I did that. He almost commanded me to put the dirty pebble into my mouth. I refused. He again almost ordered me to do what he was telling me. He had burning eyes and I had no alternative but to put the pebble into my mouth. Then he ordered me to chew it, which I flatly refused, as my teeth would be broken in the process. He raised his voice and told me that I should chew the pebble as ordered. I was under his spell and did what I was told. I could chew the pebble effortlessly as it was like chewing a candy. The pebble had turned into a sweet candy. I was surprised by this experience. I asked him to teach me the technique, but he avoided the topic altogether. I took courage to ask him whether Mahavatar Babaji was present in the mela area. He just took his own time to tell me that he was yet to arrive, but he would come in due time. That satisfied me and I sought his permission to leave. He agreed but asked me to give him Rs 10 for purchasing a woollen *chaddar*. I promptly gave him that small amount. Never did I see him again.

Such wonders are not to be confused as signs of divinity. Of course, a divine soul can create such objects for temporary pleasure of devotees. Kasturi, the author of *Satyam Sivam and Sundram*, in his interesting book '*Living God*' had narrated a similar case. Sai Baba was once returning from Hyderabad to Puttaparthy by car. The host in Hyderabad had provided some savories in tins for long journey. Baba told Kasturi to stop the car, bring a rock from the roadside, and hand it over to him. He wanted a bigger and flat stone, which was given to him. Baba handed it back to Kasturi. The stone had become a flat piece of candy of the same size, shape and weight and each one was given a slice of it. These do not prove anything except the fact of changing one object into another by the power of *sankalpa* i.e. the will power. About 90% of our brain is dormant. This is what scientists are telling us. All ESP researchers are trying to utilize the brain as much as possible. The dormant brainpower can be energized by a variety of ways. One way is to recharge the brain with sufficient supply of oxygen. Here comes the Indian

Yoga with *pranayam* as a method of providing brain with sufficient supply of oxygen. Brain is dead without oxygen.

For Sai Baba it is natural, as he never practised *Yoga* or *pranayam*. He is born with this power of changing matter into energy and energy into matter, a unique gift of an Avatar. He has explained many times that matter can be changed into energy and energy into matter by his *sankalpa shakti*. This is also a scientific theory now endorsed by scientists too.

Sai *Bhajans* in Allahabad

Soon Sai devotees of Allahabad met me. My mother's health was deteriorating, as she was mentally upset about the transfer to another place. She was admitted to a local Government hospital. I pleaded with my predecessor to vacate the Railway bungalow so that my mother could be brought back to a comfortable house. In the absence of a house, we were staying in the police rest house adjacent to Police Headquarters. My predecessor in his wisdom at last vacated the allotted house and my ailing mother was brought back to this Railway residence from hospital. A local prominent Bengali doctor looked after my mother's treatment. Her condition gradually deteriorated. Some Sai devotees came to my house in the late evening not knowing of my mother's condition. They suggested a special Sai *bhajan*. This happened when she was not even in a position to walk. While the *bhajan* was on, she started crying. I kept on applying Sai *bibhuti* on her forehead and a pinch of *bibhuti* to swallow. When the entire family came to Allahabad, I took the initiative to hold Sai *bhajans* during the daytime. My journalist brother, who came from Kolkata, spoke to many prominent doctors in Kolkata who all had said that in a case of cancer she would experience excruciating pain. That did not happen due to Sai *kripa*. She gradually went into coma. On Vijaya Dashimi day, she started breathing heavily for nearly 10 minutes, which I was told by my brother's wife was a sure sign of soul leaving the body. Incidentally, I had a premonition in the morning after bath that she would leave her body on that day. I told this to my wife. Her death on an auspicious day was the only solace I had on that day. Shri Shiridi Sai Baba left his body on Vijay Dashimi day. My mother became a deeply religious person after the death of my father while he was in service. My mother was 79 when she expired. My intuition of an impending death is peculiar. Once we visited my father-in-law in his Karol Bagh residence in Delhi. I took my wife aside and told her to bring her father to our Moti Bagh residence. I told her that this was the best opportunity to do some *seva* for him. Whenever I left Delhi for work, I requested PC Sharma, my joint director, to organize his funeral in my absence. In case of impending death of ordinary mortals, the body aura changes much before death. My mother's wish was that I should perform a special *Sradh* at Gaya, which I did years after. At Gaya, I felt that *Sradh* was genuine as I started weeping and there was spiritual vibration in the atmosphere. Once *Sradh* is performed in Gaya, there is no need to perform annual 'tarpan'.

In Gaya, many touts roam around to scout for customers only to fleece them. They are called *pandas*. I took the help of Bharat Sevak Samaj through the help of the SP. The sadhus of this organization work in low key. I asked the head of Gaya branch the significance of Gaya *Sradh*. He said that not only Indians, but foreigners too send money for salvation of troubled souls. This was a new revelation to me. I wish I had time to read those letters to find out more information on the subject.

Sai *Bibhuti*

One of my office staff in Allahabad was admitted in a hospital, which I never knew. Someone from the staff told me that clerk in the hospital wanted me to meet him immediately as he was in great agony. I rushed to the hospital and found him crying. He said his pain was unbearable in the stomach region and I should do something to give him some relief. I found that he would be operated the next day, may be for appendix. I literally felt helpless and kept on assuring him that doctors would help him out. That did not make any impact on him. He continued to cry. Suddenly, it came to my mind that I should give him Sathya Sai Baba's *bibhuti*, which I was carrying with me in my purse. I took the *bibhuti* packet and told his wife to apply some quantity on the belly and a pinch to be swallowed after every two hours. I must admit that I did sincerely pray to Baba to subside his pain. After a week or so, I asked the staff whether the operation was successful. The staff told me that the pain subsided. Next day before the operation, a second x- ray was conducted and everything was found normal. He was discharged from the hospital without operation. Mentally, I thanked Baba for the grace shown to the suffering man.

Sri Sathya Sai Baba's *bibhuti* is unique. It does work in case one has faith in God and Baba. Sunil Gavaskar narrates how he was cured of a torn thigh muscle in Australia just before first test due to start in a week's time. The physiotherapist announced that it would take three weeks of therapy before he would be able to play. The news reached the family and they sent packets of Baba's *bibuti* just three days before the test. He started applying *bibhuti*. There was marked improvement. On the D-day, he was completely cured, and he could play brilliantly. Sunil Gavaskar celebrated his 60th birthday in July, 2009 at Puttaparthy in the presence of Baba. Sai Baba has shaped Gavaskar's life from the very beginning, which is not known to many. *Bibhuti* of Sai Baba is described as *param pavitram leela bibhuti* that can give us *moksha* and we, therefore, take refuge in *bibhuti* for all kinds of afflictions.

Bhagwan Singh –a *Kriya yogi*

SK Tripathy was SP Hamirpur when I was posted in Jhansi range as DIG. He met me in Allahabad in police headquarters, and told me that Sri Bhagwan Singh, who retired, as head of UP treasury, was a religious person, and had abilities to forecast events. He did not know anything more. Bhagwan Singh was staying in Lucknow. I went to his house without prior appointment. He was gracious enough to welcome me and went inside to change his dress. I found the photo of Mahavatar Babaji on the wall as published in Yogananda's book. Then I saw a sketch of a man with seven *chakras* giving me the impression that Bhagwan

Singh was a *Kriya Yogi*. When he returned, I asked him if he was a *Kriya Yogi*. He said how did I know it. I pointed to the pictures on the wall. He was convinced that I had some understanding on the *Kriya* tradition. Then I told him my initiation into *Kriya Yog* by Swami Satyeshwarananda Giri in Kolkata. By tradition, a *Kriya* practitioner never reveals his spiritual path as per his *guru's* advice. Singh opened up. Sen Mahasaya, a direct disciple of Lahari Mahasaya, was his *guru*. He narrated many wonderful stories. On his insistence, Sen Mahasaya at last agreed to give him an opportunity to have physical *darshan* of Mataji sister of Mahavatar Babaji. In Dasaswamedh *ghat* of Varanasi mother lives in an underground cave. On the appointed day at midnight all the lights went off and he saw a slab rising above the ground. He looked into the cave and saw a beautiful lady looking at him. Soon the slab came down to its original position.

The second story was equally interesting. On a particular day, he was to attend an important meeting with the secretary of the department. As usual, he was in deep meditation in the morning. When his meditation ended the time of meeting was already over. He rushed to office of the secretary and asked the PA about the meeting. PA was surprised by this query. The PA told the meeting was attended by all including Singh. He further said the minutes of the meeting were written by him. Singh wanted to see the minutes of the meeting. He found to his surprise that it was in his own handwriting. He soon realized that God or *guru* had his own ways to come to the rescue of his devotees.

Par Kaya Pravesh

Subsequently, I had several meetings with Bhagwan Singh. He said that a householder *yogi* in Benaras, who was aging, requested him to learn *Par Kaya Pravesh*, a rare science known to a few people in India. *Par Kaya Pravesh* is the method to enter into the body of a fresh dead body by casting off his own body. This enables the yogi to continue with his *sadhana* bypassing rebirth. Singh refused, as he had no intention to prolong his soul life in another body. The householder yogi said that he had to pass on this knowledge to a suitable person. He could not find any suitable person. As per his *guru's* advice, he had to pass on this knowledge before his death. The yogi convinced Singh that it was not necessary for him to practise this knowledge. His only obligation was to transfer this knowledge. He could not refuse this argument. Per force, Singh learnt this knowledge, which he never used in his lifetime. After my deputation to centre, I lost touch with him. SK Tripathi told me recently that Singh had left his mortal body some ten years ago. I have now requested him to get in touch with Singh's son who was a conservator of forest for retrieval of any diary or writings he had left behind. Lahari Mahasaya's spiritual diary has now been published which contains his day-to-day experiences.

Swami Rama has mentioned one case of *Par Kaya Pravesh* in his book *'Living with Himalayan Masters*'. Once Swami called Bhure Baba, an old baba, entered into the body of young dead person in the northeast and became known as Anand Baba. I have not been able to locate this Baba so far. Arun Kumar Sharma, who is author of several books on spiritual science, has narrated a case of a Lama in Tibet who had performed *Par Kaya Pravesh* several times. He had met him in Tibet. Out of curiosity, I telephoned him to know if this knowledge is still available to some *sadhaks* in India. He said that he knows at least 10 such persons. As I was keen to see one of them, he expressed his inability to disclose their identities. I have not understood why this great science should be kept secret from the realm of scientific research. Arun Kumar Sharma is more than 86-year-old now. His books are based on his own experiences and not on theoretical studies of scriptures.

Bhagwan Singh's life story would inspire many households to take to the path of God or cosmic reality. To become a *sanyasi* is easy but many do not last long as they do not live a life of strict discipline and adhere to truth. I have seen many who slipped into family life without achieving anything. Their minds were vitiated by worldly affairs. Sri Ramakrishna used to say often that *sanyas* was in mind. Many *Kriya yogis* were and are householders. Lahari Mahasaya was a family man so has many disciples. It is worth noting that many police officers are *yogis* in uniform but they do not make it public. I never invited any police officer to *bhajans* in my residence or perhaps they never knew about these *bhajans*. After *bhajans, arati* used to be performed by Sri Narayanan, a long time devotee of Sai Baba. He from time to time used to narrate strange stories of his own experiences. I recall from my memory three such cases. His brother was suffering from cancer of incurable type and doctors had said that he would live another 6 months. He used to feel sad. He never brought this problem before Sathya Sai Baba. On Baba's birthday celebrations at Puttaparthy, Sai Baba made his way through the crowd, and said 'your brother is cured'. Baba just vanished into the crowd. He rushed back to his brother's house possibly in Mumbai, and found him hale and hearty. I had occasion to meet his brother in Sai Baba's Sivam temple in Hyderabad. His brother confirmed the story.

On another occasion, he left for Puttaparthy leaving the work of village seva to others. The devotees were to make smokeless chulas in a village. Special well-treated soil was necessary which was to be delivered by a contractor. On reaching Puttaparthy Baba almost rebuked Naranyanan for being callous in the matter of service. Baba told him that the contractor did not deliver the special soil and as a result, he himself had to deliver soil to the devotees. On return, he made enquiries and found that somebody else had delivered the soil.

A special 24-hour *bhajan* was organized at the residence of an advocate. He had a cardiac problem and his children objected to this special 24-hour *bhajan* at their residence. However, the *bhajan* as planned did take place. Thereafter during Narayanan's next visit to Puttaparthy, Baba almost scolded him as to why the local samity arranged the *bhajan* when the family was opposed to it. How Baba came to know of these incidents in distant Allahabad is a wonder of wonders.

22

My Audience with Sathya Sai Baba

In 1985, my family decided to have Satya Sai Baba's first darshan at Puttaparthy. Previously, I got involved in Sai *bhajans* in Jhansi and Allahabad. We broke our journey at Jhansi for a day and local devotees organized a *bhajan* where I was asked to speak. At the station, a foreigner came to me and said that he had met many spiritual persons in India. He then showed me a photograph of Sai Baba as God incarnate. That made me happy, as he did not know that we were bound for Puttaparthy.

I had requested my batch mate Sri SNS Murthy to organize our onward journey from Bangalore to Puttaparthy. Murthy and his wife are old devotees of Baba. Prabhakar, a batchmate of ours from Andhra Pradesh, was in Bangalore. On his way to Bangalore, he had dropped his wife at Puttaparthy. He readily agreed to take us by his car to Puttaparthy. In the evening we reached there. There was arrangement for our stay. Volunteers supplied food. When asked how much we had to pay for the food, he said we were guests of Baba. I thought I was just a DIG and did not deserve such treatment.

Next day, we got up early, took bath, and dressed up to take position in the *darshan* line. I was seated just facing the door of Baba's room. As soon as he came out I smiled and bowed before him. I shall never forget the smile he gave to me. I was in the seventh heaven. I mentally prayed for an interview with

Baba who alone decides who to give an audience. I was lucky to be called for the meeting along with many others. I was told that if Baba calls a particular person, the same privilege is extended to his family members.

In the interview room, there were foreigners too. Baba took his seat and looked at each one of us. Suddenly, he would produce *bibhuti* for ladies. I, being a police officer, was watching every action of Baba closely. He must have understood my mind. He pulled up his sleeves to show that nothing was hidden. He then brushed his hair to show that no transmitter was hidden there. I closely watched him materializing gold rings, necklaces and the like. I was wonderstruck by such turn of events. He said that this happens by his *sankalpa*. The objects produced were distributed among the callers. Many wept for the grace showered on them. We were not destined to receive any such gifts, but that did not matter, as his *darshan* was good enough for us.

While talking he said that he would live for 96 years and would never have gray hair. Even now, Baba has no grey hair. This is remarkable.

After the general interview, Baba often would call for family interview in a separate room. We too had the benefit of one to one talk with Baba. He promised that he would look after the family and told the career graph of my two children. He praised my daughter being studious and the son being early sleeper, both of which were true. The prediction for the daughter did not happen while the son's prediction came true. Baba promised to give medicine to my wife. Until the end of the interview the medicine was not given. At that time, we did not know the ways of Baba. When we asked people about the medicine, we were told that Baba would deliver the same at the right time. We came out of the interview room with lots of *bibhuti*. This memorable interview will remain forever etched in our minds.

As soon we returned a volunteer came to us and said Baba wanted all of us to visit the University. The University is located at the top of a hill. We decided to take the shortcut to reach the University.

At the university all the important places were shown. On return, I was amazed to find that my knee pain problem had vanished. Much later, I realized that it was Baba's grace that cured my nagging knee pain in a strange manner.

In between, whenever I got a chance I visited Puttaparthy. I was not happy in EIB for various reasons and wanted a change. When Baba called me for interview, only SP Anantpur, his wife and myself were present. Baba asked me if I had any problem. I was hesitant to speak on my present problem with EIB and wanted a change. However, I could not muster courage to speak the truth. Falsely, I said, "No problem". Baba said I was not speaking the truth. I returned without my problem being solved. However, strange are the ways of Baba, the problem was eventually solved in a strange manner.

Possibly, in 1989, my wife and I made another visit to Puttaparthy and it was memorable as Baba picked us up for interview. In the interview room, there were many persons of all nationalities. As usual, Baba asked about the health of my wife. I just said Baba 'promised' and he interrupted and said yes, 'I shall give medicine for her'. I was told earlier that Baba never forgets the promises he makes. Baba then waved his hand and out came a sparkling small Shiva Linga. He asked everyone to hold it and pass it on to next person. When it came to me, it was quite warm as if it was manufactured in a factory. Baba told my wife to put water on the Shiva Lingam and she should consume that holy water. By way of consolation, she was told that some small quantity of holy water should be given to me also. We felt happy that the promised medicine in 1985 was delivered. The Shiva Lingam is still with us in a silver container and often I consume holy water from it.

I often used to stay in Chennai for long durations for supervising the Rajiv Gandhi assassination case. My wife rang me up in Chennai to tell that Narayanan, a Sai devotee in Allahabad, had sent a telegram requesting me to visit Puttaparthy to meet Sai Baba. I ignored this telegram as I found no reason to visit Baba at that time. After some days, again a second telegram was received from Narayanan with the same request.

I decided to take the journey to Puttaparthy as I found good reasons to visit Bangalore for widening the net against the LTTE. Sivarasan managed to stay in different places to evade arrest with the help of LTTE sympathizers. In the meantime, information was received that LTTE had support base in and around Bangalore. I held a meeting with local officers with the help of my batchmate SNS Murthy.

As decided, I went to Puttaparthy not knowing whether Baba would meet me. No one can take Baba for granted. At times, he would ignore the presence of a known devotee for years. He ignored me also many times. This time Baba picked me up for interview. I was happy. Many things happened in the interview room with many people. I had no courage to ask Baba why I received two telegrams from Narayanan. All of a sudden, Baba told me that real culprits of Rajiv case would never be caught alive. It did not make any sense to me, as I did not ask any question on the case. There was nothing special about this interview. I returned to Bangalore rather dejected because of Narayanan's insistence on my meeting Baba. Naranayanan's contact number was not available. I could not contact him to find out reasons for sending two telegrams.

In 1992 my wife and I decided to visit Baba at his Whitefield residence near Bangalore by way of a farewell visit. There were many aspirants to become the Director of CBI. This was my last chance to avail LTC. The first morning *darshan* was not possible as Baba went out to address students attending summer courses. We were told to attend the evening class where we might have *darshan*. When we reached the place, the auditorium was full and we settled down outside. From nowhere a volunteer came and asked me to stand near the portico where Baba's car was parked. I said how I could stand there without Baba's permission. I may be rebuked or ignored by Baba. He told me it was my choice and he was providing a facility. I decided to take the risk and stood there as told by the volunteer. After a long wait, I found Baba emerging from a distance. I was almost restless. When Baba came near the car, he saw me and patted me on the back as I knelt down to do *pada namaskar*. He gave a divine smile, which is still fresh in my memory. Next day I was allowed to stand in the earmarked place along with DG Karnataka, Nizamuddin, a pious Muslim with his crippled Hindu wife. Baba talked to them first as they were ahead of us. Then he came to me and said, "Where is your wife". She almost jumped out of her hiding and stood before him. Baba enquired if there was any problem. 'Yes' I said. He gave us *bibhuti* by waving his hand and asked me to 'eat'. Then he went towards the vast gathering and took rounds to cover each devotee. Many gave their letters, many received *bibhuti*. Perhaps it took good 30 minutes. Again, he came back to our side away from the crowd of devotees. Straight he came to me and said, "Go in". He also invited a western couple from the crowd to do likewise. As we entered the room, we found a fat man sitting on a chair and his heavyweight wife sitting on the floor. He introduced the fat man as former Maharaja of Mysore. Then Baba introduced me as Director of CBI to him. I immediately said, "Baba I am just an Additional Director and not Director". He said very emphatically, "You will be Director in the next month". The next month was a few days to follow. I was literally taken by surprise, more because I did not ask him about my future. He was aware of my problem of tendering my papers in the event of bypassing my claim. Again, I found that Baba was all-knowing and we need not ask questions. Then Baba asked a western lady where her first husband was. She just kept quiet, as Baba was aware of her marital status. Her second husband looked a little embarrassed. The Baba told the couple that marriage was not a musical chair game. Knowing their acute embarrassment Baba by way of consolation said 'forget it'. I was called to an adjacent interview room for one on one talk. We had no questions to ask except seeking his blessings. After completion of a interviews, he settled down on a chair for general talk. All of a sudden he called us again in the interview room for the second time which was very unusual and I had never seen such a thing happening before. We went in with apprehensions, as Baba's ways are unpredictable.

The second interview was unique. Baba made us stand facing each other and he stood between us. He from nowhere materialized a seedless fruit, which I have not seen before and broke the fruit into two parts, one putting into my mouth and other into my wife's mouth. We did *pada namaskar*. I have no answer for this special blessing. We came back to main room. After sometime we were all allowed to go. Baba's prediction came true.

Abdul Razak, an amazing life story

Here, I wish to narrate a true story of Abdul Razak also his thrilling story of sliding into vices to a life of virtue. Born in 1934 in a poor Muslim family living in a hut at Jaisingpur in Maharashtra, he was almost an abandoned child at the age of two when he lost his father. Mother discarded her veil and started working with meager wages. He was admitted to a local Marathi school. Stale and cold food given to her mother by her employers was the only food he ate. He was never unhappy or zealous of others who lived comfortable lives. Deprived of a slate, notebooks, pencil, books, school bag because of poverty, he developed his own memory. He was able to recall hearing only or reading only once like Swami Vivekananda. This helped him to pass all school examinations standing first always. His friends loved him and helped him without the knowledge of their parents by inviting him to dinners when marriages were held. To earn some money he started giving tuitions to two or three boys that fetched him Rs 15 only. That was not enough; he managed to get a job of a gatekeeper of local cinema house working from 6 pm to 12.30 am. When he attended school in the morning, his eyes were red, swollen, sleepy, un-brushed teeth, without bath, dirty clothes, dishevelled and hungry. The divine power made him a graduate with honours as he continued to get concessions and scholarships for higher education on merit. Thus, a theatre doorkeeper becoming a graduate with distinction. He joined the Sale Tax Department as Inspector, a corrupt department that harassed him for being honest with false charges. He resigned from the post.

He joined a law college and passed LLB figuring in the merit list. He started his own practice and prospered financially. He joined the Gymkhana Club and Rotary Club just to increase his contacts. Prosperity made him indulge in evil and immoral activities for which he privately repented. He started hating himself. He started a search for a living guru. His list included Sai Baba, Jiddu Krishnamurthy and Rajneesh. He first excluded Baba as adverse and derogatory articles appeared in the newspapers and magazines like *Blitz*. Krishnamurthy's teachings did not touch his heart. Rajneesh's criticism of Baba's miracles confused him. I may mention here that same Karanjia of the *Blitz* met Baba for several days and came out with a book 'God lives in India.'

In the early eighties Razak had first darshan of Baba from a distance. The first visit was disastrous. After a week or so, he started thinking why so many people gathered in Whitefield and they were all educated, happy with mere darshan of Baba. After a month, he visited Baba again where there was a very brief eye contact with Baba and he felt a torch like light flashed at his eyes and electric current passing through his body. There was instant love for Baba. He continued to visit Puttaparthy or Whitefield whenever he found time for long five years without being called for an interview. This did not matter to him, as he really loved Baba. In February 1981, he visited Baba's college and hostel. A professor who was acting as a volunteer found out Razak's qualification and asked him to apply in the law faculty of the proposed deemed university at Puttaparthy. He applied for the post of visiting professor for law out of fourteen disciplines. There was a problem of selection because of numbers of applications. He thought he had no chance as very prominent people had applied. He returned home. In April 1981 he received the appointment letter from the Registrar Sri Chackervarthy, an ex IAS officer who voluntarily gave up the most coveted service to serve Baba.

Razak was keen to know how he was selected out of eighteen thousand applicants. Dr VK Gokak the Vice Chancellor answered his query. When Swami was told about the problem, he said he would select the fourteen. Swami just picked up fourteen unopened envelopes and announced their appointments, one envelope for each discipline. Razak was selected by this extraordinary process. He was taken aback by this extraordinary way of selection. Even after becoming a visiting professor Razak was not called immediately for interview by Baba or he never looked at him. In June 1982, he was asked to meet the vice chancellor who asked him why he had not claimed anything for last year's salary. 'You wrote lies in your application that you were rich and not in need of remuneration'. Swami had said that he was not at all rich and full payments should be made to him. Dr Gokak said that Swami knew everything. Again, he started thinking how Swami knew everything about him.

In July 1982, during the evening darshan, Swami came straight to him and said, "How are you sir." Next day too Swami came straight to him and asked his name. He said Abdul Razak. 'What is the meaning of Abdul', asked Baba. He said Abdul meant a devotee. 'What is the meaning of Razak', asked Baba. Razak fumbled. Baba said that Razak meant Allah. This conversation in verandah was in the presence of many people. Then Baba called him for a solo interview. Baba materialized *bibhuti* and asked him to eat and promised to meet him next morning.

Next morning in the interview room Baba materialized *bibhuti* for Razak and gave packets of *bibhuti* for the family. Again, Baba said he would meet Razak next morning. On that day, Baba in the next room gave a personal interview. Baba knew that Razak had faith in him but had doubts about creation of objects by Baba. Razak was asked if this was true and he confirmed it. He was keen to witness it by way of personal experience. Baba asked Razak for anything he would desire. He wanted Baba to give him a thing that embodied in it the entire universe and only his religion was shown on it. Baba asked Razak to look at the centre of his palm. Within few seconds Razak saw the skin in the centre of his palm open up; saw a roundish large sized object coming out of it. It was a beautiful ring that came out in octangular shape embedded with nine gems representing the universe and in the centre Islamic symbol of star and crescent in green gemstones.

In December 1982, Baba told Razak to bring his wife next month. Razak had two wives. He was in a dilemma. Baba again returned and asked him to bring his second wife. Naseem, being an orthodox Muslim, refused to go to Puttaparthy, as that would amount to idol worship. She was told that Baba had asked her to come. She ultimately agreed on the condition that she would not do *namaskar* and touch Baba's feet. They had a breathtaking interview. When addressed as '*bachchi*' [child] she slightly relaxed. 'How many children do you have', asked Baba. She said four, counting the children of the first wife. She never looked at Baba. 'Don't you want your own son', asked Baba and he gazed into Naseem's eyes. She after a while fell at Baba's feet trembling and weeping holding a corner of Baba's robe. Looking at Razak, Baba said that Nassem had just conceived and the day of delivery was announced. Not only that, Baba also said that she would have another baby. Although married for nearly eight years, she did not conceive as experts had said that she had blockages of tubes and RHO negative blood. The lady doctor of the family, when she heard story, said this could only be possible with the *sankalp* of an Avatar. She did deliver the boy and was named Sai Bakashish that means gift of Sai.

Abdul Razak wrote the book 'Satya Sai My Friend' some time in mid eighties. He lived for sixty-six years only. During this short life, he could achieve what many would not be able to achieve in several births. I have found Razak's story so absorbing that I thought it fit to be included in my life story, as it would provide inspiration to many.

Swami Rama and his Master

Elsewhere, I have mentioned about 'Living with Himalayan Masters' of Swami Rama. Now I wish to tell my readers more about Swami Rama. I must admit that a living Guru has always been criticized and admired after he leaves his mortal body. Swami Rama was not spared either. I made some independent enquires and I wish to put them on record.

His father was highly spiritual. He vanished from his home when he was over 60 years old in pursuit of his spiritual quest. He settled near Mansa Devi temple in Haridwar. As his seeking spiritual truth was intense, he was visited by a master who initiated him and said, even at that advanced stage of his life, he would have a son and made a strange request that the son should be handed over to him. After a year or so Rama was born. The master on the day of delivery of Rama arrived and held the son for sometime. Three years later master again appeared and whispered a *mantra* into his ears.

After the death of both of his parents in few years, Rama went to his guru. He was a rebel and argumentative like any other young man. In any case, the master ignored his temperamental behaviour. He as directed by guru learnt many ways of *sadhana*. He met great spiritual leaders as directed by his guru. All these have been narrated in 'Living with Himalayan Masters'.

Rama's master became well-known. Many searched for him, but failed as the master refused to come to limelight and remained at high altitude in the Himalayas. Master remained a mystery till date. Swami Rama revealed a bit about his master saying that he was born in a Bengali Brahmin family in West Bengal. He was the only son of his parents. He was orphaned at a young age. An advanced sage adopted him. Master narrated his life story with great reluctance as a renunciate never narrates his past life. The age of the Master was around sixty when the story was narrated. Deoraha Baba too never revealed his past life, and avoided when such questions were asked.

Master would remain most of the time in Sahaja Samadhi, a stage called 'Iswarleen' in yogic parlance. He used to mostly survive on milk of *shyma* [black] cow or goat's milk. He used to sing Bengali songs in his solitude. He was also called a Bangali baba. Anybody in difficulty and who remembered him, was helped by him as experienced by many including Swami Rama. There are many cases on record when Sathya Sai Baba did come to rescue not as Sai Baba but in a different body. Many westerners have recorded such cases. I have no reasons to doubt such stories, as they are scientists, engineers, doctors and the like. When I met Swami Rama, he was suffering from cancer and death was inevitable. Even in that state of acute health condition, he was kind enough to meet me. I was not in a position to ask about his Guru or any other matter of my interest.

In his book Swami Rama had revealed, which may not be believed by many, that there were few cave monasteries in Himalayas with unbroken tradition of four or five thousand years. His own master belonged to one such tradition with records of its hoary past origin including the names of all masters. Swami Rama, may be because of secrecy, did not reveal the location of his guru's cave. The book was published in 1978 and his master was never mentioned in past tense, giving the impression that he was alive at least until 1978.

When Sathya Sai Baba calls you

After retirement, I was allotted a house in Pandara Park, New Delhi. During this time, I received an invitation card for Narayanan's daughter's marriage to be performed in Allahabad. This gave me an opportunity to get his address. I was not in a position to attend the marriage of a well-wisher of mine but I used the opportunity to write to him to know why he had sent two telegrams asking me to visit Puttaparthy during my busy days in the investigation of Rajiv Gandhi murder case. He sent a prompt reply. He said that his wife was in Puttaparthy for *seva*. One day Baba called her and told her to inform her husband that the policewalla in Delhi should meet him. He had sent two telegrams to ensure my presence there. He knew nothing more than that. How did Baba know my relationship with the family of Narayanan, as we had never visited Puttaparthy together? This is one way of showing that Baba knows about the relationship between us. His omnipresence and omniscience is fully proved from this small event. It reminded me of Kolkata's Amma's case of receiving Baba's grace without seeing Baba at any point of her life. She merely did *arati* of Baba by just burning *agarbatti* in the morning and evening in her small hut. I fully realized Baba was all-knowing by this personal experience. The other reason might have been to shower his blessings on me although I consider myself as a part-time devotee.

At my Pandara Park residence, I had no work. I decided to write whatever I knew about Sai Baba. The note was based on the experiences of other prominent persons like Howard Murphet,

Dr Hislop, Indira Devi and many others. On completion of the note I lost the manuscript as we shifted to a private residence. One remarkable thing happened that in one photo of Baba *bibhuti* appeared. I did not realize why this happened. Now, I think it was Baba's message of blessing for an effort to write on him.

During my stay in Tagore Park for four years I just rested and relaxed. I almost became a recluse. I however kept my interest in studying books on Sai Baba and attended Sai *Bhajans* in the vicinity. I found university professors in many such *bhajans*. I heard many miracles of Baba from people who were highly educated. That helped me to face domestic challenges and acute difficulties. Pension was Rs 5029 only. I almost went mad. In between, I had an occasion to visit Puttaparthy, the abode of Sai Baba. I thought that Baba would call me for an interview as I was facing an acute family problem. When Baba did not call me for interview, I just started almost cursing him. All of a sudden, he looked at me from a distance and raised his hand. I returned home dejected and decided not to visit my puja room. The puja room was then allotted to a domestic help. After a few months, the domestic help left for his home town in Uttarakhand. One day, I just entered the puja room. I was stunned to find Baba's photos with lots of *bibhuti* flowing from Baba's mouth downwards. I was just in tears and called my wife to witness the miracle of Sai. I kept it a secret for fear of criticism

Visit to Puttaparthy in 1999

In 1999, we decided to visit Puttaparthy after a long gap and we never expected Baba to call us for an interview, as I was just a retired officer of no use for Baba's activities. Baba as I said knows what his part-time devotee was thinking. To my surprise, he noticed my presence and called us for the much-desired interview. There were many persons in the interview room. After the usual talks, he materialized *bibhuti* for ladies. This I have found his usual practice for which I have not found any answer. However, I have noticed that he prefers the presence of both husband and wife while visiting Baba.

He tapped my ring in my index finger. As I had never received any ring from Baba, I said that it was not Baba's gift. For years, I desired a ring gift from Baba as many of my friends had received such gifts. Baba knew my yearning for such a gift. He said, "Do you want one". "Yes", I said, all right, "you will get one". From nowhere a light green ring came to him and handed over to me to wear in the fourth finger. The fitting was perfect as if it came for me only. After another round of talks and materialization of various objects Baba looked at my wife and asked, "Are you zealous". She said, "Yes". "Alright you will get one". Baba materialized another ring that fitted her well. We were overwhelmed by Baba's grace to part-time devotees like us. We are still wearing them. Baba had told devotees that such rings enable him to receive any distress call from his devotees. The value of the stone is not known to me but many spiritual persons have asked us about this ring and one of them said it was very rare and very costly. I have never shown any interest in its value or price. It is a gift that many desire to have for Baba's blessings.

Satya Sai Baba devotees are spread all over the world. Each devotee has a personal experience. The foreigners hailing from different backgrounds have been flocking to Satya Sai Baba, not because of blind faith, but because of their own experiences. Independent of their individual faith, they all believe in oneness of God and unity of mankind. Love is the essence of Sai message to the world. As love comes out of service, all his devotees are engaged in service activities. Rightly Mother Teresa had said that 'God is love in action'.

I, once found a young Australian girl in a plane and asked why she visited India. She, without blinking, said she wanted to see Satya Sai in person. She had no hesitation to admit that she was a Sai devotee. Books authored by eminent foreigners on Sai Baba are to be read many times to comprehend him in our limited way. In 2009 during Christmas, I was in Puttaparthy as the family was already in Hyderabad for reunion of fifty-niners. The Chiristan devotees of Sai Baba visit Puttaparthy to celebrate Christmas.

Reincarnation

Once, Dr DJ Gadhia wanted *mukti* by grace of Baba. Baba said 'no mukti' as he would have to serve Baba in his next incarnation as Prem Sai. Rebirth is ingrained in various discourses of Baba. Hindus believe in rebirth as their scriptures speak volumes on the subject. As a child, Sai Baba, when confronted by his father to reveal who he was, he took out flowers and threw them on the ground and out of flowers, the word Sai Baba emerged. Nobody in Puttaparthy knew about Shirdi Sai Baba in faraway Shirdi. When Sathya Sai Baba, gifted with supernatural powers since his childhood, there was no need for him to declare himself as reincarnation of Shirdi Sai Baba. He could have established himself without invoking the name of Shirdi Sai Baba. Baba's reincarnation in future as Prem Sai in a district in Karnataka is not faraway. He, as per his own declaration, would leave his mortal body at the age of 96 years. He was born in 1926.

Madhav Dikshit was a nephew of Kakasaheb Dikshit who was a great devotee of Shirdi Baba. Madhav went to Shirdi along with his uncle at the age of eight and stayed in Shirdi for eight years until 1918, the year Shirdi Baba passed away. Subsequently, Madhav settled down in Mangalore working as an accountant in a firm. Dr Gadhia and he used to talk about Shirdi Baba. Madhav did not know about Sathya Sai Baba of Puttaparthy, who is incarnation of Shirdi Sai Baba. He did not believe it when told by Gadhia. Madhav who was hearing all this was surprised and made a journey to Puttaparthy. Baba gave an interview to him. In the interview room when Baba revealed many secrets not known to others like his headache cured by Shirdi Baba by slapping him on his forehead. Madhav started shedding tears and fell at Swami's feet. Baba further disclosed that Kakasheb did not record correctly about his rebirth as Sathya Sai Baba. He did not say to Kaka that he would come as a boy of eight years. What he had said was that Baba would come to this world after eight years of his Samadhi. Exactly, after eight years Sai Baba was born.

Rebirth is a subject of research all over the world. 'Many Masters Many Lives' written by Dr Brian is a must for those who genuinely wish to study the subject in-depth. He has cited many cases where persons could recall their previous lives in detail. Dr Brian verified many such claims by way of proof. Many took birth after a great deal of gap. Dr Brian describes various levels of soul resting. This gives credence to Hindu belief of seven *lokas*. Mahavatar Babaji initiated Lahari Mahasaya by posting him in Ranikhet and while roaming in the jungles he was called by Mahavatar Babaji by name. He said that he was overseeing him for a good length of time. After initiation Lahari Mahasaya was shown his previous life cave, where he used to do meditation. Lahari Mahasaya could recall his previous life and meaning of his present life.

The most interesting case of rebirth relates to Swami Vivekananda as reported by those who witnessed the conversation between Swami and one Nalin of Sri Lanka. Nalin came along with a group of people of Sri Lanka to Puttaparthy to have *darshan* of Baba. When they were called for the interview, Baba asked Nalin his name. He said 'Nalin'. Baba said no and said his name was Narendra, the family name of Vivekananda. Baba said he was waiting for him for 82 years. He was calculating his previous life as Shirdi Baba. Then Baba explained to Nalin that in his previous life he was Vivekananda. Nalin was spiritually high. Then Baba asked him when he would join him in Puttaparthy. Nalin's answer was after 20 years. This news spread like wild fire and since then Nalin has been keeping low profile and currently lives in Sri Lanka for *sadhana*. Many believe that Nalin would take charge of Baba's work after Baba leaves his mortal body at the age of 96 years. It is not too distant a future to witness what would happen to Nalin. If Nalin is reincarnation of Vivekananda, he will have to play a big part in the scheme of Baba's future planning.

Scriptural Understanding of Reincarnation

Hindus apart, apparently other religions do not accept reincarnation. Steven J. Rosen has attempted in uncovering the truth in *World Religions*. It is a masterly study of scriptures of all major religions to focus on how the original scripts were ignored to reject the very idea of rebirth. He guides the readers through the history of all religions, showing how the teachings of all religions are consistent with the idea of reincarnation or rebirth as is popularly understood. Quoting Socrates 'that truly there is such a thing as living again, that the living spring from the dead, and the souls of the dead are in existence.' It is believed that the ancient Greek thinkers may have derived this from their contacts with ancient India. The historic personalities like Henry Ford, Thomas Edison, Benjamin Franklin, Tom Paine, Walt Whitman and many others shared this view as the energy that animates the body, goes on into a new body after the death of the present body. The poll results show that progressively year after year people in the West started believing rebirth climaxing into 23 per cent in 1981 in America. So is the case in Europe. My English taxi driver in London, while on tour during my service, said that he believed in rebirth.

Jenson argues on the basis of Hindu concept that 'type and make' of our present body is the result of previous activities of the life before and the future body with all its attributes will be the result of present life activities. In simple terms, there is game of *karmic* theory. It is like Biblical equivalent: 'As you sow, so shall ye reap.' In the words of Plato: 'God is blameless, man has chosen his own fate and this by his own actions.' This should not lead to determinism, as otherwise life will be dull and mechanical. God has given in this life the freedom to choose between good and evil, which provides an escape route from degradation to graduation. Such a sincere effort has the divine blessings for mitigation of evils for a purposeful life here and after. There are recorded incidents of that happening by the grace of Guru and God.

Self-realization is the ultimate objective of each individual. This does not happen in one's life experience. Take the case of Arjuna, who was blessed with the divine blessing of Krishna. However, Krishna did not forget to remind Arjuna that to attain that stage he had taken many births before, of which he was not aware.of. Same is the case of Buddha as he too had to go through several births before attaining *Nirvana* i.e. the state of enlightenment. Spiritual evolution is indeed a slow process and cannot be shortened by a package course. This discourages many from meditation or embarking on practising the first two stages of *Astanga Yog* i.e. *Niyama* and *Yama* necessary for purification of mind. The great spiritual masters encourage adoption of life of virtue as a sure way for gradual spiritual enlightenment. There are many hurdles to be crossed and that should not act as a deterrent to a higher path.

Ramkrishna Paramhans once asked why two persons doing *tapasaya* did not receive the same progress. Ramakrishna replied that sixteen persons hit the same hot iron rod but the rod did not break. When the seventeenth person hit the iron rod, it broke. The efforts of all the sixteen persons did not go waste, but the time was not ripe. Only the seventeenth person was lucky, as it was the time to break the rod. If two *sadhaks* are not getting the same result, it is not because of their *sadhanas*. So one should not get disillusioned if results are different between two persons. Each person is guided by his past *karma*. We have the choice to adopt our path in this life for spiritual progress. Thus, as aptly said by Rosen: 'Reincarnation can be seen as the harvesting of the fruits of action'. There is growing acceptance in the West in the reincarnation, with growing interest on the subject of death, validity of past life therapy.

It is true that in most cases people forget their previous life. Why should it be so? There is some scientific evidence to suggest that large quantities of oxytocin, one of the hormones of the posterior pituitary gland released by pregnant mother, floods her child's system during pregnancy. This hormone flashes away memories of former life. If people recollect their previous life, the present life will be haunted with past memories with no possibility of building up new relationship in the present life. Thus, forgetting the past life is a boon to make present life more purposeful and meaningful.

The above explanation appears to be reasonable. In seventies, I happened to visit Gorakhpur as SP Vigilance and stayed with SSP Gorakhpur VK Jain as his guest. I had known that a *kriya yogi* lived some 30 miles away from Gorakhpur. I made a journey to that place by a roadside taxi. The man I wanted to meet had just come back from school where he was a teacher. He admitted that he was a *kriya yogi* of Lahari Mahasaya tradition. I just asked him if he knew his previous birth life. He said yes. I, out of curiosity, wanted to know whether he was in touch with the family he was born in earlier life. His answer was that it was of no use as that would bind him in *maya* and he would remain in confusion. This simple answer is good enough ground for forgetting the past life made easy by cosmic power by erasing that memory at the time of birth. Remembrance of past life definitely would complicate the present life. 'The soul's struggle from life to life must be isolated from the distracting influences of its past'.

Karma theory is based on the acts we do. Good *karma* in the present life assures an individual for graduation to higher spiritual life in the next birth. *Vikarma* is opposite of good karma i.e. bad *karma* which creates the reasons for rebirth in lower species of life. There is finally a category called *akarma* where spiritual based activities do not produce material reactions. This is the stage of attaining freedom from the cycle of birth and death. The person reaching that stage is free from the world of duality and the soul goes back to its original source. Hindus are therefore not fatalistic as there is a way out of the cycle of birth and death. Amarnath Yatris, in spite of terrorist attacks, do not fear death as they are bound to live again. Such deaths in such situations are blessings in disguise, as they firmly believe God's blessings for a more useful life after. Hinduism is alive, despite brutal aggressions by foreign powers for centuries. *Karmic* theory is sustaining Hinduism for centuries much before the advent of other religions. *Karma* can be neutralized largely by spiritual practices in the present life. Otherwise, the present life will be a state of helplessness or inevitability. *Karma* can be transcended by good *karma* or by the grace of Guru.

Sai Baba has enabled many to live longer than their allotted life by his mere *sankalpa*. He told Madhav Dikshit that his life was ending, but he had extended his life by ten years. Exactly after ten years he died. Brig. Bose died at the age of 80 years witnessed by thousands of people when Baba was addressing a big gathering in Puttaparthy. He came down, revived him from the clutches of death, and extended Bose's life by ten more years. Brig. Bose died at the age of 90 years. This is a well-documented case. I asked Bose's son Col. Bose in 2008 and he confirmed it. Many great Mahatmas of India had done this for the benefit of their devotees. In the recent past such Mahatmas were like Trailanga Swami, Sri Lokenath Brahmachari. Thus, Indian religion provides two escape routes to transcend *karma*, one by the grace of Guru or by God to repentant sinners. Sri Aurobindo always emphasized on the importance of 'descend of grace divine' for spiritual progress. Sri Aurobindo had no Guru. Every thing happened by the descend of the grace divine. So was the case with Anandamayee Ma. She had no Guru but the divine was guiding her from her childhood.

Indian scriptures, which many of us never read, describe birth and death in a most scientific manner. The *Bhagavata Purana* offers explanation of consciousness from foetus to death. The cosmic engineering has been explained in detail. On the first night, the semina and ovum mix. On the fifth night, the mixture ferments into a bubble. On the tenth night, it becomes a plump and thereafter becomes a lump of flesh.

In a month the head is formed and after two months the hands, the feet and other limbs take shape. By the end of three months the nails, fingers, toes, body hair, bones and skin appear as do other apertures i.e. eyes, nostrils, ears, mouths and anus. By the end of six months, the foetus starts moving in the abdomen of the mother. The right side movement indicates the birth of a male child and movement of the left side is indication of female. Sages compiled all these thousands of years ago, but Rosen asserts that it confirms to modern scientific research.

Death

Death is beautiful as per eastern tradition. Death is inevitable. Even knowing this people are afraid of death for reasons of maya, which blurs our vision and understanding. Raman Maharishi experimented with the idea of death in his own life at the early stage of his *sadhana*. He soon realized the death of his body and not his soul. All of us can try out this experiment for our own benefit.

Hindus believe that there is cycle of birth and death. This belief is based on spiritual insight of great-realized souls. The past life regression by western psychologists and psychiatrists have come to the same conclusion. There is a purpose in life. Often we forget that. There lies the greatest tragedy of living mechanically and spend our time in useless pursuits which are endless. Bread is important, but that is not the only purpose of life.

There is lot of difference in the manner of death. The way one dies indicates his spiritual attainment in the present life. In *Brihadaranyaka Upanishad* (4.4.1-4) it is said that at the time of death the area of one's heart becomes lit and by that light the soul departs through one of the apertures like the eye, the head, nose, mouth or anus. A highly realized soul departs through the top of the head and this is noticed by seeing blood oozing from the top of the head. The worst exit of soul is through anus. As the soul departs the *pranas* too follow the soul to the soul's next destination with his knowledge and deeds.

Hindus have elaborate methods and rituals just before and after death to help the dying person in the most beneficial way. A dying person is placed on the ground in the north-west alignment, head to the north due to magnetic pulls. Even after the clinical death, the *prana* still exist and may hover around the body. *Prana* makes attempt to re-enter the body.

To prevent re-entry of *prana*, the Hindus block all the apertures of entry. Thus, the nose, the ears, and the eyes are stuffed with cotton. Even lips are sealed. The lower passage that is anus is closed by tying the toes as that block the anus.

The body is burnt immediately barring great sages who often have out of body experiences. This is done because the *prana* refuses to believe he is still dead. The Christians keep the body for three days as Christ resurrected after three days. Every faith has its rationale for observing some rituals as per their own tradition.

Recorded history has proved that many spiritual personalities had premonition of their impending death. Not only that, many had announced the date and time of their death. I am only referring to cases of the recent past. Trailanga Swami, who lived for more than 300 years and left his body in Banaras, once announced his decision to cast off his mortal body, but his devotees pleaded with him to postpone the same as they wanted his statue to be installed at a place where he was living. They only wanted another month. The request was granted. Exactly, after a month, he went into his small *kutia* and told his devotees to open the door after an hour or so. When the devotees entered the *kutia* after an hour, they found Trailanga Swami dead in lotus posture. The whole story was recorded by contemporary devotees and is still available.

The second case is more recent. Ramalinga Swami, a saint hailing from Tami Nadu, was a worshipper of *jyoti* or light. He told that soon he would leave his mortal body. A day was fixed. He went into his hut and told his devotees not to open the door for a period. After the expiry of the period, his disciples opened the door only to find that he had just vanished. There was no trace of his physical body. Before opening the door, his devotees found a flash of light from the hut merging into the sky.

There was a Muslim lady saint by the name of Bibiji, who used to reside in a *dargha* in Agra. She used to remain naked. Her devotees included many prominent people. Swami Rama was one of them. Her meditation was very simple. She used to say that offer your heart to Lord with tearful eyes and the Lord would do the rest. In the presence of eminent people, she left her body and people saw a flame of light emanating from her heart region and merging into the sky. Swami Rama had recorded this incident in his book on *Himalayan Masters* and he too was a witness to this incident.

These incidents of unusual death only prove, in substantial degree, that many highly evolved souls have the ability to forecast their death or have the ability to decide their date and timing of death. For ordinary mortals or unbelievers this would appear as absurd as they have no ability to do fundamental research on the subject. Who would believe that Sathya Sai Baba had announced casting off his body at the age of 96 years? The day is approaching fast and many would be lucky enough to see that year. Sai Baba had already announced his next incarnation as Prem Sai taking birth in the state of Karnataka. His photo as Prem Sai has been shown by Baba. Those in the age group of 10 or 12 years now would be fortunate to witness this greatest miracle of the world and turn to divine power for individual salvation and relief. Rationalists will have difficulty in brushing this unique event as irrational.

2012 End or Beginning

Years ago, Sai Baba had told a devotee that from 2009 to 2011 the world would face the worst period in history of mankind. His advent is to tide over the terrific situation. Now, I have read the book called *2012 End or Beginning*, authored by a Study Centre guided by a special channel Suvahini and Guruji Krishnanda, who lives in Karnataka and he avoids publicity. The book 'addresses the changes the earth is going through' and how *saptarishis* are guiding gurus like Krishnanda and Suvahini claim to communicate with *Rishis* for guidance. Suvahini is a young lady who had worked with *Rishis* in her past lives. She has the ability to communicate with the Photon Belt, which will be discussed briefly for our understanding of the cosmos.

Much fear has been expressed about the fate of the world we know. Some predictions are disturbing, but the higher souls are engaged in averting such a gloomy future. It is said that *Kaliyug* would end by 2018. Brahma Kumaris are saying that our present stage is one of 'sangam' between the *Kaliyug* and *Satyayug*. Man and women have to change for entering the new age. Negativity in the world atmosphere is capable of its own destruction by way of a nuclear war or further degradation of mother earth.

In the realm of knowing the future, the science is incapable to apply any scientific instruments so far available to comprehend issues like consciousness. Brain dead people in many cases became conscious. How then we define death? The technique used by the living advanced *yogis* is to obtain information from highly advanced beings, which had left their mortal bodies. The instrument is the use of developed intuition to secure the source of higher wisdom. The point to be understood is that the existence of advanced beings in a realm not yet detected by science. Sri Lokenath Brahmachari and Sri Ragavendra Swami had promised that they would help people in distress if a sincere call were given to them. It is claimed that advanced *Rishis* guide us through a few channels that are capable to receive such guidance.

In this book, two channels have been mentioned. Sri Krishnanda is one of them who is said to be in touch with great *Rishis* and the second channel is called Suvahini, who is young and prefers to remain anonymous, can communicate not only with the *Rishis* but also with 'planets, stars, galaxies, energy fields, inanimate objects.'

Our solar system orbits around the sun, which itself revolves around a much bigger sun called the central sun or Alcyone. The sun revolves in its orbit through deep space. While doing so, sun encounters various fields of energy from nearby stars, which is by nature subtle and not physical. Every object in the vast universe is product of energy. Now, scientists believe that matter can be converted into energy and energy into matter. Every object has its own energy field. It is well established that moon's energy field greatly influences the human mind and the ocean. No one has found out the way to measure the subtle energy field of the moon.

It is claimed that we are approaching the energy field of a star known as Sirius. This energy field is also called the Photon Belt. It has high vibratory frequency. To withstand the high vibratory level of the Photon Belt, each one of us has to gain higher vibratory level i.e. higher spiritual level. It is claimed that we will be entering the Photon Belt on 21 December 2012. It is claimed that 'nothing negative on this earth can survive when we go through it'...Indeed, it is a dreadful proposition. For spiritual seekers little effort will bring quick and great changes when we are in or near the Photon Belt.

The world is at the crossroads of an evolution. All spiritual traditions have said that unless we evolve collectively, the destruction of the world is a near possibility. In any event, India with its past glorious record of spiritualism would play a major role in the restoration of peace and sanity in the world. Our spiritual leaders, known or unknown, are working on this evolution in a way unheard before.

There is a tidal wave of awakening at the mass level. The way they work needs to be focused. The message of Brahma Kumaris has reached all over the world. Many are practising their meditation method, which is essentially a part of Raj Yog, with faith and dedication. Many feel transformation within. They all look bright and radiate love for all.

ISCON is spreading the message of Bhakti all across the world. Ford's grandson is in it. They sing in praise of Lord Krishnsa and remain in Krishna consciousness. While travelling to Manila, I observed some foreigners of ISCON counting their beads to remain in that consciousness through the journey. Most of ISCON members are highly educated and come from wealthy families. The ISCON has been running number of schools and organizing midday meals for schoolchildren in Delhi and Mumbai under the scheme of the governments with good and healthy food.

Sri Sri Ravishanker's 'Art of Living' is now a worldwide organization spreading the message of peace. Many have left the path of violence and adopted the path of peace. Many are practising his *Suddarsan Kriya* and they all feel benefited. *Sudersan Kriya* is again a version of Raj Yog.

Coimbatore [Tamil Nadu] based Sadguru Jaggi Vasudev, as he is called, is unique in his own way of drawing people to the path of higher dimension of life. He is a mystic of 'unfathomable proportions, dwells upon life, death, rebirth, suffering, karma and journey of the self'. He, as his disciples describe, can start a powerful process of journey within into the very core of existence. His followers include highly enlightened people, who can be considered as achievers in their respective fields of work. Spiritualism starts when we cease to pray for mundane gains in life like security from uncertain future. Experience, which is beyond physical, is the first step towards spiritualism. His mysticism and clarity of thought has drawn many Indians and foreigners in his fold. I know many of them seeking the ultimate truth of life and beyond.

Kriya Yog tradition of Mahavatar Babaji is being kept alive by Sri Yogananda line of disciples and Lahari Mahasaya's line of disciples, who prefer to remain unknown like the case of already cited late Bhagwan Singh. Dayamata, a direct disciple of Yogananda now nearly 100 year old, is looking after Yogananda centres all over the world. Ranchi centre initiates many by a correspondence course. I had once visited Ranchi centre and found many in ecstasy during the period of meditation. Yoganand's book is read by multitude of people all over the world as the book has been translated into many foreign languages. Daksineswar centre of Yognanda near Kolkata is on the banks of the river Ganga. While posted in Kolkata, I often visited the place for my own pleasure.

Rama Krishna Mission, with worldwide presence, is equally engaged in spreading the message of Vedanta. It runs several schools and hospitals including one in Arunachal Pradesh. Swami Ramdev is spreading Yoga for keeping good health, prerequisite for spiritual progress. He has been able to reach every part of India by courtesy of TV channels.

Bharat Seva Sangh works without publicity. Their *sadhaks* are rendering services of all kinds to needy people. Many other countless *gurus* are rendering spiritual service to aspirants. Vipasana centres teach Buddhist method of meditation. Their retreat centres are always well attended by seekers of truth.

Often, I feel that time has now come for 'supramental evolution' as described by Sri Aurobindo in *The Life Divine*, *The*

Synthesis of Yoga, and *Savitri*. This could not be achieved during his life time [1872-1950] as people were still not prepared to receive 'divine supramental consciousness' to 'bear the pressure of the descend' of divine grace. Thus, 2012 End or Beginning projection of world events should not disturb us as Rishis, past or present, and avatars are taking care of the survival of Mother Earth. Evolution to a new era of another yoga is already visible. Those who are not in tune with the energy level are likely to suffer.

23

Ayurveda and Yoga

I must share little that I know of Ayurveda and Yoga from personal experiences. After retirement, I became a victim of eczema in right foot ankle region. I almost suffered for ten years. Constant itching in the midst of people was embarrassing. Itching was more in the night and in the process, the fluid would start oozing out. I had to cover up the ankle region to avoid attention of others. I consulted allopathic doctors, who all said that I would have to live with it throughout my life.

I tried homeopathic treatment that proved disastrous as the eczema spread all over the ankle region with lots of fluid flowing out. I had to bandage the ankle and was not in a position to wear even a shoe. A well-wisher introduced me to her family homeopathic doctor Dr Kochar. He examined the situation, gave me medicine which brought back the eczema to its original position. I continued with the treatment with no observable improvement.

In the month of June 2007, I visited Divya Yog clinic of Swami Ramdev. After examining my eczema, the Vaidya said it was curable. He asked me if I would take the medicines for a year or so. I agreed. He prescribed four types of skin disease medicines to be taken twice a day. I was cured of the terrible eczema in about a year's time. I was amazed by the success of this treatment.

A second cousin of mine told me that Arjun *chhal* powder was good for keeping blood pressure under control. One big spoonful of Arjun *chhal* mixed with water is required to be boiled for 10/15 minutes. The concoction is to be consumed in the morning much before the breakfast. His blood pressure has been under control for several years. My wife started giving the Arjun *chhal* concoction to me as I too had blood pressure problem. Arjun *chhal* powder packets are available in all the centres of Swami Ramdev. One packet is sold for Rs 10 only, much cheaper than costly allopathic medicines. Two garlic cloves to be chewed and a cup of water to be taken thereafter was recommended by Sai Baba long ago to a lady suffering from high blood pressure. I too started garlic cloves and my blood pressure is under control.

When I was a child, my mother used to give me one spoonful of lime water in the morning not knowing why she did that. Much later, I found that lime water was good for curing calcium deficiency and strengthening the bone structure. I hardly see any young mother doing it now for their children. Knowledge inherited by the elders should not be brushed away in the name of modernity. It is a fashion now to rush to a doctor for small ailments curable fully by herbal or home-made remedies.

Gomutra is prescribed for those suffering from cancer or are in the near cancer situation. When my mother developed cancer in the last stage of her life, I requested Deoraha Baba for advice through an intermediary, Baba recommended Gomutra, but that could not be administered to her, as there was difficulty in procuring it. Gomutra has even been patented in USA for enhancing the efficacy of drugs. I consume two spoonful of Gomutra everyday in the morning. I am doing this for the last five-six years. Earlier, I used to obtain it from Asaram Bapu's ashram located on the ridge that is far away from my residence. Now I get it from Swami Ramdev's clinic that is very near to our residence. A Gomutra bottle costs Rs 35 only. Apart from cancer, it tones up other organs also.

Ramdevji recommends intake of *Aloe vera* juice mixed with Amla powder and wheat grass. This mixture is also recommended for cancer patients. Col. [retd] Dalmeer Singh gave me one plant of *Aloe vera*. I planted the same in a pot. Now I have 20/30 *Aloe vera* plants in several pots. Many people have taken plants from us. I generally take a glassful of wheat grass powder mixed with *Amla* powder. I am too lazy to extract *Aloe vera* juice. Wheat grass is also called green blood. It cures many diseases. In Delhi, Omji Dua sells wheat grass powder packs. He has been doing this for more than a decade, more by way of *seva* than making profits.

I am a diabetic and used to take allopathic medicine. I gave up allopathic medicine as I found the sugar level could be controlled by doing *Kapal Bhathi* as taught by Swami Ramdev. I also take ayurvedic medicine from the Government dispensary. *Kapal Bhathi* is a good exercise for pancreas and other internal organs. I would like to mention here that Guru Gorakhnath was an expert in *Kapal Bhathi*. This I had read in *Bharater Sadhak* while posted in Kolkata. At that time, I did not know how to do *Kapal Bhathi*. It is also a spiritual exercise to arouse *Kundalani Shakti* by hitting the base of the *mooladhara chakra*.

There was a panic when several H1N1 cases were reported in 2009. Swami Ramdev recommended intake of concoction made up of Tulsi and Guduchi [Giloy] in the morning and evening. *Giloy* is available in all parts of India. My wife procured *Giloy* from our society gardner, as this creeper is available in our society garden. She has been preparing this concoction for the entire family. It is a preventive measure for building immunity and protection from flu-like conditions. We all have been benefited by consuming this concoction. She boils the ingredients by way of precaution.

Pranayama prescribed by Swami Ramdev has helped many of my friends with good results by practising *Bhastrika*, *Kapal Bhathi*, *Anulom Vilom* and *Bhambri*. *Yoni Mudra* is higher form of Bhambri where breath is held for a comfortable period by closing the nose and the eyes by fingers. The sound and light within are required to be heard and seen only to achieve a 'die-mind' stage necessary for invitation to 'descent of the grace divine' as described by Sri Aurobindo. *Yoni Mudra* is also helpful for enhancement of brainpower and eyesight. It is one of the ingredients of the *Kriya Yoga*.

I have faith in biochemical treatment as I have seen good results. In Lucknow in the late sixties, my orderly reported in the morning that he had been in toilet for at least 12 times. He was in terrible condition. I consulted Dr Darbari's famous book on the subject and based on this study, I administered a dose of biochemical medicine and gave another dose in a packet to be taken after an hour or so. I advised him to visit hospital for treatment for immediate relief. By that time, he had taken the second dose. The doctor examined him and he found nothing wrong with him, as there was no further motion. He was sent back without medicine. He came back with a smiling face and announced his complete cure.

Dr Darbari was an advocate in Allahabad High Court and met the Governor, UP, when I was ADC to the Governor. He presented the book to me for study and treat emergency cases in the absence of a doctor. I lost the book because of frequent transfers.

My daughter Sushmita almost became bald in the rear side of the head when I was DIG Jhansi. Allopathic doctor prescribed medicines that did not cure her at all. The doctor was treating her for liver problem. One day a *vaidya* from Kalpi of Jaulan district came to see me for some personal problem. After the problem was solved, I took the opportunity to tell him about the loss of hair of my daughter. He wanted to see the girl and examining her on, he asked me whether I was willing to spend fifty paisa only for the treatment. What he prescribed was unique. He told me to purchase a piece of broken conch shell [shankha] and rub it on a stone slab, the way sandalwood is rubbed to prepare the paste, which should be applied on the affected portion. She was soon cured of her disease.

For acute case of constipation, Col [retd] Dalmeer Singh gives a powder pack. A spoonful of that powder mixed with milk should be taken at night before sleep. He calls this herbal mixture 'amrit'. It has been found to be useful to many. The basic ingredient of this mixture is rose petals.

He has also developed a unique eye drop for preventing cataract. This is required to be applied twice a day. I apply it once a day. Dalmeer Singh resides in Janakpuri, in West Delhi. He is a registered homeopath doctor. He knows magnetic healing and is a Reiki master. He attends patients on Sundays in the morning and gives herbal medicines free of cost. He is highly spiritual from his very childhood. He hardly eats. Presently, he is trying to prepare Kaya Kalpa medicine from a disciple of Tapwasiji Maharaj. The problem is that nobody shares the secrets for reasons I could not fathom. Two foreign disciples, if I may use the word, of Col Dalmeer Singh, are now practising distant healing with the claim of certain degree of success.

I would like to mention about Tinny my pet she-dog and her peaceful death after spending 16 years of her life with us. Once we found blood while she was urinating. I immediately contacted Dr Yadav a veterinary doctor on phone. He was located in Mukherjee Nagar, far away from our residence in Vikas Puri. He suggested Neeri Syrup to be taken by the dog. Tinny soon recovered. When I met the doctor in person, I admired the efficacy of the medicine. To my surprise he told me, that the same medicine is useful for humans also if there is any indication of urinary tract infections like dysuria, burning sensation or any urinary disorders. In the family, we use the same medicine in such symptoms. This is a herbal Ayurvedic medicine much popular in North India.

JR Choudhury, a mechanical engineer who served various organizations in India and abroad with glory, is now above 80 years of age. He is active and alert. He is the pioneer of the foundation of Vivekananda Resurgence Foundation in Delhi. He is a Bengali from Bangladesh. Under his leadership, a school for basti children is being run in Delhi. I have visited the school a couple of times. The poor children look happy wearing school dress donated by charitable persons. Recently, Canara Bank donated the school dress to these children. The Canara Bank has a fund for social causes, which was not known to me.

I, as usual, asked Choudhury how his memory is still sharp. He told me that he has been taking *Shankhapushpi* mixed with Isabgol regularly. *Shankhapushpi* is an ayurvedic herb that acts as a brain tonic. He takes Vaidyananth *Shankhapushpi* in liquid form that has sugar in it. This is not useful for diabeties. Col. Dalmeer Singh procured for me *Shankhapushpi* in powder form. This can be taken mixed with Isabgol before retiring to bed.

Kidney stone is a problem with many. Stones can be removed by surgery, but can recur again. Yes, there is a herbal solution. Dr Ram Chandra Mondal retired as an agriculturist scientist from Indian Council of Agricultural Research,. spent most of his service tenure in south, especially in Kerala where he is now settled. Once he told my cousin Hablu, who is a publisher of books on Agricultural Science, that the juice of white stem of banana tree is useful for treatment of stones in the kidney. Half a cup of stem juice mixed with half a cup of water should be taken empty stomach in the morning. This should continue for a month. Breakfast can be taken after an hour or so. This process of the treatment is slow but the result will be positive. The stem is called 'thod' in Bengali and eaten after cooking it. Many are not aware of its benefits if taken as a raw juice. South Indians are generally aware of its benefits.

In South India, the herbal treatment is called Siddha system of treatment. Agasthaya *muni* is credited with various treatises on medicine. Herbal medicines of South India are virtually unknown to North India. Out of 18 well-reported Siddhas of South India, at least 10 or 12 of them wrote on medicines and some old manuscripts are said to be still available. There are many references to *Kaya Kalpa* medicine in ancient treatises. I wonder if the formulations are still available.

Human body is an ultimate miracle. Each cell is vibrant with intelligence, absorbs pranic energy, not known to medical science. We had and still have many non-eating saints, who survive on pranic energy that is available free for all of us. A lady called Girijabala had never taken food after her marriage. Recently two non-eating saints were subjected to medical test for a good number of days. They not only survived, but nothing unusual was found in the functioning of their bodies. This does not fall under the category of *Kaya Kalpa*. It is a challenge to modern medical science to prove the secrets of living without eating. Our *Rishis* knew this science well.

Kriya Yoga

Yoga means union with the infinite for obtaining a stage of bliss and realization of self. Credit goes to Patanjali for formulating *Astanga Yoga* i.e. the eightfold path of *Raj Yoga*. The basics of eightfold path are;

1. *Yama* means moral conduct like purity of mind and body.
2. *Niyama* means non-injury to others, truthfulness, non-stealing.
3. *Asana* i.e. right posture where the spinal column is held straight
4. *Pranayama* i.e. control of breathing process for higher intake of prana for energizing the body.
5. *Pratyahara* i.e. withdrawal of five senses from external objects.
6. *Dharana* i.e. holding the mind with one thought only.
7. *Dhyana* i.e. meditation attempting to reach a die-mind stage.
8. *Samadhi* i.e. a state of evolution to superconciousness stage merging with the cosmic reality.

In the spinal column and beyond there are seven *chakras*, which may be called psychic centres, each with the possibility of opening up by practice. The base of the spine is where the *mooladhar chakra* is located. Just above it is *chakra* called swadisthan. In the navel region is located the Manipur *chakra*. The *chakra* in the heart region is called *anahat chakra*. The *chakra* in the throat region is called *visudhi chackra*. Then comes the *agya chakra* between the eyebrows. The last *chakra* is called *sahasra chakra* on the top of the head. The *kundalini shakti* is the hidden power arousal of which is what is required in *Raj Yoga*. The *Yogis* of India knew how to activate each *chakra* for progress in the path of self-realization.

The process described above is a long process. Even observing *Niyama* and *Yama* would take a lifetime. Therefore, the spiritual scientists have devised new methods for faster growth. In this category, I consider *Kriya Yoga* as a route to faster progress. This I feel is *Raj Yoga* with modification. In *Kriya Yoga* all the five senses are withdrawn from material objects and drawn inward by some practices. In *Kriya Yoga*, the most essential element is *Khecheri Mudra*. This is difficult but achievable under the guidance of a guru. This is what I have heard from some advanced Kriya Yogis.

Other paths are equally fruitful as was the case with Krishna Prem discussed elsewhere. Bhakti, Karma and Gyan are to be merged with *Raj Yoga*. Look at Brahma Kumaris. They practice Raj Yoga with concentration on the *Agya chakra*. Nevertheless, they love God and sing in his praise. Only an adept can initiate into the right path. Adepts are those who have realized the cosmic power.

Conclusion

While narrating some incidents of my police career, I have shown how the CBI had solved some of the complicated cases. It is my experience that every case can be solved if there is proper utilization of men and material. In the Rajiv Gandhi murder case there was no clue in the beginning, but could be worked out by proper application of mind and chasing every lead by a team of officers, which included the Director, the Additional Director, a Joint Director, three DIGs, a number of SPs, Deputy SPs (DySP). The entire conspiracy was worked out. The culprits were punished. The same was the case with the Security Scam. If there is proper investment, there will be results.

This leads to a question of adequacy of officers in the CBI for investigation of cases. The yardstick was that each Investigation Officer (IO) was supposed to handle three cases in a year. In addition IOs are also supposed to make verification of information, attend court cases as IOs or holding IOs in the absence of the original IO having been transferred or retired from service. For fruitful investigation, each case needs to be investigated by a team of officers, at least four IOs in each case. The yardstick fixed by the government needs a re-look.

The state anti-corruption organizations would require similar strength if states are interested in tackling the growing corruption. Corruption is the greatest internal and external threat to India. Corruption has subverted all the institutions of governance, including the police, administrators, the defence and even the judiciary. All the five hijackers of IC- 814 obtained Indian passports, ration cards, driving licences without any semblance of field verification, as is the case with ordinary citizens. In Mumbai, in serial blasts cases of 1993, the customs officers allowed smuggling of RDX and firearms in lieu of huge payments made to them. Corruption has made the Indian system porous and vulnerable.

Corruption is a low risk and high profit enterprise. Are we as a nation shown any concern? Bribe money, as said elsewhere, has not been calculated in any black money studies. It was argued that income could not be calculated twice as bribe giver's money was already taxed. This is a fallacious argument as bribe is given out of unreported income. Time has come to mount pressure on the government to calculate generation of bribe money annually by obtaining inputs from the CBI and state agencies and sample checking of ground reality by surveys. Corruption should be the first task for every government to tackle.

Stashing away Indian stolen money abroad by Indians is said to be around 1.7 trillion dollars in Switzerland alone. This, if true, is more than the annual National Income. I have cited elsewhere where Indian foreign accounts in Switzerland were found and the Swiss authorities refused to divulge the names of the account holders on the principle of dual criminality by classifying such offences as fiscal offences by Switzerland and such offences are no offence in that country. The recent case of Hasan Ali speaks volumes about his having 10 bank accounts in Switzerland. While the Indian government publicly sought help from Swiss authorities, it is claimed by Swiss that some forged documents were sent. It has been reported by a well-respected journalist that since April 2007, the Indian government has kept mum on Swiss request for proper documentation.

As I have said earlier the India's stolen money abroad should have created a storm in the country. Politicians of all hues have lost credibility, may be due to a perception that in this game of hide and seek many are involved. The political class as a whole should have demanded action for the sake of their own credibility.

I strongly believe that time has come for another commission like Santhanam Commission to study corruption comprehensively and come up with new ideas to deal with corruption, money laundering, stashing away India's stolen money abroad. The Santhanam Commission was constituted at the initiative of Sri Lal Báhadur Shastri in 1963 and the report was submitted in a year with revolutionary ideas, one of which was to make possession of disproportionate assets as a substantive offence for public servants.

For beginners in the spiritual path, in which category I place myself, my attempt has been to inspire young people to explore and derive satisfaction from the achievements of highly educated people like Vivekananda and Sri Aurobindo by reading their books. Let the beginners not wait first for a Guru to arrive at their doorstep. Guru or a guide comes at the appropriate time when the seeker is ready for forward movement in the path of virtue. Observance of *Niyama* and *Yama*, the first two stages in *Astanga Yoga*, is very essential. Otherwise, it will be like a game of ladder and snake, where a person goes up and slides back repeatedly.

One should allow his intuition to develop by just practising a bit of meditation by remaining silent and watching the breathing process. Mind will remain focused on breathing only. No other thought will emerge during that duration. Duration of deep silence without any thought will gradually increase and this stage has been described by Sai Baba as die-mind stage for attaining various spiritual experiences leading to stage of *Samadhi* or communion with the Superpower for those with past good *karma* and *sadhana*.

One need not to be confused on the path to be adopted. One can adopt any path of his choice like *Bhakti*, *Karma*, *Gyan* and *Raj Yoga*, as all of them ultimately merge into one reality. Life is not to be wasted by pursuing only mundane affairs as life is too precious to be wasted. Career and spiritual quest can mix. One need not be sacrificed for the sake of other. This misconception has to be removed.

Let me assure the readers that there are great souls still living in India and many of them avoid publicity. Search and you will find them. Avoid those who are milking money in the garb of a sadhu.

Let me end the long story of my life by quoting a self-composed hymn, which I have been singing alone often since sixties:

'I have no birth, no death and no decay.'

So I say,

"I am He, I am He, and I am He."

Index

18 Siddhas, 199
AB Lala, 53
Abdul Rahim, 116
Abdul Razak, 229
Acharya Kripalani, 48
Adi Shankaracharya, 31
Advani, LK, 174
Afghan Jihad 1979-1989, 191
AG Office fraud, 86
Akhilesh Singh, 142
Akhtar, Abdur Rehman, 192
Al-Qaeda, 196
Altaf Gauhar, 176
Amod Kanth, 150
Anandamayee Ma, 199
Anti-Terrorist Coordination Cell, 132
Art of Living, 247
Astrom, Prof., 89
Author,
- as ASP, Aligarh, 28
- as Battalion Commandant, 41
- as DIG Jhansi range, 96
- as DIG Kolkata, 83
- as DIG Police Headquarters, 120
- as DIG Railways, 118
- as SP Deoria, 47-56
- as SP Vigilance, 57
- as SP, DIG, CBI Kolkata, 59
- at Wardha Ashram, 48
- Faith in cosmic powers, 44
- in spiritual quest, 199
- Last tenure in CBI, 131
- on bonded labour, 55
- on disproportionate assests, 60-61
- on Hawala, 131-32
- on Lal Bahadur Shastri, 36
- on Netaji's mystery, 53
- on Pandit Nehru, 34-35
- on police image, 50
- on political interference, 85
- on Voluntary Disclosure scheme, 63
- training at Mount Abu, 15-20
- training at Moradabad, 24
- visit to Badrinath and Kedarnath, 31-32
- visit to Taj Mahal, 13-14

Autobiography of a Yogi, 58
Avtar Singh, 67

Baba Mustaquim, 99, 102
Babu Gujar, 99
Bachchan, Amitabh, 114
Bachchan, Jaya, 114
Badrinath and Kedarnath, 31
Bahadur Shah Zaffar, 203
Bajpai, Uma Shanker, 96, 107, 211
Balwan gang, 99, 101
Banerjee, Purnendu Kumar, 176
Banerjee, Shushital, 114
Bank Frauds, 69
Barua, Paresh, 160
Basu, Ajoy, 51
Behamai Massacre, 97
Bhagwan Das, 91
Bhagwan Singh, 220
Bharater Sadhak, 207
Bhattacharya, Dileep Kumar, 24
Bhopal Gas Leak Case, 145
Bhrigu Samhita, 45
Bhullar, Devinder Pal Singh, 133
Bhutto, Zulfiqar Ali, 186
Billa and Ranga, 92
Bitta, MS, 133
Bombay Serial Blast Cases, 171
Bonded labour, 55
Border Road Organization, 31
Bordoloi, Gopi Nath, 47
Bose, Subhas Chandra, 52
Brahma Kumaris, 21

Capt. Ranade, 39
Captain Gopal Krishna, 23
CBI, history of, 76
  political interference and, 85
  system of checks and balances in, 77
Central Economic Intelligence Bureau, 125
Central Fingerprint Bureau, 88
Central Police Training College, 15
Chand, IP, 100
Chandrana, 70
Chandrashekar, 149
Charan Singh, 47
Charlu, 71
Chaturvedi, JN, 92, 120
Chaturvedi, Rajendra, 111
Chelliah, Prof., 64
Chidambaram, 130
China-India War 1962, 176
Chopra children murder case, 91
Choudhury, JR, 254
Col Tandon, 23

Dalal, Sucheta, 165
Dalmeer Singh, 203, 254, 255
Dalvi, JP, 177
Das, BN, 33, 204
Das, DN, 93
Dawa-wal-Irshad, 179
Death, 242
Delhi Special Police Establishment Act, 77

Deoraha Baba, 12, 204
Desai, Morarji, 86
Dhani Ram, 92
Dhar, Anuj, 53
Dharna encounter, 107
Diamond merchant kidnapping case, 139
DIG Lahari, 73
Dikshit, Kakasaheb, 237
Dikshit, Madhav, 237
Dikshit, Sheila, 30
Dikshit, Vinod, 30
Dikshitlu, 90
Dixit, JN, 29, 34
Dulles, Allen, 186

Edgar, Cayce, 215
Enlai, Zhou, 176
Eric Stracy, 16

Fake CBI officers, 84
False Medical Reimbursement Claims, 72
Field Marshal Manekshaw, 22

Gadhia, DJ, 237
Gandhi, Indira, 133
Gandhi, Rajiv, 11, 149
Gen. Ayub, 186
Ghose, Samarendra Nath, 44
Ghulam Mustafa Khar, 139
Gill, KPS, 133
Giri, Uma Shanker, 111
Gopal Krishna Handoo, 16
Gopinath, 201
Goswami, Chunni, 175
Gulauli encounter, 108
Gumnami Baba, 52
Gupta, Ranjit, 43
Gupta, Shekher, 152
Gurmukh Nihal Singh, 21

Hafiz, Mohammad Saeed, 180
Hakim Singh, 112
Hamid Gul, 180, 192
Howrah station car parking scandal, 66
Hussain, Ahmed, 121

Inderjeet Singh, 91
Indian Communists, 210
IPKF, 149
Iskander Mirza, 186
ISCON, 247
Islam Ahmed, 38
Ishwarchandra Vidyasagar, 48

Jackson, Jacob, 17
Jaggi Vasudev, 247
Jagram, 99
Jaiswal, Gyan Prakash, 143
Jamaud-Dawa, 180
Jaya Bhaduri, 113
Jayprakash Narayan, 48
Jeans, James, 199
John Lobo, 73
Joytirmoy Basu, 85
Justice Khosla Commission, 52

Jyoti Basu, 22

Kaldor, Prof., 64
Kamakhya Devi, 203
Kamakhya Tapaswiji, 203
Karthikeyan, 149, 152
Katre, MG, 131
Kennedy, John F., 37
Khalid Mohammed, 172
Khan, Qurban Ali, 76
Khan, Roedad, 178, 190
Khan, Yahya, 187
Khosla Commission Report, 92
Khushwant Singh, 102
Kohli, DP, 9, 60, 76
Kripalani, Acharya, 48
Krishna Prem, 202
Kriya Yoga, 256
Kusma Nain, 108

Lala Ram, 97
Laljit Singh, 150
Lashkar-e-Toiba, 179
LTTE, 153, 154, 156, 157, 160

Madeleine Slade, 49
Malabar Special Police, 19
Malkhan Singh, 101, 110
Mallah, Vikram, 97
Man Singh Yadav, 99
Management Information System (MIS), 73
Manekshaw, Field Marshal, 22
Maulana Masood Azhar, 116
Mayawati, 49
Mazumdar, Charu, 58
Mehta, Harshad, 165
Menon, Krishna, 178
Mira Bhen, 49
Mitra, SP, 95
Modi, Syed, 11
Mohd. Iqbal, 151
Mohd. Sharif, 138
Mondal, Ram Chandra, 255
Mool Chand, 101
Mount Abu, 21
MP Singh, 73
Mukherjee, Ram, 114
Mukherjee, Sasadhar, 114
Mullick, BN, 90, 186
Musharraf, Parvez, 180
Mustaquim gang, 99, 102
Myrdal, Gunnar, 50

Najm Sethi, 193
Nawaz Sharif, 180, 194
Nayyar, KK, 182
Nehru, BK, 21, 134, 178
Nehru, Pandit Jawaharlal, 42
Nehru, RK, 123
Nikson, Ronald, 202
NSG, 159
Nuss, Bela, 116

Omar Sheikh, 115, 116
Operation Blue Star, 132
Operation Gibraltar, 179
Osama bin Laden, 196

P Chandrasekharan, 151
Pakistan, coup in, 180
Pakistan: From Jinnah to Jihad, 185
Pandey, Satish Dutt, 28, 202
Par Kaya Pravesh, 221
Patel, SD, 92
Peter, Harkos, 214
Phoolan Devi, 11, 98
Police,
  image of, 50
Prabhat Kumar, 58
Pradhan, RK, 133
Prosad, Shanti, 38, 41

Qamrul Hasan, 24

R Documents, 82
Radhakrishnan, S., 21, 33
Radhavinod Raju, 164
Radu, Livio, 136
Raghunath Mallah, 99
Rahat Latif, 190
Raja Vijay Karan, 140, 152
Rajender Shekhar, 144
Rajesh Pilot, 156
Rajagopalachari, P, 211
Rajiv Gandhi Murder Case, 149
Ram Autar, 99
Ram Singh, 36
Ramakrishna Dev, 22
Ramchandran, SK, 22
Ramzi Yousef, 172
Rao, Narasimha, 49
Rehmat Ali, Chaudhuri, 183
Reincarnation, 237, 238
Renison, 78
Ribeiro, Julio, 134, 148
Roy, Purabi, 53
Roy, Raja Ram Mohan, 48

S Ramani, 149
Sahai, Inder Mohan, 25
Sai *Bhajans*, 218
Sai *Bibhuti*, 219
Samra, 173
Sanjay Singh, 142
Santhanam Commission, 260
Santham Committee Report, 60
Sardar Gurmukh Nihal Singh, 21
Sarvepally Radhakrishnan, 21, 33
Sathya Sai Baba, 12, 210, 212, 224
Saxena, GC, 24, 28
Saxena, NS, 57
Security Scam Case, 165
Sen, D, 9, 58
Sen, Santanu, 77, 174
Shahid, 116
Shahnawaz Committee, 52
Sharma, Asoke, 92
Sharma, PC, 89, 219
Sharma, Rajeev, 181
Shastri, Lal Bahadur, 36, 187
Sheopuri, RN, 25
Shirdi Sai Baba, 219
Shukla, Rajiv, 100, 103
Simla Agreement, 188

Singh, NN, 173
Singh, Vikram, 109
Singh, VP, 103
Singhal, BP, 100, 109
Sitaram, 51
Sleeman, 104
Sorkar, PC, 19
Special Police Establishment (SPE), 76
Special Task Force (SIT), 149
Sri Lanka, 149
Sri Ram Gang, 97
Sri Yogananda, 58, 213
Swami Rama, 12, 201, 232
Swami Sivananda, 33
Swami Vivekananda, 48, 238
Syed Modi Murder Case, 141

TADA, 161
Tapaswaiji Maharaj, 202, 204
Tariq Ali, 180
Tarun Bhaduri, 113
Telephone Exchange Trunk Call Fraud, 71
Telgi stamp paper fraud, 136
Thakur, Meera, 107, 108
Tiwari, Narain Dutt, 47
Trailanga Swami, 207
Tripathy, Tripuresh, 58
Tyagi, Mahavir, 179

Vardarajan, Perumal, 158
Varma, AP, 22
Vijay Karan, 140, 152, 159
Wadehra, RK, 68
Watts, KL, 40, 48, 57

Yadav, Dhrub Lal, 99, 105, 106, 115

Zakir Hussain, 37
Zalim Singh, 51
Zhou Enlai, 176
Zia-ul-Haq, 189

We Convert Fighters into Writers

New and Bestselling Books by other IPS Officers

Title	Author	ISBN
Manas Police & Security Yearbook 2010-2011 (Fully Illustrated)	Ajit Doval IPS, BR Lall IPS and other Top Cops	978-81-7049-366-2
CBI Stands Firm: Power Games to Demoralise	BR Lall, IPS (Former: Joint Director, CBI, India)	978-81-7049-396-9
Intelligence Tradecrafts of Spy Warfare	MK Dhar, IPS (Former Joint Director, IB, India)	978-81-7049-399-0
Comman Man's Guide to Police & Criminal Laws	Dr DV Guruprasad, IPS (DGP - CID, Karnataka)	978-81-7049-385-3
Industrial Security: Mgt & Strategies	DC Nath, IPS & Capt SB Tyagi	978-81-7049-308-2
Financial Terrorism: Black Money and the Indian Elite	BR Lall, IPS (Former: Joint Director, CBI, India)	978-81-7049-368-6
Intelligence for Management	DC Pathak, IPS (Ex Chief – IB)	978-81-7049-377-8
Inside IB and Raw: The Rolling Stone that Gathered Moss	K Sankaran Nair, IPS (Former Head: Research and Analysis Wing (RAW)	978-81-7049-305-1
Intelligence: Corporate Success and Vigilance	DC Pathak, IPS (Ex Chief – IB)	978-81-7049-289-0
Operation Triple X: An Indian Spy-Run in Pakistan	A Novel by MK Dhar, IPS (Former DGP, Punjab)	978-81-7049-301-3

The Undisclosed Punjab: India Besieged by Terror	Birbal Nath, IPS	978-81-7049-323-5
Combating Communal Conflict	VN Rai, IPS	978-81-7049-340-2
The Folds of Insurgency	AP Maheshwari, IPS	978-81-7049-331-0
Who Owns CBI: The Naked Truth	BR Lall, IPS (Former: Joint Director, CBI, India)	81-7049-293-9
Long March of Islam: The Future Imperfect	RK Ohri, IPS (Retd.)	81-7049-186-X
Open Secrets: India's Intelligence Unveiled	M K Dhar, IPS	81-7049-216-5
Threat to Security: How Secured is India from within	PC Dogra, IPS (Former DGP, Punjab)	81-7049-304-8
Fulcrum of Evil: ISI-CIA-Al Qaeda Nexus	MK Dhar (Former Joint Chief of IB)	81-7049-278-5
The Bell Tolls: Tomorrow's Truncated India	RK Ohri, IPS (Retd)	81-7049-294-7
The Peace Keepers: Indian Police Service (IPS)	SR Arun, IPS	81-7049-107-X
Human Rights: International Challenges-in (Set of 2 vols)	Dr S Subramanian, IPS	81-7049-068-5
Human Rights Training (Set of 2 vols)	Dr S Subramanian, IPS	81-7049-108-8
Industrial Espionage: Causes and Cure	Dr S Subramaniam, IPS	81-7049-079-2
Executive Protection	Dr S Subramaniam, IPS	81-7049-079-0

Notes

Notes